the Joy of Words

For Ingrid Frances Spiegl,
my wife – who understands me

Fritz Spiegl

the Joy of Words

"A Bedside Book for English Lovers"

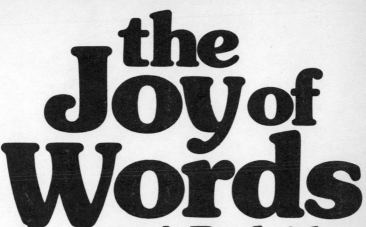

Fancy a bit of verbal intercourse?

Try reading between the lines..

ELM TREE BOOKS
LONDON

Design by Craig Dodd

First printed in Great Britain 1986
by Elm Tree Books/Hamish Hamilton Ltd
Garden House, 57–59 Long Acre, London WC2E 9JZ

British Library Cataloguing in Publication Data

Spiegl, Fritz
      The joy of words.
      1. English language – Usage
      I. Title
      428   PE1460
      ISBN 0-241-11877-8
      ISBN 0-241-11753-4 Pbk

Typeset by Rowland Phototypesetting Ltd,
Bury St Edmunds, Suffolk
Printed and bound in Great Britain by
Billing & Sons Ltd, Worcester

Contents

Introduction

During the last war recruits who were colour-blind found themselves rejected from the armed forces. After all, a sailor or airman unable to tell whether a craft was coming or going because he could not distinguish red from green (that is, port from starboard) would not have been of much use in battle. But then it was discovered that a colour-blind person taken up in an aeroplane was able to see through the enemy's camouflage in a way the normally-sighted man could not.

Someone who has learned English instead of picking it up at his mother's knee is in a comparable position. At first the language seems to have been specially devised to confuse him. Because everything – vocabulary, grammar, syntax and usage – has had to be consciously acquired, he is likely to take things literally, and hears absurdities which the native accepts because he instinctively knows what is meant. But the foreign-born learner can turn his disability to advantage when he finds himself questioning what he hears, and may even see through attempts to pull the wool over his eyes – by the great deceivers, the purveyors of clichés, the habitual presenters of anything from half-truths to convenient distortions and downright lies, like some journalists, politicians (both national and local), trades unionists, merchants and marketing men.

The (often praiseworthy) growth of the welfare state and of the industry concerned with equality (both racial and sexual) has brought in its wake a wondrous profusion of jargon and job titles; and feminists, too, in an attempt to attain what they see as equality, have gone overboard ('Wie, in das Wasser gesprungen?') trying to change the language.

But people who go overboard are sure to get wet and may end up looking very bedraggled.

This is a time of change in communications. The British newspaper industry has at last been forced to start abandoning Gutenberg's 500-year-old technology, but journalists' style is still a mixture of florid 19th-century hyperbole and juvenile punning, while the spelling, vocabulary, grammar and general competence of 'print workers' has kept pace with the decline in elementary education. Even the brightest, youngest journalists adopt the foolish traditional jargon, which they use in order to keep up with their peer group. They may be civilised, articulate, intelligent and urbane in ordinary conversation – but as soon as they wind a sheet of paper into the typewriter, things that would normally fall start to 'plunge', 'hurtle' or 'plummet'; they do not eat and drink but 'tuck into' and 'quaff'; and police never arrest but 'swoop' or 'pounce' (except in the *Guardian*, where they have been known to 'ponce'). Things are not 'expected' but 'set' to happen. They weep 'openly' or 'unashamedly', for 'heartbreak' comes easily to them, and 'horror' or 'terror' are mercilessly devalued. And although they write about 'heartless thieves' they think nothing of pestering the newly-bereaved with questions like, 'How do you feel?'

There is a well-beaten path from Fleet Street to the radio and television stations, and many newspaper journalists enter broadcasting without wiping their prose. The proliferation of radio stations, local and (the great buzz-word of the times) 'community' radio, has brought a dramatic increase of broadcasting and given us a variety of alternatives to the alleged 'dinner-jacket' style of the BBC (those announcers' dinner-jackets were in any case a myth). But unfortunately 'more' is seldom synonymous with 'better'.

Then there are certain academics, doctors (even musicians), who feel they need to clothe their statements in a sort of verbal fancy-dress, a secret language whose meaning they try to keep from the outsider. However, this is a book meant to be read (or more likely dipped into) for fun rather than instruction, intended for people who love words but do not hesitate to turn them inside-out – a book for English-lovers (and in one or two sections for English lovers). It does not pretend to have anything very serious to say about language or linguistics. It is, moreover, full of bias and prejudice – a result perhaps of the author's having reached a time in life when we all believe that what *we* were taught at school is 'correct' and will remain so for ever; and a time when one no longer feels the need to leap on every latest band-wagon of trend and fashion.

But the book also tries to reflect a growing interest, throughout the English-speaking world (including America, where new words enter the dictionaries every day) in the preservation of standards in communication. Perhaps it is only another manifestation of those 'old-fashioned values' people seem to long for. (Perhaps the nostalgia wave of the 1970s and early 80s is beginning to include the English language as an example of fine craftsmanship worth preserving). Many people, especially listeners to Radio 3 and Radio 4 who write to broadcasters as well as to the BBC itself, see a threat to the language as tantamount to a threat to the established order. That there is a gentle revolution in progress is shown by the fact that these letters no longer come exclusively from middle-aged, middle-class listeners but also from the young, many of whom feel that they were deprived of proper teaching by the misguided progressivism rife in schools a generation ago; and almost everyone deplores the abolition of Latin.

Words are precision-tools. You *can*, in a makeshift sort of way, use a chisel as a screwdriver; but eventually you will ruin the chisel, and it may not do the screw much good, either. I would not presume to 'correct' the mistakes, foibles and quirks of others. You can tell someone his flies are open, and he will thank you for it; but point out a habit of speech and pronunciation (such as we all acquire at various times without noticing) and he may never speak to you again.

Some of the material in this book is based on talks given on BBC Radio Three and Radio Four. I have also made use of, and amplified, articles and book reviews which have appeared in *The Listener*, as well as my *Endpieces* from that magazine. The fact that *Endpiece* used to share a page with the crossword brought a response from delightfully unexpected quarters, most notably some touching, unsolicited words of encouragement from Leonard Bernstein — a true maestro of words as well as music and a life-long devotee of *The Listener*, which he rightly described (in his letter to me) as 'the best-edited paper in our language'. A few of the subjects in the following pages were previously touched on in *The Liverpool Daily Post*; and in one or two sections I have had second or additional thoughts about material used in *Keep Taking the Tabloids* (Pan Books, 1983) or in *Music through the Looking Glass* (Routledge, 1984).

My thanks go to the many listeners and readers — too many to list them all — for their stimulating, helpful or encouraging comments, but I must single out Julian Budden, D. J. Enright, Professor Peter Fellgett, Roy Fuller, Daniel Jones, Robin Lustig, John Lyons, Robert S. Morrison, Robert Orledge, David Pollak, Daphne Russell, Dorothy Stanton and Dr D. T. Whiteside. Also the editor and deputy editor of *The Listener*, Russell Twisk and Richard Gilbert, and their team of virtuoso sub-editors, who generally kept me in check and spotted errors or inconsistencies. There is nothing worse, in a book of this kind, than to get one's facts wrong. But mistakes there are sure to be, and I have therefore left a page or two blank for readers to add their corrections, improvements and additions. At Elm Tree Books, Kyle Cathie and my editor, Caroline Taggart, are owed gratitude for steering me into the right paths and saving me from my own over-enthusiasm.

Among members of the BBC, thanks are due to staff and producers who have added their suggestions (or have patiently allowed themselves to be questioned about trivial points), among them Gillian Hush, Fraser Steel, Kay Jamieson, Graham Melville-Mason, Dr Janet Morgan, Mark Rowlinson, Dr Ernest Warburton, Reg Brookes; and Piers Burton-Page and Jim Black (who are in charge of announcers on Radios Three and Four, respectively). Also to *The Liverpool Daily Post*, which in spite of its recent slide into tabloid style still offers a unique coverage of events on Merseyside, that nationally so much maligned area, a service no full-colour, new-technology, mass-circulation national paper can provide.

The cartoons for chapter openings are by Marie-Hélène Jeeves; cartoons on pages 98, 136, 143, 149, 175, 209 and 210 courtesy of *Punch*; photographs on pages 186 and 189 courtesy of the Photo Source Ltd. The poem by A. P. Herbert on page 215 is quoted by permission of A. P. Watt Ltd.

Community, *environment*, *neighbourhood*, *project*, *action*, *interaction*, *consciousness* . . . and of course *ethnic* (from a Greek word meaning 'of the people' but which has now been twisted into 'belonging to a non-white minority group which is, or thinks it is *disadvantaged*' – and there's another word to conjure with . . .)

Shuffle and combine a few of these buzz words and you, too, can write advertisements for your sharing, caring equal opportunities council. It is an industry that is fast getting out of hand, a giant inverted pyramid of highly-paid appointments, usually politically *orient*[*at*]*ed* (the jargon is catching), vague as to actual function – and a job for life. For example, the egregious 'Deputy' Leader of the Militant Liverpool City Council, who made such misery for the city in 1985, held a full-time social-worker's job with another council, for which he received a vast salary while seldom if ever making an appearance there, let alone visiting many claimants. Applicants for such a sinecure must be *committed*, *motivated* or *involved*, all in a cheerfully intransitive way: no matter whether they are committed *to*, motivated *by* or involved *in* anything. But they must be *positive*. Some, like those seeking out injustices, are even required to be *aggressive*, or *abrasive*. Above all, their politics must be well to the left of the left.

To judge from my cuttings file there is no shortage of jobs in the industry. Soon there will be more people looking after people than there are people to look after. Wanted: COUNSELLORS to counsel, doubtless in a one to one situation and about anything from marriage to grief. Sheffield employs BEREAVEMENT COUNSELLORS (jolly decent and caring, but this is a job which used to be best done without payment by a member of the family); and I hope Rochdale Borough Council got the DELINQUENCY MANAGER they were looking for, and that he is managing nicely. Also wanted, STIMU-LATORS to stimulate, 'COORDINATORS' to co-ordinate and ACTIVATORS to activate: whom or what is seldom stated. OUTREACH WORKERS must not only be able to reach out but to 'relate': the object is no object. 'Workers' must also, of course, be 'conscious', in the customary, intransitive manner. The Inner London Education Authority wants (or wanted) a NEIGHBOURHOOD SPORTS MOTIVATOR (who provides the 'motivation' for kids to kick a ball around?), a MOTHER TONGUE INSPECTOR (say 'Aah'?) and armies of EDUCATIONAL PSYCHOLOGISTS, now springing up in every education authority. These are required to deal with what we used to call duffers but are now euphemised as 'underachievers'. After all, you must not let a duffer know that he is a duffer, in case he feels disadvantaged by his disadvantage – or might decide to make an effort after all and put a psychologist out of work. At the end of it all these poor, over-fussed-over children are still unable to 'achieve' (let alone ask awkward questions about transitives); but they will have learnt to call splashing about in puddles 'creative waterplay'. Paddington – the council, not the bear – would like to hear from you if you are a potential TENANT LIAISON OFFICER, perhaps a person whose job is to snoop out illicit liaisons among 'unwaged claimants'.

As farm work in the fields declined, so openings have multiplied for FIELD WORKERS who, however, trudge city pavements; and although it is heartening that the state cares so deeply, the number of children battered to death by brutish parents seems to be increasing, not diminishing. This system has evolved its own language, too tedious to describe in detail. A social worker, speaking on the BBC, sharply interrupted her interviewer. 'We do *not* call it "baby battering",' she reproved him. '*We* call it "non accidental injury".' They also speak of some evil, tattooed bully as 'my client', while he, in turn, refers to 'my probation officer' as proprietorily as if he were speaking of 'my lawyer' or 'my bank manager'.

Much verbal rot emanates also from the appointments departments of academe, where, after all, sociology was invented.* I see from my pile of cuttings that Sheffield Poly offers a post described as MA IN WOMEN'S STUDIES (and in these punctuation-starved days one must, I suppose, be grateful that even if ma gets no full-stops, the women are given a possessive apostrophe). Cranfield College of

* 'Sociology' is not as recent a coinage as one might suppose, though the word was almost immediately considered suspect: *Blackwood's Magazine*, 1843: 'These are to constitute a new science, to be called Social Ethics, or Sociology . . .' and in 1851 *Fraser's Magazine* already attacks the word: 'The new science of sociology, as it is barbarously termed.'

Technology can give you a POSTGRADUATESHIP IN REMOTE SENSING (perhaps they should get together with the new chair of Parapsychology at Edinburgh); and our Liverpool Catering Training College offers a TWO-YEAR SANDWICH COURSE IN FOOD TECHNOLOGY (a steak-and-kidney course would doubtless take much longer). The Scottish university of St Andrews wants to appoint a suitable applicant to its CHAIR OF LEARNING DIFFICULTIES. 'We used to call it the Dunce's Stool,' writes the reader who sent me this example. Closer study of the advertisement reveals that it is a very worthwhile project, for the chair has been endowed by a charity devoted to research into mental handicap. Only the title seems to be somewhat unimaginative ... ('Darling, I want you to meet Hamish, he's our new Professor of Learning Difficulties'!) University advertisements from all over the country are now calling for NEW BLOOD LECTURESHIPS; but if you are a haematologist they're not for you. It is some newly-invented term the population at large is not supposed to know, or perhaps enquire about. Even the student unions are at it: Reading University Students' Union Community Action Group (and there's another sharing-caring mouthful for you) is looking for a FULL-TIME CO-ORDINATOR. The blurb that goes with it is totally incomprehensible, but it suggests that among Reading University students 'community action' (whatever that is) comes before studying.

When English words fail, there is always pseudo-French or needless German: 'Lincolnshire and Humberside Arts wish to appoint a DANCE ANIMATEUR' (whereas East Midlands Arts, not an Equal Opportunities Employer, it seems, would be satisfied with a mere DANCE FELLOW); and 'Recording Engineers', or 'Studio Managers' as the BBC has long called them, are not good enough for Sussex University: there you can learn to become one in the Department of *Tonmeister Studies*. After all, why use a simple English word or two when you can dazzle someone with a foreign one? There is a job for you as DEPUTY HEAD PAINTER at the Yvonne Arnaud Theatre, unless the job has been filled and there already is a person busily painting heads.

There is a job for an ADVISER TO THE CHIEF DRAUGHTSMAN. Now, if the Chief Draughtsman is any good he shouldn't need anyone to advise him in his own trade. (But is it not a well-known fact that every politician who is anybody, from the Prime Minister downwards, employs one or more 'Political Advisers'? I wonder who is Sir Yehudi Menuhin's Musical Adviser?) There are jobs for CASEWORKERS, CARE-WORKERS, RESOURCE WORKERS, LEISURE WORKERS and DRAMA WORKERS. At the ILEA there is a vacancy for a DETACHED YOUTH WORKER. And COWORKERS (not the kind of 'field work' they may suggest at first glance), who get much money but no hyphen. Too much work and no play may make Jack a dull boy, but he could combine both if he applied for one of the many jobs of PLAY WORKER. There are, needless to say, hundreds of jobs for RIGHTS WORKERS, hired to tell people of their 'rights'. But, equally needless to say, no Duties Workers.

Job creation seems to have invaded every field of human endeavour. Not so long ago, the London Philharmonic Orchestra was administered by the principal trumpeter with the help of a girl secretary. The orchestra manager and librarian, too, were playing members of the orchestra. Now, every orchestra seems to employ not only a General Manager but also Concert Managers, Orchestral Supervisors, Registrars, Financial Controllers, Programme Conveners, Sponsorship Administrators and other splendidly-titled officers in full-time positions. Even the humble Orchestral Porter who carries the drums and pushes the piano into place (in the Liverpool Philharmonic for many years a Scouser called Wagner) has been elevated to the rank of Platform Manager; there are never fewer than two of them. And when publicity is needed for a concert there are, of course, Press Officers and Publicity Managers to talk to the press. In the overmanned National Health Service, too, when a hospital bulletin about a patient is called for, an official, properly unionised by NALGO or NUPE or one of the other conflicting bodies, is available to deal with enquiries. It used to be the medical superintendent or the nearest available doctor or matron who would give what information they could. All this now falls to the task of a specialist spokesman – who, when an especially news-worthy person is being treated, suddenly achieves nationwide fame through television exposure. *Punch* once carried a cartoon showing a parent leaving a toy shop with his small son, who is proudly clutching a box labelled 'Little Doctor Set'. The caption reads, '. . . and – who knows – maybe one day even a Hospital Administrator.'

Advertisements for a 'Girl Friday', which used to be a favourite euphemism for ill-paid jobs that involved unskilled duties like making tea or acting as receptionist, are no longer merely silly, they are illegal. These are now Persons Friday. The Equal Opportunities industry itself has to employ more and more caseworkers, fieldworkers, etc. to deal with complaints from aggrieved (or publicity-seeking) women who want to sue for damages because they were not interviewed for the post of masseur to Chelsea Football Club. The obligatory shibboleth which appears at the head or foot of almost every public or private appointments offer, 'We are an Equal Opportunity Employer', is itself often belied in the text. Thus Harrow Borough Council, seeking an Allotments Officer, qualifies the 'Equal Opportunity' line with the ominous warning, 'This post is subject to LMGSC ringfence procedure. Applications are restricted to employees of the GLC and London Local Authorities.' Many Equal Opportunity Employers state ingenuously, 'Preference will be given to applicants of ethnic minorities' (by which they do not mean Swedes, Italians or Greeks, but blacks). Some equality!

Another curious, slightly sinister, phenomenon has emerged from the race relations industry (and heaven knows there is plenty of discrimination, both overt and covert, against minorities): when members of 'ethnic' groups are selected and engaged for their jobs they automatically qualify for the description of 'Community Leaders'. I was under the impression that in a free country 'leaders' were elected, not engaged as paid employees?

Even the BBC Singers, advertising a job for a Soprano, have to add, 'The BBC is an Equal Opportunity Employer', thus implying that applications from castrati (or Boy George) will be sympathetically considered. Some unions insist on there being paid EQUALITY OFFICERS on industrial premises, so that any suspected injustices may be sniffed out: there are even SEXUAL ORIENTATION OFFICERS in some union-dominated establishments to ensure that applicants or

Following expansion we now require a
MARKET DEVELOPMENT EXECUTIVE
to join our team to implement a sales strategy

Business Development Officer
(Business Advice)

ADMINISTRATIVE AND
CUSTOMER SUPPORT
TRAINEE

CO-OPERATIVE
DEVELOPMENT OFFICER

MEDIA RESOURCES ASSISTANT

British Museum (Natural History)

Head of Visitor Resources
to be responsible primarily for the Museum

DIRECTOR OF LEARNING RESOURCES BRANCH

MANAGEMENT EFFECTIVENESS UNIT
The Council is establishing a small group of officers with the skills and
experience required to carry out efficiency and effectiveness reviews of

CITY OF PETERBOROUGH
(Equal Opportunity Employer)
DEPARTMENT OF LEISURE
AND AMENITIES
require a

COMMUNITY
WORKER

Leisure & Recreation — Parks
Resources Manager

COMMISSION FOR LOCAL ADMINISTRATION IN ENGLAND
COMPLAINT EXAMINER
ocal Ombudsman investigates complaints alleging maladministration by local

CITY OF YORK
LEISURE SERVICES DEVELOPMENT OFFICER

LIAISON/INFORMATION OFFICER
Person with experience of information work required to help strengthen links
with 31 GLAD borough associations. Background in voluntary organisations

Research & Monitoring Assistant

COMPUTER LIAISON OFFICER

Bradmore Kids Workshop
Playleader in Charge
£5,841-£6,138 p.a. inc.
(plus unsocial ho—

Ref.: RAP. 44.
Recreation Assistants

COMMUNICATIONS MANAGER
required in headquarters of international charity. Can you—
the challenge of this demanding and varied posi—

RECREATION DEPARTMENT
ASSISTANT CHIEF RECREATION OFFICER

CLWYD COUNTY COUNCIL
County Planning and Estates Department
COUNTRYSIDE INTERPRETATION
AND INFORMATION OFFICER

COUNTRYSIDE INTERPRETER
£7,815-£9,339
Scale 5/6
Inclusive of London Weighting.
To be responsible for developing and implementing an ambitious and
comprehensive countryside interpretation and information programme
aimed at "Opening up the Park" to the public. Applicants must be good
communicators with considerable relevant experience.

Knitting Technologist
Negotiable salary   North Notts
This is an opportunity to join a leading knitwear producer as a cut
and sew technologist fully conversant with flat bed machinery.

YVONNE ARNAUD THEATRE
requires

DEPUTY HEAD PAINTER

ASSISTANT DIRECTOR OF LEISURE SERVICES
Culture Division
£15,573 — £16,626

TAMPAX
LIMITED

CREATIVE
COMMUNITY ARTS
WORKER

MALE BANK CLERKS
We are looking for aggressive young men to join
our expanding branch operations. Applicants

PROJECT ENGINEERS

Applications are invited from qualified
engineers, preferably with an electro-
mechanical bias, who have an analyti-
cal approach to industrial problems
and experience in line-management.

COMMUNITY HOUSING WORKER

ERECTION SUPERVISORS
We have vacancies for Erection Supervisors and Forem
for men, preferably with a Drawing Office Training, who have
experience in the erection of all classes of Structural Steel
work and in Site administration and the control of labour.

HOUSING ADVISER (2 posts)

Temporary Part-Time Intake Social Worker

SPECIAL NEEDS OFFICER

Development Worker
Under 5's

PRIVATE SECRETARY TO THE NATIONAL SECRETARY
The National Secretary of the NUM requires a private/confidential

MAINTENANCE ADMINISTRATIVE OFFICER

ENERGY CAMPAIGNER

ASSISTANT PROGRAMMED MAINTENANCE OFFICER

CHURCH ARMY HOUSING
requires
TWO DEVELOPMENT OFFICERS

EMPLOYMENT
DEVELOPMENT WORKER
(APS £7791)
Wanted for community employment project
in Sparkbrook, Birmingham, to develop
employment initiatives, especially on

NEW ENTERPRISE ADVISOR
An individual capable of motivation
at all levels and with a broad

CITY OF WESTMINSTER
Housing Benefits Section
**Team Leader
(Housing Benefits)**

SMALL BUSINESS
CO-OPERATIVE DEVELOPMENT OFFICER
REQUIRED IN CARDIFF

EXPERIENCED
HOUSING RESEARCHER
to work for the Tenants of Brent.

RESEARCH ASSISTANT
Tool Support for Requirements Analysis

ETHNIC ARTS DEVELOPMENT OFFICER (Ref. 843)
A new and highly challenging position in developing the existing policies

7

WELFARE/EMPLOYMENT RIGHTS SPECIALIST

We are seeking:

Two Committee Co-ordinators

£10,638 — £11,2

Support Group Co-ordinator

To take over the running of 2 of th
plus subsidiary committees and group

Information Services Co-ordinator

Management Consultancy

EMPLOYMENT LIAISON OFFICER

required immediately for challenging

VENDOR INSPECTION CO-ORDINATOR

TOURING EXHIBITIONS CO-ORDINATOR

ELECTRICITY NEGOTIATOR

Work Experience Co-Ordinator

DELINQUENCY MANAGEMENT – INTERMEDIATE TREATMENT

JOBMATE CO-ORDINATOR

SOUTH LONDON

NEIGHBOURHOOD HOUSING OFFICERS (ETHNIC)

NEIGHBOURHOOD YOUTH AND COMMUNITY WORKER

CO-ORDINATOR – INTERMEDIATE TREATMENT

NEIGHBOURHOOD WORKER

COMMUNITY RELATIONS OFFICER (Education)

Alone in London Service

RESETTLEMENT WORKER

COMMUNITY RELATIONS OFFICER (Employment)

COMMUNITY RELATIONS OFFICER (Social Policy)

AP4-SO1: £8,523 — £11,166
(inclusive of London Weighting)

The three successful applicants will be members of a team under the
direction of the Senior Community Relations Officer and will be

COMMUNITY RELATIONS OFFICER
(COMMUNITY DEVELOPMENT)

To be responsible for implementation of policies and activities to promote equal opportunity in the
spheres of education and social welfare and health. Also to encourage the development and
strengthening of self help initiative amongst the mainly Pakistani and Bangladeshi minority
communities.

The demanding post is suitable only for those with initiative and an acute social awareness. The
appointee should have had experience of race relations work related to education and

NEIGHBOURHOOD OFFICER

COMMUNITY RELATIONS OFFICER

officer, who will be the sole officer of the Council, will be
responsible in the Executive Committee for implementing

YOUTH AND COMMUNITY SERVICE
Kestrel Project

YOUTH AND COMMUNITY WORKER

SENIOR COMMUNITY WORKERS (3 posts)

ADVISORY OFFICER
—WEST MIDLANDS (Based in Birmingham)

NORTHERN RACE TRAINING UNIT
An Equal Opportunity Employer

RACE TRAINER

IMESDOWN (SWINDON) & DISTRICT COUNCIL
FOR RACIAL EQUALITY

RACISM AWARENESS TRAINER
AP4 – SO1 (£7545-£9231)

Applications are invited from people, probably in their late 20s and upwards,
interested in developing a new field of work on racism awareness and related

busy neighbourhood advice centre
in Peckham serving a multi-ethnic
community requires experienced

ADVICE WORKER

ETHNIC MINORITIES HOUSING PROJECT WORKER

MINORITIES' ARTS ADVISORY SERVICE
North West

RESOURCE WORKER

required to work with artists from the ethnic
minorities, specialise in non-Western art
forms and administration to acquire, dips

Inspector for Mother Tongue (Bilingual Education)

Development Officer with Ethnic Minority Senior Citizens

WELFARE BENEFITS ADVISER

CAMBRIDGE AND DISTRICT CITIZENS' ADVICE BUREAU

WELFARE BENEFITS ADVISER

1 ADMINISTRATOR
1 OUTREACH DEVELOPMENT WORKER
All positions are 18 hours per week.

SHELTERED HOUSING AND SPECIAL PROJECTS OFFICER

To be responsible for the establishment and supervision of a Central Control
alarm system for residents in our sheltered housing, and for advice and

Outreach Worker

PLASTICS PROCESSING INDUSTRY TRAINING BOARD

TRAINING ADVISER

We require a Training Adviser to provide a wide
range of advisory services on manpower and training

SYLHETI-SPEAKING WOMEN'S RIGHTS WORKER

TENANT LIAISON OFFICER

HOUSING BENEFITS ADVISER
circa £8,500

ADVICE WORKER

An experienced Advice Worker is required for this
busy inner London Bureau. Post is for dave's week

EXPERIENCED SOCIAL WORKER
Salary Scale £8,712 — £10,242

to join a small team where increasingly the emphasis will be on
Non-Accidental Injury situations.

INFORMATION OFFICER/CASEWORKER
—WOLVERHAMPTON TRIBUNAL UNIT

FURTHER AND HIGHER EDUCATION ADVISER
£14,865 – £16,059

HOUNSLOW LAW CENTRE
requires an Asian language speaking

ADVICE WORKER

COUNTY PERSONNEL DEPARTMENT

ETHNIC RELATIONS/EQUAL OPPORTUNITIES ADVISER
£14,148 to £15,198 per annum

A new post to support the work of the County Council to
promote equal opportunities among the existing workforce
and job applicants and ensure that unfair discrimination is
not practised in the provision of the Council's services in
general.

Action Aid Programme Director

Full-Time Advice Worker
PLAISTOW CAB

ADMINISTRATIVE AND CUSTOMER SUPPORT TRAINEE

Project Officers
Department of Lands
and Physical Planning

ASSISTANT DEVELOPMENT EXECUTIVES

NEW TECHNOLOGY TUTOR

LIBRARY PROJECT LEADER

Development Engineer (Export)

8

employees know which way to turn if the much advertised promise 'This position is open to persons of all races and sexual orientations' (*All?* Rubber Fetishists and Underwear Stealers?) is transgressed. But there also lurk SEXUAL HARASS-MENT OFFICERS, waiting to inform Big Brother if any calendars of nude women are displayed in the workshop; or of a male paying a robust compliment to a female worker, like saying 'Hi, gorgeous!'

Beware of accidental discrimination. A Police Authority wants to pay good money for a DARK ROOM ASSISTANT, adding ominously, 'No Colour'. Similarly, Nordico Ltd has a vacancy for a THIN FILM TECHNOLOGIST; Liverpool Health Authority seeks a STERILE SUPPLY MANAGER, the City of Newcastle a SMALL FIRMS OFFICER (will candidates be passed through a ring until one of suitable size is found?); and there are ambiguous calls for a RADIOACTIVE WASTE MANAGER (get out your geiger counters) and an EDIBLE OIL ENGINEER (yum-yum). Hyphens seem to be in short supply everywhere. The firm of Bolton and Paul need an ERECTION SUPERVISOR (sex not stated); and Tampax Limited PROJECT ENGINEERS, without stating the nature of the projects.

Clwyd County Council wants a TEACHER OF MUSIC SCALE 1 (keep it simple, bach), Monmouthshire County Council is looking for DUTCH ELM DISEASE INSPECTORS - TWO POSTS (and if the disease has got that far would they have much left to inspect?) Workers of the World, unite. You have nothing to lose but your splendid titles. There is no shortage of work in all manner of 'workshops' – an overworked word meaning a place (usually straight out of Pseuds' Corner) where anything but manual work is done: my cuttings collection of advertisements starts with a BIRTH CONTROL WORKSHOP and ends with an invitation from Bradford Diocesan authorities to a WORSHIP WORKSHOP: jobs to look after us, not so much from the cradle to the grave, or even from womb to tomb, but from the erection to the resurrection.

Applicants for any of the positions and openings listed above may wish to consult a Dissertation by R. D. Carter of the University of Michigan which propounds the fascinating theory that people who go for interviews and *smile* generally get on better than those who scowl and sulk. His paper is called 'Gazing and Smiling and the Communication of Interpersonal Affect in a Quasi-Interview Situation'. He explains (somewhat tautologously in view of the very explicit title), 'This Dissertation deals with the nonverbal communication of interpersonal affect ("liking-disliking", "approval-disapproval", "warmth-coldness", "friendliness-unfriendliness"), in face-to-face interaction. In experimental research, affective non-verbal behaviors treated as independent variables are described as serving an influence function (influencing through their stimulus value the behavior of a subject). As dependent variables they serve an indicative function (indicating something about the affective reactions of a subject to experimental manipulations). A conceptualization is proposed that links the influence function to the behavioral notion of a generalized conditioned reinforcer and the indicative function to the idea of operant performances.'

What did we do before we had an 'environment'? This apparently now indispensable word has acquired so many meanings as to be itself almost meaningless. The provenance is sound enough, from the French for 'round about'; and to environ meant to form a ring round, surround or encircle. But when you read in the press or hear someone say on the radio (I may be imagining this but it's usually in a nasal kind of local-government voice), 'The environment we breathe . . .' he clearly only means air. 'Environing' to the town planner means making a place conform to his idea of pleasant surroundings. On Merseyside we have warning notices saying ENVIRONMENTAL AREA: NO MOTORS, which presumably means an environment where pedestrians can breathe fume-free air – I mean *environment*. Officials we used to know as Health or Sanitary Inspectors have been given such imposing titles as 'Environmental Health Inspector'; perhaps understandably, since 'sanitary', the ancient word meaning healthy, had been gradually going down the drain (so to speak) and become associated with the general disposal of human waste. So a new euphemism was in any case overdue. On the other hand, the Department (and Minister)

for the Environment – well, one would hope they are *for* it – are not concerned with health but represent what was for several hundred years known as the Ministry/Department of Works, dealing with public parks, buildings and ancient monuments. Then again, what used to be known as Parks and Gardens has in the headlong rush for municipal renaming been grandly christened the Department of Recreation and Open Spaces. Where I live it includes the cemeteries as well as playgrounds: plenty of open space but not much chance of recreation, unless it is in hope of re-creation on the day of judgment.

What did we have before acid rain? Whatever it was there must have been a lot more of it about than there is now. I have an aerial view of the centre of Liverpool taken in the 1880s, or rather, an attempted aerial view. Factory chimneys sprout from streets that have long since become not only environmental but strictly residential, and belch even more black smoke than the thousands of domestic coal-burning fires. (As a result the artist sitting in his balloon moored over Bold Street was able to save himself a great deal of work by obscuring the detail with clouds of swirling black smoke.) But no-one complained of acid rain, for it had not yet been named. The citizens were presumably as healthy as anyone was in Victorian days. But now that we are so fortunate as to have a great deal of environmental control (that includes smokeless zones), grassland, crops and woods everywhere are said to be dying of acid rain. German environmentalists have even coined a poetic word that could come straight out of a Schubert song: *Waldessterben*, 'forestdyings'. But elsewhere scientists have been forced shamefacedly to admit that what they identified as yellow rain had in fact been bees' poo. A few years back there was a spray-can scare. The propellant used in deodorants, scents and shaving-foam was supposed to rise heavenwards, clog up the Van Allen belts and condemn us all to living in a hazy 'greenhouse effect environment'. But this particular environmental craze seems to have fallen by the wayside. And how did we manage to live all these years with the killer asbestos? Not so long ago I used to saw, drill and file the stuff, as would any handyman householder; lie under my car to wrap asbestos cloth round the exhaust and get its dust in my eyes and hair. Every housewife had her frayed ironing-board pad, and no doubt liberally breathed in clouds of asbestos. Are we all under sentence of death? There is no doubt that many unfortunate people working in asbestos factories with the blue variety (actually grey, just as on ironing-boards) have developed a dreadful disease, and too many have died a painful death from it; and that the industry was for far too long either ignorant or careless of the dangers. Asbestosis was in fact described and so named as long ago as 1927 in the *British Medical Journal*, and 'recognised as a serious industrial disease' in the *Lancet* a year later. According to my reference books there is also Cork Worker's Lung, Farmer's Lung, Furrier's Lung, Pigeon Breeder's Lung, Mushroom Worker's Lung, Cheesewasher's Lung, Fishmeal Worker's Lung (and even Thatcher's Lung, caused by straw dust, not Parliamentary Question Time). Yet in 1938/9 the Government was happy to issue every civilian with a gasmask containing an asbestos filter. Are we now to believe that even if the Germans didn't get us, the asbestos would have? I very much doubt it. But the warnings have gone out: Wrap up your Wartime Gas Mask and hand it to (yes!) your Environmental Control Officer. Someone finds a bit of old asbestos lagging, and schools, hospitals and underground stations are closed. Not long ago the entrance hall of Broadcasting House got the full environmental treatment, with workers in space suits chasing away would-be visitors as if they had inadvertently entered a nuclear reactor. I don't blame the unions: the temptation must be great to screw a little extra money out of employers for real or imagined dangers. And . . . I hate to worry you . . . but this book, like many others, is printed on stock containing a proportion of recycled paper. It is good environmental practice – but you never know where it's been.

How we laughed when we heard a NALGO official, interviewed on Radio 4, say 'Our members have been scapegoated . . .' But then it rang a niggling little bell somewhere in my *déjà-lu* subconscious. Sure enough, the little *Dictionary of Psychiatry* by H., L. and B. Thakurdas (M.T.P.

Press) reveals that it is an accepted term of that particular medical discipline, coined in 1943: 'Scapegoating is a phenomenon wherein some of the aggressive energies of a person or group are focused upon another individual, group or object.' *Journal of Abnormal and Social Psychology* (Veltfort and Lee). So now we know that the NALGO man had the full weight of medical, if not linguistic, authority behind him; though inclusion in a dictionary merely records precedent and makes it not one jot less ugly a back-formation.

Even as I write this, the *Today* programme brings on an expert who says 'We want an urban development agency that will laserbeam resources . . .' All he meant was 'concentrate', and although he may make *Out-takes* in *The Listener*, like our scapegoater, I hope it won't get into the dictionaries for some time yet; and I was delighted to hear Brian Redhead giving him a proper tut-tutting for it. Yet it is no worse than 'pinpointing', only newer. When gold-hunters first went 'prospecting' in 1848 people complained bitterly, even though it was merely a revival of an old word ('Man being a prudent and prospecting creature, hath the advantage of all other creatures in his foreseeing faculty', 1681). Nouns-turned-verbs, like 'to engineer' or 'to motor' have all been attacked in their time. Now, when services are 'axed' and people are not shot but 'gunned down', no-one complains. Being scapegoated is no worse than being disadvantaged, fancied, targeted (often with a superfluous t, supposedly to aid pronunciation, like rivetted or facetted), or – thanks to computers – accessed, even randomaccessed.

Rubbishing has had a good innings lately. Almost everyone accused the government of 'rubbishing' the churches' report on inner cities (why inner? what's inner about Tottenham or Handsworth?), and a very satisfying word it is, too, coming from a noun already used in a dismissively exclamatory way: *rubbish!* But too many people leaping upon a new word always gets one's goat, or even scapegoat.

Other compounds and back-formations which have been decried at one time or another are carpetbagging, wirepulling, logrolling, etc., perhaps by traditionalists who then solemnly say 'I must go and deadhead my roses.' There has been a lot of ratecapping about recently, but people who in previous ages went pickpocketing or footpadding became muggers instead. I've heard back-formations like whipping-boyed; and those who in the 19th century were shanghaied are now hijacked or skyjacked. Seajackers have so far, however, remained plain pirates.

Debriefing still worries me. Briefing was at first restricted to lawyers, the action of their being given instructions. During the last war air-crews were briefed before going on their missions; and when they returned they were questioned about what they had seen and done, which became known as debriefing. It struck me as a rather loose term, as you can't really have your earlier brief removed, taken away or cancelled out, which is what the *de-* prefix implies. It was really the other way round: air-crews returning with whatever useful information they had gleaned in fact briefed those who had earlier briefed *them*. Debriefing was soon in general use, but now has been strained too far, meaning nothing more than an interrogation, e.g. of eye-witnesses who had never been briefed in the first place, such as survivors of a hijack or other disaster. (Of course, you *can* still be debriefed in the sense of being debagged or, if a priest, unfrocked.)

A correspondent of mine was recently discombubulated ('disturbed, upset, disconcerted', 1834) by my harmless comments about 'bombshell' (see page 164). I do not question the ancient pedigree of the word; merely deplore the fact that journalists seem unable to find any other synonym for a big surprise, while the rest of us do. Which in turn reminds me of a story about Noah Webster. The great lexicographer was – or was supposed to be – at work on his dictionary, when Mrs Webster unexpectedly entered his study and found him in the arms of their housemaid. 'Oh Mr Webster!' she exclaimed, 'I am surprised!' Webster raised himself up on one elbow and said, with all the dignity he could muster in that position, 'No, my dear. *We* are surprised. *YOU* are astonished.'

It is a brave man who makes statements like: 'Haydn was the first composer to use the cor anglais in a symphony.' Someone, somewhere, is sure to find an earlier instance. In the same way I have learnt not to pick on some verbal coinage new to me and declare: 'There's no such word.' There are few original inventions; and, anyway, the coiner can always retort: 'Well, there is now.' I was once unwise enough to state in something I wrote for the *TLS* that 'the Royals' was a faintly anti-royal neologism. Someone quickly pointed out what I could have learnt from the *OED* had I bothered to check: Fanny Burney used it in 1788, though in a factual, not a dismissive way. Call little Prince Harry a 'Royalet' and you may be accused of being twee, like some tabloid's women's editor. But you could ward off critics by quoting Thomas Fuller (1650) and several other ancient precedents.

Someone wrote to *The Listener* taking issue with the use of the verb 'to craft', only to be righted by another reader, who had bothered to look up the word in the *OED*. In the sense of 'to make or devise skilfully', 'crafting' goes back to the early 15th century. I purposely used 'righted' above because if anyone complained I could quote the *OED* in my support, for it gives usages in this sense from AD 971 to 1440. But as 'righting' afterwards became associated more with setting something or someone upright than aright, I would normally avoid it. All the same, I could not bring myself to speak (as people on the BBC now do all the time), still less to write, about someone 'hosting' a chat show or 'guesting' in a concert. Or to say (as someone recently did), 'He programmed the symphony in London': life is not so hectic on Radio 3 that one needs to skimp a couple of words.

English is grammatically simple. There are no endings to learn as in French or German. But the way one can turn nouns into verbs tends to make things harder, not easier, for the foreigner. Add to this the curious way identical words change their meaning according to the placing of the stress ('he was dogged by misfortune in the face of dogged determination') and the learner gets hopelessly confused. Some of this confusion is shared by natives. Even famous actors and producers have failed to note Shakespeare's distinction between '*con*jure' (as in magic tricks, to rhyme with 'sponger'), and 'con*jure*' with the stress at the end and rhyming with 'pure'. A perfectly entrancing notice in a Greek tourist spot warns: 'It is forbidden to entrance the monastery in shorts or indecent clothing.' Regularly on the BBC nowadays, newsreaders '*dis*count the possibility' instead of dis*counting* it, as if they were talking about cut-price socks; they tell us that some country has been '*ann*exed' by another, and generally ignore useful noun/verb stress differences: *es*cort/es*cort*, *ex*port/ex*port*, *pro*test/pro*test*, *con*test/con*test*, *orn*ament/orna*ment*, *re*ject/re*ject*, etc. I suspect they are products of 'free-expression' English teaching and have little experience of real poetry. A person who has read aloud Matthew Arnold's lines: 'Too fast we live, too much are tried,/Too harass'd to attain/Wordsworth's sweet calm, or Goethe's wide/And luminous view to gain' will never put a thumping stress on the *ass* of harass.

Newspaper sub-editors live too fast to bother about verb/noun distinctions, and tell us in their hastily devised headlines: FLIES TO HAVE TWINS IN IRELAND, or IRA BOMB GUTS FACTORY, something which is made worse by their reluctance or inability to punctuate: DO YOU WANT A WOMAN VICAR? Word-blindness and -deafness seem now to be almost endemic among the young. People who use 'row' (to rhyme with 'cow') as a verb (as in 'the couple rowed all the way across the Atlantic') see words better than they hear them in their mind's ear.

I was going to have a tilt at the neologism 'mix'. An American abomination, I thought, which is no improvement on 'mixture'. But luckily I checked, and of course it was there in the *OED* all along. At first it meant 'dung, filth' (like the related German *Mist*), but was already used in its 'new' sense by the Countess of Pembroke in 1586 to praise a broken consort: 'O make harmonious mix of voice and string.' According to Nancy Mitford, 'writing-paper' is to be preferred to 'note-paper', which she condemns as a crude, non-U Americanism. Well, it was good enough for Mrs Carlyle in 1849; the Hon. lady would have been horrified to hear that Charles Lamb wrote of a 'notelet' in 1824.

But now I stick my neck out and state there is no such word as 'importantly', over-familiar from the gaspingly adverbial opening noise: 'More importantly . . .' which is so trendily epidemic among today's communicators. A pompous councillor may strut importantly, but there the adverb ends. 'Importantly' is would-be posh, a nob's adverb, first introduced by those vaguely aware that words are somehow more impressive if they have a -ly at the end, by people who would ruin the expression 'box clever' by genteelifying it into 'box cleverly'.

It is now fashionable to say that there is no right and no wrong way, that usage determines correctness. This may be so for vocabulary. If someone decides to call a small furry creature with a long tail a camel, and a big animal with a hump a mouse, and enough people do likewise, that's what these quadrupeds will be called; though for a time confusion will reign, and some Arabs may try to mount mice. I deplore the trend, not because I'm against progress, but because words are precision tools. You *can* use a chisel as a screwdriver, but it will never be the same again. However, where word-stress is concerned, there is usually only *one* right way. Once again I blame some of our pathetically inadequate teachers who make their charges produce home-made doggerel instead of learning and, equally important, reading aloud poetry by the old masters; and only *then* encourage them to write in their own manner.

My guess is that the false-stress revolution began with 'our own correspondents' abroad, when long-distance lines were always bad and reporters had to shout to make themselves heard. What we now get is a kind of spoken shouting, with the strongest stress reserved for the last word, regardless of the fact that this usually turns the sense upside-down. It is much cultivated by ITN reporters, and even more by some local-radio newsreaders who think that a Dalek monotone makes their report sound important (though the real urgency is to get on as quickly as possible with the next commercial or pop 'dedication').

It's hard to describe this last-word-stress intonation: something like a crescendo followed by a final dropping of the pitch on the last word or syllable, which is somehow elongated into a sort of downward-infected moo – and I mean no disrespect to cows. Think of the accomplished Alan Whicker. His reports are always neatly divided into phrases all the same length, each with an identical intonation in the form of an arc, each last word landing up on the same note, though he uses a final diminuendo, not a moo.

Try saying aloud a few of these BBC/TV gems: 'He is not a household name to most *men*' (. . . but dogs, cockroaches and women always swear by him?); 'He is looking to his colleagues to support his *case*' (a TV reporter, as a group of Ministers was seen filing into 10 Downing Street, each carrying his official briefcase); 'The Duke of Edinburgh is very fond of wild *life*'; 'She bought the property with royalties from her children's *stories*' (or was it *children's* stories?); 'The thieves got away with several mail *bags*' (which would suggest the gender of trousers, not sacks belonging to the Post Office); 'The captain of a Royal Navy vessel which collided with a German tanker has lost his master's *certificate*' (careless of him, but one hopes the captain won't suffer hardship from the mislaying of a piece of paper; or, as we often hear, hard *ship*); 'His name has been on the most wanted *list*' transfers the wanted-ness from the man to the list; 'A guard of honour was *mounted*' (I do hope not, for his sake); and 'Tits like *coconuts*' suggests a vulgar comparison, not an ornithological fact.

'Sound *Archives*' (I believe the BBC also has *Written* Archives) has become almost standard reverse-stress (like school-*leavers*', 'pry*minister*, 'head*quarters*', 'thanks*giving*', 'West*minster*', and, contrary to how the Finns say it, 'Hel-*sinki*'). 'Stable *lads*' suggest the lads' stability, not their calling. 'There'll be rain in *places*' (everything happens in 'places'). It's the *qualifying* word, usually the penultimate one, that needs stressing – the feminine ending in verse or music. I've heard: 'Berlioz's *Harold in Italy* is based on Byron's child, *Harold*' – at any rate that's what it sounded like. And 'Bach's Organ *Works*': most Radio 3 listeners probably don't need that reassurance, knowing that he fathered 20 children on two wives.

Yet when a final stress *is* called for, it is often missing. From China we heard that 'Mrs Thatcher adopted the Chinese custom of *applauding* herself'; when what was meant

was '. . . applauding *herself*'; and 'The burden of this programme falls almost entirely on the *shoulders* of the parents'
(not their elbows or knees). If you say 'The weather has
affected thousands of *people*' you are by implication excluding the sheep and the goats; 'a green*grocer*' emphasises his
curious colour. If one were to formulate a rule (perish the
thought!) it would be: when you say 'rabbits' ears', stress
ears if your subject is rabbits; if it's ears you're on about,
stress *rabbits*'.

Dr Robert Burchfield, in an interview on Radio 4, said
wryly that although he had recommended '*con*troversy' in his
pamphlet about BBC pronunciation, people went on saying
'con*trov*ersy'. He wasn't aggrieved, merely illustrating a point
he made that although lexicographers can prescribe till
they're blue in the face, the public will decide what's what.
*Con*versely (not con*vers*ely), he probably recommended 'con-
*trib*ute' (which is the posher way), but people continue to say
'*con*tribute' if it pleases them. I doubt if there is such freedom
and flexibility of pronunciation and syllable-stress in any
other language. You can say either 'eether' or 'eye-ther', and
no one will think the less of you. Pauline Bushnell, on the
6 a.m. news, tells us that 'the pound has had a little respite',
which she pronounced to rhyme with 'despite'. Half an hour
later, Brian Redhead says it the same way; but then it's John
Timpson's turn to read the headlines, and he makes it rhyme
with 'cesspit'. What discussions, if any, then took place
behind the scenes, or how many listeners rang in, I do not
know. But next time the story came round, Mr Redhead used
a neat circumlocution: 'Pressure on the pound has eased,' he
said; and in the subsequent news, Miss Bushnell again
avoided the issue by saying that the raised interest rate had
'given the pound a little encouragement'. But by 7.17 a.m.
Mr Timpson firmly made it 'res-pit' again, and after that the
word was avoided altogether. The dictionaries appear to side
with the Timpson version and give no alternative, although
the big *OED*'s citing of archaic forms 'respyght' and 'respight'
would favour the Bushnell/Redhead line. But Shakespeare in
Measure for Measure has 'O injurious law/That respites me

a life . . .' – which probably supports the 'cesspit' version if the scansion is to work.

A day earlier, the experienced presenter of *Science Now* used in his items-to-come menu a pronunciation I had never encountered before: 'polijamy' and 'monojamous'. Why he did so became clear when the pre-recorded insert tape of the contributor was put on. The speaker was a distinguished scientist with the now so familiar polytechnic lecturing delivery, and it was he who pronounced those 'g's soft as in 'squidgy' and 'podgy'. So the presenter tactfully did the same in order not to appear to be correcting his guest. Eccentric perhaps, but not 'wrong'. One could, however, fairly conclude that as a dedicated single-minded academic, the expert hadn't read the old Bloomsbury jingle, 'Higamus hogamus – woman's monogamous/Hogamus higamus – man is polygamous'. On the same programme I have heard '*gay*-see-us' for gaseous, which would appear to have more relevance to gays than to gas. Experts on *Medicine Now* seem to prefer to '*die*-sect' cadavers than '*dis*-sect' them; and here I would risk saying they're wrong, unless they really mean to talk about 'cutting-across' (disect, cf. bisect) not 'cutting asunder' (dissect). You can hear doctors talk about 'res-*pirra*tree', 'respi-*ray*-tree' or 're*spy*-rat-ree' problems; or 'respir*ratory*' if they're under American influence. Tories tend to talk about '*statu*-tree' obligations, but Labour prefers 'sta*tutory*' ones (the Americans again stressing the -*tory*); and the same class/regional differences exist in *com*munal and com*mu*nal. On rational (not emotional or political) grounds, I here side with the Tories: there are *stat*utes and *com*munes, not stat*u*tes and com*mu*nes.

Scholars of ancient art say either 'by-*zan*-tine' or 'b'*zan*-teen', with a preference for the former. There is no reason why there should not be a third form, '*bizz*'n'tine' – but the man who said it that way was a radio reporter, and all he revealed thereby was that he didn't mix much with art historians and had probably only seen the word written down. Some classicists speak about 'my-thology', as if they were speaking of their own 'thology', not about myths. Peter Heathfield, of the miners' union, in the course of a single

sentence, said first 'Nay-cods', then 'Nack-ods' and then

'Nay-cods' again. You can be an 'egoist' or 'egotist' as you prefer – and what does it matter so long as you love yourself? And say 'privvacy' and 'pirracy' or 'pry-va-cy' and 'pie-ra-cy', as you wish. On Radio 4 they seem to prefer 'rabbid' dogs to 'ray-bid', having presumably taken the Pronunciation Unit's advice. But I still prefer the latter, party because the noun is rabies, not 'rabbies' and partly because the BBC version sounds too much like 'rabbit'. *Classical Music* recently printed a defamation of James Galway by calling him an 'ex-patriot', a pardonable spelling mistake, for that is how the BBC recommends 'expatriate' should be pronounced. I insist on saying 'ex-pay-tree-eight' just to be on the safe side. Do I say '*con*troversy' like Dr Burchfield, or 'con*trov*ersy' like most BBC reporters? I say 'argument, disagreement, debate, quarrel, dissension'; perhaps 'wrangling' or 'row'.

Linguistics experts talk knowledgeably about the 'Great Vowel Shift' which took place, I believe, at some time in the Middle Ages. Not being an expert, I don't pretend to know what happened, or which vowels got shifted where and by whom. But I doubt if people got together one day and said, 'It's time we moved our vowels', and from that day onwards English was never the same again. In ages past, such changes took lifetimes, but today, constant repetition on the sound-meeja makes them discernible to the naked ear, so that they are soon almost universally accepted, if not adopted. As I'm not a phonetician either, I don't know all the right terms, but I have a feeling we're in the middle of a Great Lingual Shift. A hundred or more years ago, Mr Punch occasionally commented on the more leisurely changes obtaining in his day, as well as on regional accents, publishing snooty, class-conscious cartoons (illustrated jokes, really) headed 'POOR LETTER H' ('appy 'Arry hand 'is huncle). 'POOR LETTER W' (as in Samivel Veller), or 'POOR LETTER K' (ridiculing the cockney glottal stop) – cartoons smugly aimed at the lower classes, who, Punch maintained, did not know how to speak. Today, it is the poor letter s that seems to be suffering mutation, but it is no longer a class thing. We're all doing it (though for my part I confess I'm not exactly rushing to catch up): s into sh, s into zs (as in Zsa Zsa Gabor) especially when the s happens to be adjacent to a y (or 'frictionless palatal continuant or glide', I believe the experts call it). The fact is that our tongues are getting lazy, and instead of two tongue-movements – the first with the tip against the bit behind the upper teeth to make 's', the second with the middle against the top of the palate to formulate 'y' – we seem to make only one movement. Thus 'Today's *You and Yours*' often comes out as 'Today-zhoo'n'Jaws', for the elision applies also when the tip-of-the-tongue 't' and 'd' sounds are followed by a vowel – as in the once-universal 'lit-e-ra-t-yoor', which has now become 'litch-e-cha' (similarly, 'pro-ceed-you-are' for 'procee-ja' would now sound affected). What is happening is, I think, merely a speeding-up of a process has been going on for many decades. 'Stayshun' is now the rule, although I remember as a child hearing older parsons preaching about the 'Stass-y-ons of the Cross'. Every news and current-affairs programme today is full of 'ishoos', which are tossed back and forth with such vehemence that you'd think the speakers were suffering from sneezing-fits. We get used to it, but for me they will remain 'iss-yoos' for the rest of my days. It would be loath-some if Iago said (*Othello* III, iii); 'I am to pray you not to strain my speech/To grosser ishoos'; but I bet they already do, over at the National Theatre. I still wear a 's-yoot' as I was taught to say 40 years ago, but will eventually, no doubt, adopt 'sooht': I can already hear myself sounding quaint, and people will soon be giving me funny looks. I used to know a pseudo-posh, officer-class type who called his sister-in-law, Sue, 'S-yoo', and *he* sounded a right twit. But when I hear a Radio 3 announcer say, 'Bach was very fond of the loot', I bridle, muttering, 'What musician isn't?' I will also stick to 'rezz-yoom' and 'ass-yoom' instead of the currently fashion-able 'rezzoom' and 'as-soom'; and worry what the blind think when *In Touch* refers to them as 'vishly handicapped': they are the very listeners who are aurally the most acute. Older women called Ursula may resent being called 'Urshla' by the young, especially if they're also diabetic and told they use 'inshlin'; and on *Home-ing In* they sometimes recommend loft 'insh-lation'. It is almost a tradition among workmen, who have long called asphalt 'ashfelt' (although the *OED* seems not to admit it). 'Association' has shifted from the old, clerical-posh, 'as-so-see-a-see-on' to 'as-so-see-ayshun' (the standard educated way until recently) and latterly to 'as-so-shee-ay-shun' – a veritable Schweppes advertisement and a major risk if it comes from a wet talker addressing you face to face. Unions are also at risk, from the 'trayjoonions' to the 'Soviechoonion'. If you think all this is very deplorable, as I do (vainly paddling against the tide a-shoo-szhoo-all), look up some of the words in a pronouncing dik-sh'nry. Or perhaps we could start a Home for Sick Shears? Not thishear or neckshear . . .

'And do you know,' said an Archbishop of Canterbury complaining to Winston Churchill about the upkeep of Lambeth Palace, 'we have 42 bedrooms!' Churchill replied, 'How very inconvenient.' Then he added, '. . . especially when one reflects that you have only 39 Articles.' Doubtless part of the Winston Book of Apocrypha; and in any case now so dated that the story has to be explained to most people under the age of 40. We are more likely to talk about Clause Four, the Five Principles, or Resolution Two-O-Two than the constitution of the Church of England; and the social history of sanitation has made the honest English pisspot, euphemised first as chamberpot, then 'night vase' or 'an article of bedroom furniture', into an almost ubiquitous plant-pot.

I don't know about Lambeth Palace, but on meeja premises the shortage of articles is now so acute that they may eventually die out altogether. And the awful thing is that the telly-literate young, potty-trained as they are by newspapers, disc-jockeys, radio and television announcers, no longer notice the absence of either the definite or the indefinite article. But the practice of leaving out 'the' or 'a' is much older than its breathless media urgency suggests. In fact it goes back to the Germans and their obsession with titles. Emigrants took it to America, where it was lampooned by Mark Twain as early as 1869 in *The Awful German Language*, where he calls it the 'compounding-disease', which had by then spread to the American press. He writes: 'This is the shape it takes: instead of saying "Mr Simmons, clerk of the county and district courts, was in town yesterday", the new form puts it thus: "Clerk of the County and District Court Simmons was in town yesterday."' But it is only since the 1950s that the English press has adopted it, and little more than a decade that it has become so obtrusively common on radio.

In print, judiciously used, '. . . an article by Scottish actor Jock McCoy' sidesteps the subtle distinction between '*a* Scottish actor' and '*the* Scottish actor'. But most young writers seem to have developed an immunity to the Article Deficiency Syndrome and newspaper journalists are taught to cram in as much information as possible about a subject before they get to his name (and, of course, to give his age after it). It is the sensible way of the teleprinter. But unfortunately writers without the time or inclination to rewrite adopt this jerky, telegraphic style. In the Fleet Street Bible, 'The mighty God, the Everlasting Father, the Prince of Peace' would become 'Mighty God, Everlasting Father, Prince of Peace Jesus (32)'.

The Article Deficiency Syndrome has also eroded the possessive pronoun: 'Black soul singer Marty Brown was accompanied by live-in girlfriend Belinda Green, son Darren and daughter Samantha.' It looks bad enough in print; but in real, living speech it produces awkward and angular mouthfuls that are actually harder to say: 'I asked British Frozen Farm Food Federation Chairman Reginald Boreham' instead of 'I asked Reginald Boreham, the Chairman of the . . .' Where ordinary people would say: 'The Bill was introduced by Mr John Smith, one of the abolitionist MPs,' newsmen say '. . . by abolitionist MP John Smith.' And this wretched ugliness is taken to ever greater lengths. Say a member of the European Parliament has several initials: 'I talked to MEP R. F. E. Burton.' It makes English sound as silly as German, in which grand-sounding titles are awarded at the drop of a *Pickelhaube* and continue to be enjoyed, yea, even beyond the grave. For example, a deputy station-master, or *Bahnhofsvorsteherstellvertreter*, leaves his widow with the title *Frau Bahnhofsvorsteherstellvertreterswitwe* ('Mrs Deputystationmasterwidow'). It's not such a far cry from 'Special guest will be award-winning actress Janet Doe.' I don't know whether Miss Doe has won any, but in an age when awards are handed out to everyone like going-home presents at a children's party, 'award-winning' has almost become a definite article in itself.

Satisfactory speech rhythm needs the 'the' or 'a' to serve as a barely articulated springboard – almost inaudible but quite indispensable (except, of course, with speakers who make *every* 'the' into 'thee' and every 'a' into 'eh', but that's another subject). The difference is surely self-evident between '. . . the defection of the former Russian KGB chief, Oleg Gordievsky', which is how people talk to each other; and 'the defection of former Russian KGB chief Oleg Gordievsky', which is how they don't.

When Article Deficiency is combined with the Bogus News Possessive, which sometimes comes piled up in multiples, e.g. 'Westminster's Coroner's Court's decision to record a misadventure verdict on mother-of-six . . .' or 'We'll be talking to BBC Television News's Kate Adey' (try saying it aloud, like 'Paris's Orly Airport'), it is time to turn over to Radio 3. But alas, articles have been disappearing even there: 'Soloist will be flautist Richard Adeney with composer Malcolm Arnold conducting . . .'

My friend Ben Trovato, the well-known pundit on Latin America, once told me that when Eva Peron took a salute she complained to the old general standing next to her that one of the soldiers marching past, his head turned stiffly towards her, had out of the corner of his mouth muttered the word, 'Whore!' The old soldier said, 'Don't let it worry you, madam. *I*'ve been retired 25 years and they still call me General.'

The cut-off point at which military titles are carried over into civilian life (does one have to ask permission?) seems to be the rank of captain (you never hear a country pub landlord say, 'Ar, the second lieutenant'll be in soon . . .') and none of my friends who reached the rank of lance-corporal has felt the need to have it printed on his visiting-card. After the last war, there was a spate of MPs bearing military rank but they appear to have died out, though here there must be an upper cut-off point. Those who harboured ambitions of high office knew that military rank could in this country prove a disadvantage. Only banana republics and military dictatorships have generals as Prime Minister or colonels as head of state. Everyone knows they are self-awarded chevrons, as there is no one of higher rank who could possibly promote the boss; just as Idi Amin pinned a VC on his own chest. (Has Jerry Rawlins given himself any more stripes, by the way, or is he still a Flight-Lieutenant?) Even impertinence sometimes pays off in post-colonial banana republics. Did not a Caribbean dictator award himself first a doctorate and then a knight-hood – and eventually get a genuine dubbing from the Queen?

It must be about 20 years since Dr David Owen last practised as a neurologist. When he was Minister of Health, the doctorate was apt and bore witness to practical expertise most Ministers do not possess. But if he gets to 10 Downing Street, he will surely have to abandon his doctorate (which, as with most medics, is in any case an honorific overstate-ment: he is actually MB and BChir). He wouldn't want to put himself on a nominal level with Dr Jonas Savimbi or Dr François Duvalier (Papa Doc), would he?

Some people assume that all educated foreigners must be doctors of philosophy, at the very least. There's a story about a correspondent watching early Israeli settlers at work passing bricks along a line, from whom he heard a continuous, low mutter. A prayer chant, he thought – but when he got closer he found they were saying to one another, 'Danke, Herr Doktor – Bitte, Herr Doktor . . .' Even I, English-educated if not -born, find myself occasionally doctored in letters from readers and listeners, when all I could ever aspire to would be a 'Dus. Moc.' In Austria the coveted title of professor is in the personal gift of the president, like Kammersänger ('court chamber singer', some 70 years after the last emperor's abdication). The veteran conductor Karl Böhm was allowed to be called 'Professor' only at the end of his life. But in this country the title is automatically given not only to incumbents of university chairs but to instrumental teachers at the music colleges who may be highly qualified and experienced trombone players but have never passed an academic examination. 'Laurie-Taylor-Professor-of-Sociology-at-the-University-of-York' (as we are so used to hearing him an-nounced in one breath), has, I hear, been taking a prolonged sabbatical so that he can better occupy the Chair of Acute Observation at the *Stop the Week* table. In the last few years, Professor Roland Smith has been constantly in the financial news. His entry in *Who's Who?* reveals that he is Professor of Marketing at the University of Manchester Institute of Science and Technology: at least as useful a qualification, I'm sure, for boardroom battles and takeover wrangles as is MB/BChir for a Minister of Health. But does Prof. Smith find as much time as he would wish to teach his students? But beware of political ecclesiastics, from Archbishop Makarios to Bishop Abel Muzorewa and the Reverend Josiah Chinamano.

Lord Winstanley wrote an engaging letter complaining about split infinitives and sent it to, of all papers, the *Guardian*, that delightful repository of old puns, free spelling, creative typesetting and (on the appropriate pages) socio-trendy gibberish. It was like asking a football manager to do something about the use of swear-words on the terraces. Sure enough, the *Guardian*'s defenders of the anything-goes school swung into action. Although one correspondent quoted Fowler's excellent advice, most seemed merely to object to Lord Winstanley's strictures on the principle that rules are a bad thing. Now, I have been writing and speaking English for many years but I can honestly say I have never split an infinitive, either written or spoken. Not because I'm a blind observer of rules, but because I have never needed to. It sounds insufferably smug, yet I talk normally and ordinarily just like everybody else and certainly don't choose my words with particular care. But English is so rich in simple alternatives that one can always find another way round. Shakespeare could have written 'To be or to not be . . . 'tis a consummation to devoutly be wish'd . . . to sleep, to perchance dream . . .' Far from being the natural thing to do, splitting makes for awkward jerks that hold up the flow. And that, surely, is the valid objection, not the breaking of some ancient rule.

People get bothered also about plural confusions, sometimes with reason. When *You and Yours* asks (or, as they would doubtless have it, ask), 'Are the Foreign Office always as helpful as we might expect?' I am tempted to mutter: 'Well, are it?' We get used to plural idiosyncrasies. 'The couple was divorced . . .' would have been standard usage a generation ago, but no longer sounds right; 'were divorced' does not offend me, but I don't use it. Like a split infinitive, it might worry someone, so I quickly rejig: 'the two were divorced . . .'

'There is roadworks on the M4' sounded wrong because it was formally said. If, however, the announcer had thrown it away ('There's roadworks . . .'), it would have passed as normal colloquial communication. 'Two men and their dismasted yacht was winched aboard' sounds right from a sailor telling yarns on the seashore (imagine it in a West Country burr, and the right formation sounds wrong), but was to me unacceptable in Radio 4 news. Then again, footballers and on-the-spot commentators are justified in telling us 'The team were short of attacking power . . .', whereas I would expect 'The team was . . .' from the sports reporter in his prepared account after the match. Otherwise Radio 3 will soon be announcing the Housman/Vaughan Williams song as 'Are my team ploughing?'

The other day a Radio 4 announcer told of some road hazards and ended with the warning, 'In a word, be careful.' It must have swelled the *Out Takes* postbag, but as an informal throwaway line I found it perfectly acceptable. On the other hand, another traffic announcement, given formally and with great emphasis, 'The situation can be summed up in *one* word – *absolute chaos*', was laughable because the three words were so heavily stressed. 'Their feelings are one of shock and anger' in a prepared news script is indefensible, as is 'there are a variety of such books on the market' – especially when said on a book programme.

'The drug seemed to be responsible for the deaths from liver failure of at least 31 people' doesn't work for a different reason: there is only one death per person, thank God. In the same way 'A million pounds were given to the fund' is right only if individual notes were handed over separately, and '. . . the flock were moved to new pastures after the threat' suggests Bo-Peep took her sheep one by one. Where confusion is possible, rules is rules.

I cannot get used to plural confusions of the verb-object kind, as in 'These sort of happenings . . .' But a history book of 1551 has, 'These sort of people are named of the greke Cosmographers . . .' and this apparent mismatch continued happily down the centuries until Ruskin, in 1872, has: 'Do those sort of people know what love is?' After that, I suspect, the Victorian grammarians laid down their laws, including the one against splitting infinitives, and we avoided it until the meeja gave it its blessing. And for me 'the media' can be singular only if pronunciation and spelling reflect the current usage: 'the media are . . .' but 'the meeja is . . .'

———◆◆◆———

The other day I heard a staid newsreader say that Sir somebody or other was to 'head up' some new committee. I thought things through, looked up (and checked out) my notes; and now weigh in with the conclusion that colloquial English is getting ever more prepositional. Again, one can at least partly put it down to the old triangular traffic: the influence of German on American, and American on English. When you think it over, you may agree that the German *ab-* is often forced by uneasy translation into -up. For the last 20 years I have dabbled in amateur printing, but only in the last ten or so have people said to me: 'Will you print me *up* some notepaper?' It suggests the German word *abdrucken*. 'Balls-up' and 'cock-up' appear to have become acceptable on Radio 4 and even in Parliament. 'Pissed-off' (formerly, 'browned-off') is still a little way-out; but the prepositional vulgarism with which Philip Larkin sounded off against parental influences is still considered crude enough to have made him miss (out-on) the laureateship. You may look up to, or talk down to, someone; do him down, do him over; and, as a last resort, do him in. You may do up your house, so that it can be knocked down at an auction, unless it falls through.

Years ago, calling on a schoolfriend, I would one day be told by his mother 'He's not up yet', and the next day, 'He's not down yet': both meaning he had slept in. Later on he took to sleeping out, and, later still, to sleeping around (which has little or nothing to do with sleeping) and playing up his mum something dreadful. She was not only fed up but felt put out when he was put up by the girlfriends whom he would often look up. When he got home she laid into him with a firm put-down. I used to meet (now people say meet up with) him in town. We would perhaps live it up one day and not live it down for weeks. (He was later sent down from Oxford for sending his professor up.) We hoped that getting on with a girl might lead to getting off with her (i.e. from hitting it off to having it off) unless, of course, she told one where to get off. Though again, you might invite a bus-conductress to *tell* you where to get off. (Don't take all this too seriously: I'm only having you on.)

Time off has become 'time *out*'; even the Prime Minister is now invited in Question Time to 'take time out . . .'. Each time the Bishop of Durham speaks, he seems to speak out against her, or up for minorities. Little Boy Blue is now told to blow *up* his horn, just as a football referee alarmingly 'blows up' at the end of a match, when all he does is blow *down* the end of his whistle. Cuts have become cut*backs*: a paediatrician on *Woman's Hour* said: 'We've seen a consider-able cutback in this kind of operations on boy babies.' We have carve-ups, spin-offs and shoot-outs. There is feedback but, we hope, no fallout; things no longer merely balance but balance out. We have to face up to difficulties, or we may lose out, but never down, under, across or over. I dimly remember a sand-filled box outside the headmaster's study which said, 'This box is for putting cigarettes out in.' The purist cannot afford to look down on such things, or he will miss out on a stock of useful expressions; yet the foreigner cannot look them up in dictionaries.

As my command of the vernacular increased, I learnt to distinguish between our sports master's old van breaking down and, finally, breaking up (though hearing him say, 'We're going to be dead on time' was alarming); and not to laugh when someone said, 'Would you mind putting the cat out if it doesn't put you out?' But even the native sometimes nods. In Britten's *The Little Sweep* the boy-hero has to sing, 'Please don't send me up again!' But they do, mercilessly. And in *Owen Wingrave*, I am told, Janet Baker, rejecting the cowardly Owen whose courage deserted him when he failed to stay in a haunted room, had to sing the line, 'I will not marry you because you couldn't stick it out.'

As anyone who has anything to do with the BBC soon finds out, the Corporation was among the first in the use of professional abbreviations. Newcomers soon adopt the jargon and may quite unselfconsciously mention that 'Aitch Camp' (i.e. H.CAMP, the Head of Current Affairs Magazine Programmes), XSMO (External Services Music Organiser) and H.Cop (Head of Copyright Department) are about to see the 'Dee Gee' (Director-General) about some matter; and when a secretary holds a hand over the telephone mouthpiece and urgently whispers to her boss, 'I've got the HOTS for you,' he shows no surprise but takes a call to the Head of Office Training Services. It is said that many years ago the post of Assistant, Regional Services, Engineering, had to be renamed, and, for all I know, there is an H.Abbr. whose job is to avoid such pitfalls. But no. The idea that anyone in the BBC would stoop so low as to juggle the designation of a post in order to produce a memorable acronym is unthinkable.

Most BBC abbreviations are functional and unmemorable, like POMXP Ops. or HTFWS, or cumbersome, like MH&OSMS for the Monitoring Department! Contrary to popular belief there is no EIEIO, but it is true that the Chief Assistant, Talks and Documentaries, Radio (CATDR) is known as the 'cat doctor'.

The outside world, however, has gone crazy on abbreviations and acronyms. Everywhere, men and women anxious to foster worthy causes with support groups, action committees, movements For this or Against that, rack their brains to invent a name whose initials make a word. I sometimes think they choose the acronym first and then search for a good cause to fit it. It might be a new word or an old one misused, like CLAPA (the Cleft Lip And Palate Association) or ICE (Inner City Enterprise), CATCH (Campaign Against Tolls on our Culture and Heritage), DOG (Doctors against Overpopulation Group), CACTUS (Campaign Against Cable TV Under Swindon), or GASP (Group Against Smoking: in the acronym game you can bend the rules). Don't be afraid of FEVER. It's only the Friends of the Educational Voucher Experiment in Selected Regions. Sometimes you look in vain for meaningful initial letters: MIND stands for what should really be the Mational Issociation for Nental Dealth, and CRUSE is an excellent body that helps widows (1 Kings 17). If it catches on, the new acronym soon becomes a bogus upper-and-lower-case word. People write earnest letters to the *Guardian* in support of Blac (whatever that is, and for once it's not a misprint) and radio reporters bring urgent news about Unifil: I thought it was some patent cushion-filler but it turns out to be the UN Force in Lebanon. A Mr George Wilson, in a letter to the *Spectator*, claims to be 'Director of Radar', which is, of course, the familiar wartime acronym for RAdio Detection And Ranging. Now it appears also to stand for Royal Association for Disability and Rehabilitation. The crass stupidity (whose?) of reinventing a good existing word is mind (or MIND)-boggling. On the other hand, Miss Henrietta Ayres is named as 'Secretary of SODPRO' and no thanks, I'd rather not know what that means. The Acquired Immunodeficiency Syndrome AIDS (*not*, as usually written, 'Acquired Immune Deficiency) was inaptly chosen by a bunch of American doctors to make a word that suggests help is at hand, which it isn't. And they must have quite ruined the market for a certain slimming preparation: try asking your chemist, 'Have you got Ayds?'

I know I have a low irritation threshold where the media are concerned. But I can't be the only man who feels like kicking the set when I hear newsreaders, presenters, Ministers of the Crown and other grown-ups discuss solemn issues while using nursery words like Neddy, New Pee and Eat Poo. (Nupe is, in fact, the name of a West African tribe and their language.) As soon as another acronym is added to the unlovely list, speakers immediately drop it into conversation, generally bandy it about as though it had been in the language since Shakespeare, and assume as a matter of course that we are familiar with its meaning. When one of the dreaded print unions, the Society of Allied and Graphical Trades reorganised itself in 1982 it solemnly decided to enshrine the fateful year in its acronymic name: 'SOGAT 82'. Though I suspect there might have been a little internecine bitchery, or at the very least a brotherly tongue in cheek, when a typesetter from a rival union described its General Secretary as 'Miss

Brenda Dean of SOGAT, 82.' But the media dutifully kowtow. On radio and in the papers, 'SOGAT 82' it is.

The rulers of 'emergent states' (which is what we now have to call those that used to be 'backward countries', usually military dictatorships) have taken the acronym to their be-medalled bosoms in a big way, taking as their model previous totalitarian practice, from the Russians' OGPU, Comecon and the Gulags to the Nazis' Gestapo, the Stalags and Oflags. So, like children copying the latest playground craze, the African rulers, too (who are like children by turn innocent, greedy and vicious) had to have their Zanu, Zapu, Swapu, Swafu, Zippra, Ziffra and Zupo and Zeppo* – with the amazing exception of the un-lamented Idi Amin, whose tor-ture squads gloried in the name of 'State Research Bu-reau'.

*Sorry, he was a plant. Zeppo was the fourth Marx Brother, the one who had to sing because he could not make people laugh . . .

The papers tell us that 'the wine trade was represented by Harry Sheehan, Secretary of VULVA' (which I take to mean something like 'Vintners' and United Licensed Victuallers' Association'), so perhaps SOGAT 82 is a fine vintage? I can only pray that sogat means something filthy in Armenian. Remember the Amgot scandal of 1945, when the Allied Military Government of Occupied Territory had to be re-named because it made Turks fall about laughing? *Am* and *göt* in their language mean what my small daughters used to call 'front-bum' and 'back-bum', respectively. So watch out, DIG, FLAG, WWOOF, CLODO, PIE, KANUPP, WEEP, WAVAW and the rest: nemesis may yet overtake you.

I don't know if the Russians have a word for Information Technology but I doubt it. They are envious of the spread of the home computer in the West, yet at the same time terrified of it. Micro-chips mean information, and information is what they do not want to give to their people, let alone the means of spreading it. You need a licence to own even a typewriter; and a specimen of its work has to be deposited with the authorities so that *samizdat* authors can be traced. The simp-lest spirit duplicator is a potential subversive weapon, and privately-owned copiers (let alone offset-litho office printing-machines) such as are used by the rest of the world, unheard of. A word-processor with unlimited printing-out facilities would be a godsend to any dissident.* And while the Chinese are looking outward and moving towards the Roman alphabet, the Soviets cling to their Cyrillic characters, which make communication with the outside world that much harder. Yet ordinary Russians are as enthusiastic learners of colloquial, idiomatic English as the Chinese, which is surely good news all round for an eventual understanding.

* 'Dissident' is not as new a word as its recent over-use would suggest. Thomas Carlyle, in 1837: '. . . unconquerable Martyrs according to some . . . chicaning Traitors according to others.' The older preferred form was the rather more satisfactory 'dissentient'.

I remember seeing Mr Khrushchev questioned on BBC Television by a young interviewer who asked (as he might have asked any British minister), 'But aren't you baying at the moon, Mr Khrushchev?' As the interpreter translated, the Russian leader's face visibly darkened. The interviewer stammered something to the effect that 'baying at the moon' was an English figure of speech and no, he hadn't meant to call the Soviet leader a dog. Some things simply do not translate, like the Chinese 'drunken hare' description they applied to a British diplomat some years ago. It apparently referred to an old folk-tale of theirs which, not surprisingly, was unfamiliar over here.

Russian propaganda language appears not to have changed since the revolution and is as absurd and stilted as ever. This has always struck me as odd when you think of all the expensively public-school-educated British defectors and spies who could so easily have cleaned up their new masters' propaganda English; or at least prevented howlers or double-meanings like those occasionally produced in Eastern-bloc English-language publications. But no, it almost seems as if Burgess and McLean had taken with them a copy of *Nineteen Eighty-four* and omitted to tell the Russians that Orwell was being satirical. I have a cutting somewhere which fulminates against someone who '. . . has already discarded the fig-leaf which had covered his nakedness and now stands exposed as a tool of the West . . .'; and there was the famous Stalinist edict to the Russian media: 'The organ of the party must penetrate the most backward parts of the proletariat.'

The Russians have 'good' words, like 'solidarity',* 'proletarian', and 'unific-ation' (which means the same as 'annexation' in English or 'liberation' in American double-speak) and you must be 'peace-loving' but at the same time prepared to engage in 'class warfare'. The good Russian is 'freedom-loving' but must be prepared to be locked up in a state lunatic-asylum for saying so in the wrong context. From all these words you can construct ran-dom sentences of almost any length (just as English poli-ticians do in their own language): '. . . the solidarity of the proletarian freedom-loving peoples of this great union . . .', etc. which has the masses cheering in Red Square by the mere sound of the words, not their meaning. And, of course, the technique is widely copied by demagogues in the West, as I attempt to show elsewhere. The 'bad' propaganda words are even more varied and often ludicrously archaic and stilted. It is surely the Russians who have kept 'lackeys' alive in ordinary English speech by their constant reference to them. We would prob-ably now say 'flunkeys'. The Russian lackey was imported under the czars from the German *Lakai*, just as the sinister *likvidirovat* – the action of making persons into non-persons by 'liquidating' them, dated 1924 in the *OED* – began as early German communist bluster: *liquidieren*, related to *auflösen*, 'dissolving'. (There probably aren't many Russian

* This has lost neither validity nor credibility since the emergence of the Polish Solidarity movement, for it should be remembered that the West loves it only because of the old principle 'My enemy's enemy is my friend.' Lech Walesa and his *Solidarnosz* are a long way to the left of Arthur Scargill and his National Union of Mineworkers. The Polish battle of wills is a struggle between two extreme factions of the hardest 'hard left'.

housewives who use a liquidiser in their kitchen, but if they do I would be interested to know what they call it.)

The Soviet vocabulary of international abuse is strong on animals. Capitalist 'running dogs'* (suggesting Dalmatians trotting between carriage-wheels, a footman or lackey standing on the axle) and imperialist 'hyenas' are still going strong: poor maligned hyenas, but they do often have the last laugh. Jackals sometimes do duty for them.

I used to think that 're-visionist' and 'reactionary' were simply loose terms of communist bluster (meaning 'bolshy'?), but both words have precisely defined dictionary meanings. Reactionary goes back to John Stuart Mill, who called Coleridge one in 1840. Revisionism is not unrelated to it, being the advocacy (by one Edward Bernstein, in the 1890s) of evolutionary rather than revolutionary socialism, thereby opposing orthodox Marxism.

* I was perhaps a little over-imaginative in supposing that these had anything to do with the footmen or lackeys of noblemen. The OED quotes an example of 1628 which reveals that this was then a term for sheep-worrying dogs: 'That no man sall keip runnyng doggis that runnes fra hous to hous or throw the cuntrie slaeing thair nychtbouris sheip.'

The good old standby 'bourgeois' (an indispensable term of opprobrium in any decent dialectical argument) is interesting, because the poor middle-classes who, with the sale of more and more council-houses, are growing in numbers by the hour, get the abuse both from above and below — just like the SDP-Liberal Alliance. The French upper classes and aristocracy before the Revolution used to spit 'bourgeois!' at those beneath them who gave themselves airs (as in Molière's *Le Bourgeois Gentilhomme*) whereas post-revolutionary worker-comrades turned the word into an upward sneer at the middle-classes as seen from their viewpoint.

Do the Russians know that the Roman *proletarius* was the lowest class of citizen 'who contributed nothing to the state except offspring', a kind of Stakhanovite begetter of children not fit to work either with his hands or his brain? Trotsky gave the Soviets an -ism swear-word to bandy about after he had fallen out with Stalin, when he was written out of the 'good' parts of the reference books and transferred to the negative side, under 'Trotskyism'. But today's 'Trots' (the British ones at any rate) have moved so far away from his teachings that many of them have only a hazy idea of who Leon Trotsky was. It is not inconceivable that if his comparatively civilised ideas had prevailed in the power-struggle against the peasant-brutish Stalin the world might be a better place today.

A fascinating discovery: the communist Russians do not admit the word 'Nazi', preferring 'Hitlerite' or 'fascist' and for a very good reason: a child who enquired 'Comrade-daddy, what does Nazi stand for?' would have to be told it was the German acronym/abbreviation of 'National-sozialistische Deutsche Arbeiterpartei' – National Socialist German Workers' Party – which is, of course, uncomfortably close to home. Unswerving nationalist socialism is exactly what is expected of the Russian worker, too. ('Working classes' and 'the workers' have almost lost their meaning in the West – as many of British manual workers are not working because of unemployment, while those of us, like freelances, who toil with their brains and on their own without union protection, often work a great deal harder but are denied the right to call themselves 'workers'.)

'Stalinist' appears not to be quite such a dirty word in Russia as it is among orthodox communists in this country. If there *are* any orthodox communists in this country, thanks to the wondrous profusion of dialectic deviants. There is not just the 'hard left' and the soft left (and for all I know also the *al dente* left), as well as the broad left, but all manner of splinter and sub-groups, and sub-sub-splinter-groups. As a correction in the London University paper *The Sennet* was obliged to explain: 'Last week we described . . . Val Furness as a "Communist Party candidate". She feels this description is ambiguous and needs to be clarified. She is a member of the Communist Party of Britain (Marxist-Leninist). She is not a member of the Communist Party of England (Marxist-Leninist) or the Communist Party of Great Britain, the Communist League or the Communist Federation of Britain (Marxist-Leninist). She would like to say that she is not in the Broad Left either.' But that was a few years ago. She may even have grown up by now. Or perhaps she has joined the Workers' Revolutionary Party. Yes, but which faction? The Healy-Redgrave Wing or the Banda Splinter Group?

Surrounded as one is in central London by foreign tourists, some with phrase-book in hand, others remarkably fluent in broken English, I often wonder what *they* make of our newspapers. News-write bears little resemblance to what the visitors would have been taught at language-school, nor to the everyday talk of the Britons they hear around them. I also wonder who the people are who write the repetitive bilge which we accept as normal journalese. Headlines as well as text are compounded of a mixture of mock-archaic, stilted expressions, juvenile puns or obscure stock allusions to forgotten book titles or TV soap operas. Nothing ever falls but 'plunges', 'plummets' or 'hurtles'; every attempt is a 'bid', every mundane decision a 'vow', every journey a 'dash' – 'mercy dash' if someone is helped. Things are never expected but 'set' to happen; and police do not arrest but 'swoop' or 'pounce' (except in the dear *Guardian*, where they have been known to 'ponce'). What would a Japanese Professor of English make of 'Death Dice Jeeves in Upstairs Downstairs Drama'? Why *not* 'Butler risks Life to save Employer's Child?' Day after day they grind them out: 'Take-away thieves last night ransacked a Chinese restaurant . . .'; 'It was a black day for coalman Ted . . .' Teachers who don't get what they want are caned, butchers get a roasting, maritime projects are sunk, scuppered or torpedoed – unless they succeed, when, improbably, they 'ride high', as cyclists always do unless *their* aspirations 'fall flat'. Musicians always strike notes – high, low, discordant or sour.

Newsmen are overtaken by a great coyness when they describe women or matters sexual, and women have legitimate cause for complaint. Those with big breasts are described as 'shapely', 'curvaceous' or 'well built' (as though they were some piece of machinery). Hair colour ('attractive buxom blonde', etc.) is always stated (as are age and marital status) whether germane to the news item or not. According to hacks, people go in for kiss 'n' cuddle, slap 'n' tickle or horseplay. Many innocent words like 'saucy' (formerly meaning 'cheeky') are given sexual connotations; and euphemisms abound. But then they assume a virginal coyness, as when they reported the gruesome murder of a woman whose body had been discovered chopped into several pieces

– 'but she had not been interfered with'.

'Biscuit hopes crumbled last night . . .' was the jolly start to a story about yet more unemployment on Merseyside. Presumably because journalists know they bring only out-dated news, seen on TV the night before, they feel they must become buffoons and 'entertain' readers by turning everything into a crude, predictable quip. But which NGA or NUJ or SOGAT rule prescribes that the messenger of doom should invariably come as a red-nosed clown doing a tap-dance?

All headlines, even those surmounting serious news items, are made into jokes, puns so feeble that they would be laughed out of a nursery-school class. I have before me a sober evening-paper article (as sober as the once influential *Liverpool Echo* gets now in its new, sub-tabloid, bottom-of-the-market style), an article about hip replacement. It is headed 'HIP HOORAY!' The *Daily Telegraph* still avoids much of this tedious rubbish, though even there smart young hacks just out of training feel they must copy their peer-group and play the idiots' game; while the *Guardian* tries to be cleverer than the rest and sometimes succeeds: I forgive them almost anything for heading a bad review of *Antony and Cleopatra* 'The Biggest Asp Disaster in the World' – but not 'Chink in the Bamboo Curtain' (twice), and 'Hot under the Cholera' for an epidemic.

During its loony reign the Greater London Council, which poured money into thousands of 'minority' projects and made an idiot of itself many times over (e.g. by resolving in solemn committee to black the word 'blacked' from its industrial relations vocabulary) for some reason failed to stop photographers from attending multi-racial gatherings. For the black-and-white camera lens has a deplorable, but apparently unavoidable, built-in colour prejudice when photographing very black people next to the very pale. This can work both ways, as the lens aperture may be adjusted to favour either blacks or whites (and we know who would have been favoured by the GLC's trusty photographers). For example, a picture in the *Nairobi Standard* of Milton Obote meeting

Pope John Paul II naturally favoured the former. Thus his features are visible, but His Holiness could just as easily have been a complete blank, white, cardboard cut-out. (Perhaps the Pope should have been advised not to wear his away-colours under such circumstances.) The best-known pictures of Idi Amin, conversely, show only his eyes and the gleaming highlights of his face. But then almost all English newspaper pictures, excepting those using the 'new technology' come out as a dirty grey mess. It often makes nonsense of the captions hopeful sub-editors append to the pictures. 'Agony is etched on the face of Steve Ovett after dropping out of the race' says the caption. But Ovett's face is a shapeless grey blob which has nothing etched on it except perhaps a smudgy dot-screen. The press photographer in a hurry always seems to have time to arrange his subjects in a limited number of poses, in accordance with clichés that have developed over the last decade or so, coinciding with the general trivialisation of the English press.

GETTING THE JOYFUL NEWS: The subject is shown on the telephone, even if the joyful news in fact arrived hours earlier, when the photographer was miles away and on another job.

THE THUMBS UP: The signal of success, or at any rate optimism, which has the subject giving the well-known sign, possibly leaning out of a car window. This is an obligatory pose demanded of every political candidate, when he will wear an outsize election rosette (and incidentally, when did politicians start this idiotic horse-show practice?). The V for Victory sign used to be an alternative but has now been discredited by terrorists, freedom-fighters, etc., who also go for the raised fist, originally the communists' answer to the flat-handed Hitler salute.

THE OPERATIC TENOR GESTURE: Facing the camera, both arms outstretched, like a singer hitting what the press invariably calls a 'high note', the subject poses in front of whatever is relevant to the story, e.g. the building he has just bought, won, or where he is about to take up a job.

SHARING A JOKE: The standard caption when two or more people stand talking at a function, probably with a drink in one hand and looking glumly at each other. A favourite of the glossy society magazines.

Mr Bernie Grant pictured yesterday

LORRAINE CHASE

Robin Cook: "arms control agreement undermined"

UGANDA President Apollo Milton Obote meets Pope John Paul II during a private audience at the Vatican. At left, Mrs. Obote looks on.

The unknown man waiting to be recognised

Waiting for change: The watchful faces of an Indian mother and child—Alan Garcia offers an ambiguous message

Agony is etched on the face of Steve Ovett after dropping out of the race.

THE SIDEWAYS-ON KISS: The subject is shown full-face, being pecked on the cheek by way of congratulations, by one, possibly two, pouting friends, relatives, employees, runners-up, etc., who are seen in profile.

THE UNSEEMLY GRIN: Difficult to avoid if only old picture material is available, but the greater the tragedy reported in the accompanying story, the more incongruously joyful or smiling is the face that stares out at one.

THE FUNNY HATS CLICHÉ: The subject, either a child or a glamorous female, is posed wearing an inappropriate hat (policeman's, sailor's, parking-warden's, etc.) when the story involves some uniformed person. Hats also figure in:

THE HEAD-SCRATCHING POSE: 'Puzzlement for proud dad David — suddenly a father of five', says the caption, and 'David' (tabloid rags do not usually admit surnames) dutifully scratches his head, though he must have been perfectly aware of what it was that caused his wife to become pregnant.

THE CHORUS LINE: The subjects — the more unlikely the better, e.g. OAPs or politicians — link arms and stick one leg outwards and upwards. Like Mr Kinnock's now famous 'Dancing in the Rain' routine it shows that people will do anything to get their pictures in the papers or publicise a cause dear to them. Not long ago even the Controller of one of the BBC Television channels was seen doing it. It is clearly not a pose people strike naturally, but when requested by a press photographer many of us are willing to make idiots of ourselves. Indeed one can imagine Leonardo da Vinci saying to his models for 'Christ and the Disciples at the Last Supper', 'I say, fellows, would you mind all crowding round the far side of the table so I can get a better picture?' Why else would a dozen people make use of only one side of a long table?

THE FORESHORTENED PERSPECTIVE: The subjects are photographed from above and all look up at the camera. They come out triangular, with big heads and tiny feet. A favourite trick of what is now called 'corporate advertising', i.e. advertising the firm, not its products. But there is, conversely,

THE BIG FEET POSE: This also makes use of the camera's inbuilt exaggeration of perspective, often when photographing sportsmen who have performed, or are about to perform, some newsworthy accomplishment with their feet. These are shown in alarming close-up, with the subject's grinning face small in the distance.

THE FISH-EYE LOOK: By means of an extremely wide-angle or 'fish-eye' lens, the photographer is able not only to photograph their subjects as though they lived in a goldfish-bowl but also give them fish-like eyes. A favourite of Sunday colour-supplements.

GRINS AND GRIPS, or the Presentation Cliché: Subjects shake hands while handing over a cheque, gift, cup, etc., but do not look at each other (as you would do when handing something to another person, if only to make sure not to let go prematurely) but look out in front at right angles to each other, straight at the camera. And of course –

THE CAT-FLAP: Otherwise known as 'cropping', this involves cutting down a photographed face to remove everything but the eyes, nose and mouth, thus giving the impression that the subject is trying to enter by the cat-door.

THE BOXERS' NOSE-TO-NOSE POSE: This shows the contestants in an impending fight apparently trying to out-stare each other so as to give the impression that theirs will be a 'grudge-fight', which always helps to bring in the audience. (Not to be confused with the nose-rubbing pictures often shown when royalty and other important persons visit parts of the world where this is the standard form of greeting.)

THE ANNUAL POLAR BEAR: Or whenever there is a cold spell during the winter, when every headline-writer manages to get a BRRR! headline into his tabloid, a press photographer is invariably sent to the nearest zoo to take a picture of a polar bear. 'Sandra (5) feels right at home in temperatures like we've been having . . .' etc. Usually an 'expert' comment is solicited, too: 'Said zoo-keeper Jeff (23) . . .' In summer weather, conversely, photographers make for the nearest public park, office roof, etc., to picture some office girl sunbathing, and the headlines read PHEW WHAT A SCORCHER! or 83 AND STILL RISING! (so much for decimalised temperatures – see page 135).

THE PHOTOFIT, formerly Identikit: The putative facial characteristics of wanted criminals on the run (are there any unwanted ones?) are assembled from the description of

Gathering of the clan, Jimmy's brothers and sisters drink to his success

The jobless—jumping for joy in Devon's "Doleish".

Home again then shock

Dr Jonas Savimbi, the rebel Angolan leader, sharing a joke with a woman at his bush command post of Jamba after his Press conference at which he appealed for American military aid to defeat Marxist forces in the country.

KISSES for Dr Richards, from daughter Susan (left) and his son's fiancée, Joanna Harris.

victims or witnesses and published in the newspapers. There seem to be only three sorts of picture: when clean-shaven, the culprit usually looks like David Frost; when bearded, like Rolf Harris; and when clean-shaven and wearing glasses, like Sir Robin Day.

THE ARTIST'S IMPRESSION: When no photographs are available or allowed to be taken (as in court hearings or parliamentary reports) an artist is engaged to draw the scene of whatever event it being described. This is a speciality of Sunday newspapers. For maximum entertainment such drawings or plans ('explosion here', 'assailants enter by skylight', etc.) should always be compared with those appearing in rival papers. They seldom if ever agree.

I have an old comic coloured postcard showing a lady amiably caricatured as Jewish who is taking part in a seance. Above her a disembodied pair of gesticulating hands is materialising. She says, 'Oi! Oi! Look, it's Abey trying to speak with me!' Ten or fifteen years ago, if you saw two people conversing in the street, you could always tell from a distance that they were foreigners. Englishmen took Hamlet's counsel, 'Do not saw the air too much . . .' and kept their hands still while speaking. One was always told it was good manners, and the nanny-educated probably still heed it. The Duke of Edinburgh, for example, keeps his firmly behind his back. Prince Charles is taking after his father, and the little grandson princes are comically doing the same. Or else, the Englishman keeps his hands in his pocket. Royalty, however, always having to be aware of protocol, generally avoids this, as do British diplomats on important official occasions. Foreigners would soon comment adversely, as many British people did when they were shocked to see, on a formal group photograph of the Queen with a Commonwealth Prime Ministers' Conference, that one of her Prime Ministers was smoking a cigarette.

Television chat shows have removed some of the reluctance of British people to use their hands. Gesticulation is no longer equated with bad or foreign upbringing but with sincerity and enthusiasm – real or feigned. I maintain that the emergence in recent years of a large number of gifted young English conductors is related to the way the young have overcome some of their inhibitions about waving their hands about in order to express themselves. (Did not Sir Adrian Boult teach that a good, flexible wrist-joint was all a conductor needed?) Imagine a foursome discussion between, say, David Bellamy, Jonathan Miller, Magnus Pyke and Germaine Greer, all hand-cuffed together. I do believe they would be struck dumb; or else would resort to the actions of television news reporters, who follow their instructors' directions by keeping their hands still, but instead emphasise points with manic nods of the head like a hungry chicken or, when reading from an autocue (which for some reason means a sideways-cocked head), looking like a coy budgerigar.

English discussion gestures are on the whole still rather stiff and awkward. There are, for example, the RIGID PALM GESTICULATORS: palms upwards and flat, fingers together, they mime back-handed downward slaps, hands usually alternating; or else swat sideways as if attacking an unseen mosquito. Feminists and other females with strong opinions often turn into TWO-HANDED BOSOM PLUCKERS: fingertips bunched, palms hollow, they emphasise points by plucking imaginary bits of fluff from their cleavage. This can be done either symmetrically with both hands or alternately, one at a time. The WOOL-WINDERS horizontally rotate their hands round each other, as if winding wool or exercising them inside a fur muff. Sometimes speakers gesticulate two-handedly with interlocked figures, palms vertical: we'll call it the CAT'S CRADLE effect.

PALM THUMPERS punctuate their statements by knocking the fist of one hand into the palm of the other; and there's the KARATE CHOP, single or double: points are emphasised with fierce downward movements of the edge of the flat palm (one or both) which are guaranteed to knock out anyone unwise enough to get underneath it. This is quite intimidating, and an unfair aid to any argument. Then there are the ENUMERATORS. They appear to be making counting movements by bringing the index finger of one hand down on successively extended fingers of the other; though they are

48

not in fact making numerical points at all. Even the TOP HOLERS are no longer thought to be typically French: the tips of thumb and forefinger meet to form a circle, meaning 'A1 – top hole'.

Other television chat show conventions dictate that host as well as guests should make their entrance by lightly tripping down one or two carpeted steps, although everybody surely knows by now that in order to do so they have to climb some rickety stairs at the back of the set. Michael Parkinson pioneered the WATER SIPPING APPLAUSE ACKNOWLEDGMENT. As soon as the audience starts clapping he reaches for the tumbler. Some kind of allergy to studio lights seems to have given him a distressing, recurring itch on the right-hand side of his nose, which he periodically strokes with a forefinger. I used to think it was a secret signal for the autocue to get a move on, but am told this is not so. Lately, the chat-show HAND ON KNEE gesture denoting absolute, total sincerity has been both overdone and parodied. One need hardly say that chat-show participants always kiss on entering the set as if they had just met, when we all know that they probably spent most of the day together – deciding what they should say to each other. Kissing is OK man-to-woman and woman-to-woman; man-to-man contact is generally but not always restricted to a firm handshake.

Politicians are a subject on their own, though it is clear that the further left the opinions expressed, the more extravagant the gestures. This needs closer study by an expert, so I will mention only the SCARGILL FINGER WAGGLE and the LENIN FIST. Scargill's body language seems to be as limited as his vocabulary (why didn't someone find him an alternative to the inevitably recurring 'butchering this industry?') and he always underlines every syllable with a furious forefinger, every so often relieving the monotony by changing hands: one jab per syllable. Hitler did exactly the same thing, and of course, all demagogues not only practise their gestures before a looking-glass but know full well that the best way of getting their message across is by the endless repetition of slogans. The LENIN HARANGUE STANCE is based on a familiar, idealised painting and needs hardly be described. The posture strictly requires a waistcoat into whose arm-hole the left thumb has to be hooked (though in this age of the two-piece suit it may be mimed); the body leans far forward, the right arm is bent at right angles, and the fist clenched. Again, the fist emphasises the syllables.

A 102-year-old lady had been attacked and robbed by thugs, the news-reader told us, and they had stolen (he said) 'her *life savings*'. According to my calculator she would have had to put by 58.82352p in each year of her long life. But of course she didn't. It was just another example of knee-jerk news-speak. To the hack, every sum, however small, stolen from a working-class person, constitutes that person's 'life savings'. You'll never read 'thieves attacked and robbed retired National Coal Board chief Ian McGregor of £856,000, his life savings.'

News-speak operates rigid class-distinctions. (Where are those famous Equality Officers the NUJ appoints to each chapel?) Every female child of a rich man is automatically described as an 'heiress', even if no details of her father's will are known, or that he drew one up. Never is a son described as an 'heir' in the financial sense, only lineally. That poor old lady may live in a terrace-house belonging either to her or the local council and worth, say, £20,000. No figure will be given in her case. But go a few notches up the social scale and we shall be told 'the couple returned to their £125,000 bungalow in Essex in their £43,000 Rolls Royce, having collected their son from his £2,800 a term public school.' Whether the house really belongs to them or the Halifax Building Society, or the car to a finance company, is immaterial. Your average Daily Hack may not have many values but he knows the price of everything, with subtle distinctions: illicit drugs are apparently valueless indoors. They only have a 'street' value. He knows his optics, too: no binoculars are ever less than 'high-powered'; and his explosives. One glance at a few bits of twisted metal and we are told with categorical certainty that it was 'a car-bomb containing 130 lb of TNT'.

The obligatory condition in which one returns from holiday is 'bronzed and fit', unless carried from the plane on a stretcher; and the uninjured in an accident are twin-termed 'alive and well'. The task of recovering or identifying dead bodies must always be preceded by the word 'grim', but the fortunate people who survive unhurt invariably 'walk away'. I once saw a man 'walk away' from a burning wreck at a speed that would not have disgraced Steve Cram. But acquitted from a prosecution you 'walk free' from court – even if your feet hardly touch the ground before you are taken – sorry, 'whisked' away in a car, usually a 'fast' car.

A young journalist who recently covered a murder trial tells me that when she returned to her office the editor asked, 'Was he dragged screaming from court?' She replied, 'No, he just looked a bit upset and a policeman led him down to the cells.' The editor replied, 'You will write, "A man was dragged screaming from court . . ."' If tears are shed, there are only two ways of weeping: 'openly' or 'unashamedly'. 'Heartbreak' is the standard additive for sad mothers ('heartbreak mum').

'Heartless thieves' is probably how our hacks would start the story about the 102-year-old woman. But they don't consider it heartless to hound a newly bereaved person, till they get some sort of 'story' from him, or her.

Press headaches are always figurative, and come in two sizes: 'giant' and 'outsize'. Every planned robbery which is not a snatch is 'daring', and the bank that is robbed gets the obligatory prefix 'high street', even if it is situated in the market square. Stores and big shops are also 'high street'; but smaller establishments are always 'corner shops', even if they *are* physically on the high street. A courtship taking less than six months or so is 'whirlwind', followed perhaps by a 'tempestuous' marriage. Ex-wives (seldom ex-husbands, curiously enough) are described as 'estranged', an archaic word never used in any other context.

New babies as invariably 'bounce' as Goodwood is 'glorious', even in a rainstorm. I was under the impression that this knee-jerk prose was spread insidiously, like AIDS, from news-person to news-person. But no, it is *actually taught* in at least one polytechnic in the South of England, which has a faculty of journalism where the students are set exercises and examinations in the correct use of clichés.

Bring back capital punishment. If only so that thugs who rob old ladies can 'enjoy' the traditional 'hearty breakfast' on their last morning. But I fear they're more likely to 'walk free'.

<hr>

'. . . and you're an inveterate writer to the press,' said John Dunn when we recorded *It Makes Me Laugh*, a programme on Radio 4. I denied it vehemently, and hoped the exchange would be edited out. But he confronted me with the evidence: the sneaky BBC had apparently for years been keeping an embarrassing cuttings dossier on me. And there they were, the letters, usually to *The Times* and printed in the bottom right-hand corner, where the quips go. I suppose the man who raises serious issues and wants to change the world carefully pastes his published letters into an album. I have forgotten most of mine. If I have kept any it would have been by sheer accident; for I always feel uneasy about writing, afraid of being labelled an exhibitionist bore. In truth I'm a reluctant letter-writer, have tried many times to be methodical about filing and answering letters but never succeeded. I appear to be unable to put finger to typewriter unless someone has commissioned something from me and it's almost past the deadline. I did once have occasion to write to the *Daily Telegraph*, because I felt I could add to the story of another reader's experiences with HM Customs. My tale was of some imported textbooks that had mysteriously disappeared after a Customs inspection. The reply came from the topmost man of HM Customs and Excise, who leapt into print as hastily as would any press attaché of a foreign embassy, indignantly denying everything, of course. Fed the wrong information by one of his lying minions he got all his facts wrong – and the *Telegraph* gullibly printed them. I left it at that, and ruefully decided to stick to quips in future; and to *The Times*, the Newspaper of Record, if it will have them.

There are some strange myths that have grown up over the years. For example, that three letters published in *The Times* assure the writer an entry in *Who's Who?*. Or that letters written as it were *ex cathedra* from a clerical address such as a vicarage or rectory were more likely to be published than those from Acacia Avenue. However, 'The Bishop's Palace' at the head of a letter must be a sure passport to print, and I doubt whether many emanating from the House of Lords get turned down. Letters written under an assumed name, or those giving no address, are said to stand no chance of being published. However, by some remarkable oversight *The Times* recently published one from an obscure political extremist organisation written over an anonymous-sounding name over a British Monomark 'address', i.e. a confidential, untraceable box number: the nearest thing to an anonymous letter from a fictitious address.

You can always judge a paper by the quality of its correspondence columns, the way the letters are selected, and the manner in which it responds to them. Every letter to the Editor of the *Telegraph* and *The Times* is acknowledged, not only out of courtesy but as a safeguard against impostors. These acknowledgments are, however, marked 'Personal'; after all, some correspondents may not wish to let their secretaries, servants or wives to know that they had written a letter, let alone that it had been rejected.

Like many readers I turn to the letters page first when I open a paper, but always glance at the signature before reading a letter. If it is from a foreign embassy it is seldom worth reading. It will more often than not contain a 'categorical denial' – in other words be full of lies. After all, the sole function of a press attaché is to lie abroad for his country (see p. 179). No letter signed 'Prospective Parliamentary Candidate, Eatanswill (or whatever) Constituency' is likely to be anything but a desperate attempt to keep the candidate's name before the public. People who read more than one newspaper soon get to know the passionate campaigners for this or that cause, the self-publicists and the bores. These tend to resort to a form of saturation-bombing by sending the same letter to every paper in the hope that one, at least, will score a hit. It is rather like writing the same love-letter to several different women.

But during the long miners' strike, when the press was so full of ugly news of pickets, burnings and intimidation that one hardly bothered to read about them, I scored a rare letters double. Its double effect would, however, have been missed by any but compulsive multi-newspaper-readers like me: a kind of private joke meant more for the letters editors than the public.

From Mr Fritz Spiegl
Sir, Thank you for helping to revive attractive and apt old English words, e.g., the miners' "stoggage"(my – early – edition, June 27).

On checking with the OED I find that to be "stogged" means "to be stuck in mud, mire, bog or the like."
Yours faithfully,
FRITZ SPIEGL,

Sir,—Thank you for helping to revive attractive and apt old English words, eg your apology for a "two-day stappage" (first edition, July 13). On checking with the OED I find " stap (17th Century) . . . exclamation of surprise, anger, etc., or as an asseveration." — Yours faithfully,
Fritz Spiegl.
Liverpool.

The Times, 30 June   *Guardian*, 17 July

Guardian letters have a flavour all of their own. Many start with the Jewish/American, hands-on-hips-indignant, 'So . . .' – as in 'Sir, – So Ms Johnson thinks single-parent women should . . .' You get a high concentration of the buzzing 'Ms' in that paper; as well as letters from couples who write from the same address but sign with different surnames: either live-togethers or married couples where the female partner insists on remaining a Ms with her own name. 'Sir, Oh dear . . .' is also a favourite *Guardian* start (but not as favourite as it is with radio listeners who send complaints to *Woman's Hour*, where letters beginning 'Why, oh why, oh why . . .' and 'I'm sick and tired of . . .' are received by the sackful). The *Guardian*, which led the field with f*ck, recently had a letter coyly starting with 'Cripes!' a word which is to Christ what 'gee!' is to Jesus, 'golly!' to God, and 'bally' to bloody. Another *Guardian* speciality is the cumulative letter joke, in which correspondents take up and elaborate on themes from previous letters. Thus if there have been separate correspondences about, say, short people, old men, monkeys and sex, someone is sure to write a letter starting 'As a four-foot-two septuagenarian who enjoys sex with chimpanzees . . .' The further you go towards the political left, so correspondents' forenames contract. Militant letters are often signed by people called Ros, Liz, Maggie, Les, Des or Dave, with Dave an easy winner.

The 'As . . .' opening, establishing the writer's qualifications, is an old stalwart. A writer to *The Times* began engagingly, 'Sir, – As the surviving son of the first Diocesan to dispose of his episcopal palace (Chester, in 1919) and, later, as partner in a firm of architects who had much to do with the housing problems of several bishops, two archbishops and a host of parish clergy, I hope that I may be allowed to add a postscript . . .' *Times* readers used to beg with old-fashioned courtesy permission to 'trespass upon your valuable space' but don't so much now; but many still have the honour to be the Editor's obedient servant. The chummy 'Yours sincerely' close, now increasingly common, never seems to fit well with the formal 'Sir –' opening, but when I put 'Yours faithfully' to a paper I really mean it. On the other hand, 'My attention has been drawn to . . .' is a way of saying 'I wouldn't normally be seen dead reading your rag . . .'

Unlike foreign noblemen and dignitaries, Britons are usually modest about signing their own titles, honours and other qualifications, especially peers, who sign their surname only. A letter on House of Lords paper signed 'Yours faithfully, Jones' will have the letters editors scurrying for Debrett to check which one he is; or if he writes from home, which address of one particular Lord Jones tallies with that given on the writing-paper. Then they can put 'From Lord Jones of Llanfairynghornwy' between the letter and its headline. The *Daily Telegraph* used not to put 'From . . .' in this way unless the writer was somebody important or titled, but has now accorded the courtesy to every correspondent. *The Times* has long adopted this practice. However, one can almost sense the distaste with which its letters staff put 'from Mrs Jane Smith' above the letter of a woman who signed herself 'Jane Smith' without divulging the forename of her husband; they would in accordance with old custom wish to put 'from Mrs John Smith'. Only John Smith's widow or ex-wife has, by this convention, a right to be 'Mrs Jane Smith'.

Many papers now omit both the 'Sir' opening and the 'Yours faithfully/truly/etc.' subscription, making readers' letters into small, signed articles; which I think is a mistake.

They also ignore time-honoured conventions of address. If Lord Jones's wife Sally signs herself 'Sally Jones', they will put 'from Lady Sally Jones', which she is not, unless she is an Earl's or Duke's daughter. Perhaps there is something to be said after all for the informality of 'the Old Codgers', which is how the letters editors of the *Daily Mirror* sign their comments.

I like the informality of radio today, the asides and the neat ways in which slips are sometimes turned to advantage. Captured on tape, somewhere, I have an announcer giving the weather on Radio 3 (where the work of meaty-logical experts is given in standard English): 'Many areas will be dry and warm, with some sunshine. It actually says "shoeshine" on my script, so with any luck you might get a nice light tan.' It would have been unthinkable in the John Snagge days. But unfortunately some radio informality can turn into matey-ness, which in my old-fashioned view is best left to local, 'community' or downright junk radio.

'In the early 1960s,' wrote G. M. Miller in the first edition of the *BBC Pronouncing Dictionary of British Names*, 'the BBC felt that it would be more realistic to throw the stage open to the men behind the scenes, so that newsmen participated personally in news broadcasts, meteorologists gave us our weather forecasts, policemen enlisted our aid direct from Scotland Yard, and the BBC Motoring Unit kept us hourly aware of traffic problems. Their prime advantage is that they are informed and articulate on their own subject . . .' And so it came to pass. But Miss Miller went on, 'They hold the interest and sympathy of the listener because of their expertise . . . (and are) consequently easy to follow . . .' and here some may disagree. Newsmen certainly lend immediacy to their reports, provided you can understand what they say over a bad telephone line against the sound of gunfire or other noises they call 'actuality'. One hears no policemen on Radio 3 and few on Radio 4; but even though the Inspectors Knacker of the Yard often have a certain parodiable quality, their messages are usually clear. It is after all part of their job. They may 'proceed' where others go, talk about 'elements' when they mean people, and about 'helping with inquiries'; but they are used to, and trained in, talking to their own men and the public. All the same, traffic news seems to have been taken away from the traffic experts and given to announcers. As it is aimed at thousands of motorists in charge of potential murder weapons called 'vehicles', the clarity of the speakers is more immediately important than their friendliness. And the BBC Shipping Forecast, even more a matter of life or death for seafarers, is invariably read by the clearest speakers, the professional announcers.

Only the weather information for ordinary folk is still in the hands of the weathermen and women apparently considered part of the entertainment industry (witness their habit of thanking announcers for handing over to them!). They are by no means ordinary folk but highly trained in their particular science (and are surely more often right than wrong in their predictions of something so unpredictable as the British weather), usually cheerful, jolly and friendly (except those who have been told to be, and put on a kind of bedside manner). The only trouble is that, like so many scientists, some of them may not be too good at communicating; and as a result I, for one, often cannot understand what they are saying. Or if I can, I get distracted by their idiosyncrasies, begin wondering how they spell some of the curious sounds they make – and lose the thread of what they were trying to tell me. They fail to hold my interest and my sympathy, and what set out to be information has become, at best, a friendly sort of rustic folk noise in the background.

That is where the 1970s idea falls down. Why not also throw open the job of designing traffic-warning and other road signs to the men who mend the motorways, or even to the civil engineers? Of course, the spelling may be haphazard, and some of the z's and s's back-to-front, and by the time you've figured it out you may have hit a bollard. Who cares so long as they have character and friendliness? I do, for a start. All I want for my alas imperfect ears is information intelligibly presented. I am aware that as an ex-foreigner I shouldn't be criticising the locals. But if 40 years ago I'd had to ask the way in halting English, I would have hoped not to chance on a charming rustic speaking in the broadest Mummerzet.

So, for the enlightenment of other middle-aged ex-foreigners with ears that no longer respond to all frequencies, here's a glossary of Weather English. *Bitsa rain*: rain now informally falls in pieces, though in the old days I believe such 'bits' would have meant hail. *Icelated*: as in 'icelated *shahs*'. These may be *scat*(tered), or *winchy*; and may lead to *grind* frost *here'n dare*: one is tempted to ask, 'Where and where?' *Wince*: these may reach *gaah* force, but when they blow southerly the weather may turn *mahda*, with higher *temchas*. At least for a *whaa*. The *Bishiles* include places like the *Ahlamahn* and the *Ahlawite*; and *Eyeland*, which is divided into two parts, *Norden* and *Sudden*. Far *to* the north (prepositions suffer much stress) is a cold place called *Arseland*. But *derby* is not a place: 'Derby bright periods . . .' *Courage-ways* are the areas used by *roh jewsers*. *June* is not a month but a preposition: 'June the early part of the evening . . .', though the weather may improve '*tords* morning . . .', ending with the dreadful plague of gnats: '*gnats* it.'

I can't remember the exact words of the news-reader as it was some years ago, but they went something like this: 'Marjorie Anderson, who was presenter of the BBC's *Woman's Hour* programme for 21 years until her retirement in 1973 . . .' And as soon as that rather tortuous sentence had got under way I, as I am sure did thousands of other listeners who remembered her with affection, felt that the ending would be '. . . has died at her home in Kensington.' Fortunately we were all misled, and Miss Anderson is well and enjoying her retirement. Indeed the news was good, for the sentence ended something like '. . . has been left a legacy of £20,000 by a listener whom she had never met.'

What had died was the famous BBC Black-Edged Voice, and it has now almost completely disappeared – whether for lack of technique or as a result of a conscious move towards a more detached news style I do not know. It was a simple device first heard, I think, when there was much bad news during the war: a sympathetic octave drop between the first couple of words, or the subject's first and second names, prepared listeners for the worst. (Try saying someone's full name aloud to yourself and you'll see what I mean.) A year or so ago, every announcement I heard of the death of George Howard, the former Chairman of the BBC, seemed to be delivered in a manner so matter-of-fact that (had I not known he had been gravely ill for some time) I would at first have thought he had been given some award or distinction.

One does not expect anything so subtle as a sympathetic inflexion from the daleks who rattle through the news on your friendly local Radio Rubbish; after all they have to get back as quickly as possible to the commercials or the pop music that are the reason for their existence. But at the BBC style still matters, and the broadcaster is constantly impressed with reminders that he must not offend listeners. It is probably haste, combined with the occasional lack of imagination, that makes even some of the most distinguished presenters come out with ludicrously composite, unpunctuated information such as '. . . he was aged forty-six and leaves a wife and three children the time is twenty to eight.' A little less dependence on the gruesome style of Fleet Street, where they positively delight in bringing bad news, might go a long way to help. For example, if you cannot (or will not) use the sympathetic inflexion, why not try inversion? 'The death is announced in London of . . .' at the beginning of the item would spare friends and relatives that agonising wait through a convoluted sentence that starts with a person's name and then insists on going through a list of his qualifications before coming to the real point of the story. Has he died or just been awarded the OBE?

News items about airliners are often cast in a singularly clumsy way, taking no account of the thousands of listeners who have loved ones in the air at that very moment. As surely everyone will confirm, one's heart stops before the gist of such an announcement is arrived at. It could often be reached with more sensitivity. When some unfortunate tourists went missing after being abducted in Zimbabwe the BBC news-reader said: 'Zimbabwean radio has said that three bodies of Europeans have been discovered. But the government in

Harare has denied this report.' That, too, was surely both insensitive and the wrong way round. I could imagine the anguish their parents (who at that time would have had some hope that the young people were still alive) must have felt at hearing the stark report about bodies having been discovered, and their (alas, only temporary) relief at hearing the government's denial. I would have put, 'The Zimbabwean government has denied reports that . . .' After all, news-editors do not hesitate to take their inversions to an absurd degree when it suits them, as in sentences they feel should end (in the manner of the show-business barker) with the name of the reporter: 'Following the course of events at the scene of the extensive police operations has been BBC Home Affairs Correspondent Chris Underwood.'

I planted a verbal tease in the foregoing paragraph. When did people start to 'go missing'? Until about fifteen years ago people merely disappeared. Now one often reads or hears melancholy news-items like, 'The murdered woman went missing on Saturday after a shopping trip to Margate . . .' It appears to suggest that she purposely and knowingly decided to go missing, and in order to have herself murdered, too – just as she decided to go shopping to Margate. I put it down as another German-inspired Americanism, related to *verlorengegangen*, i.e. 'gone lost'; and perhaps even related to the injunction one might well address to the action of going missing – 'get lost!'

'Questioning,' said Johnson to Boswell, 'is not the mode of conversation among gentlemen.' And he added, 'There may be parts of his former life which he may not wish to be made known to other persons, or even brought to his own recollection.' Today's interviewers on radio and television have no such compunction. Their brief is to be abrasive and searching, to take up an opposing stance even if they privately agree with their subject. They prefer 'putting' to asking: as in, 'Let me put it to you . . .' (when they get home after a hard day at the microphone, do they say, 'Put it to your mother to get me a cup of tea'?) and may even accuse him of make-belief ('Aren't you living in Cloud-cuckoo-land?'). They usually start off by telling him what he already knows: his name, what his job is, where he hails from, and why he is being questioned: 'Jim Thwaites, you are a farmer from Kent and you're expecting a record harvest.' It is an old broadcasting convention to impart information to the listener by bouncing it off an interviewee or colleague. (On *Start the Week* we used to call this device a 'Well Richard Piece' – because Richard would give you your 'in' by asking some pre-arranged question to get you going; and you'd start off on an equally contrived piece that appeared to be addressed to him, and which always began, 'Well, Richard . . .') No worse than addressing the chair, I suppose, but the listener may wonder whether he isn't eavesdropping.

Another convention is that the interviewer shows no reaction to his subject's answers, which is sensible enough. One would hardly expect him to interject, 'Is it really?' or 'You don't say!' or even whistle sharply through his teeth; though it can be disconcerting for the interviewee not to get any audible feedback from his questioner, even to jokes, apart from silent 'noddies'. These are a television phenomenon – occasional shots of the interviewer nodding sagely and encouragingly. And surely everybody knows by now that these noddies (and often questions, too, to answers already in the can) are recorded when the interviewee has gone, and edited in? Few interviews get the luxury of two cameras.

Interviewers are now over-fond of prefacing questions with the word 'just', which sounds like a foolish demand for exact quantification and often is. When Edward Heath left London for Bonn to take part in a concert, the interviewer said, 'Mr Heath, you are conducting in Germany. *Just* how important *is* this in terms *of* the Common Market?' The former Prime Minister, an old hand at *not* answering questions, brushed it aside and said what he wanted to say. I wished he had played the interviewer at his own game and replied: 'In terms of the Common Market, if you want me to quantify, just 3,984 semiquavers.'

It is strange how many interviewees seem to be too over-awed to answer back – or are such retorts always cut? To questions like that put to Mr Heath, there simply are no answers; or to questions like 'Just how disappointed *are* you

61

not to have been re-elected?' In an item on *You and Yours* about gifted children, some obnoxiously smart nine-year-old, who had a pert little answer to everything, was effectively silenced by: 'How clever *are* you?'

Where you or I would ask 'Why did you do it?', the interviewer says, 'Just what was your motivation?' Whenever a reporter comes out yet again with the stock question 'How do you feel?' I long for someone to snap back 'How the hell do you *think* I feel?' Many tear-stained bereaved are asked such foolish questions, at a time when none should be asked at all. Also, conversely, 'Just how did you feel when you heard your son was safe?' What *do* they expect? An impromptu Ode to Joy in heroic couplets? There is equally no reply to questions like 'Just how disappointed *are* you not to have been re-elected?' On *Midweek* we had, 'Michael Selby, you work in the prison service. *Can* murder be fun?' (Though I should add that the 'theme' was detective fiction.)

But one can enjoy the occasional put-down. When a reporter said, 'Mr Hattersley, you were hit over the head by a chair,' the deputy leader of the Labour Party, evidently a stickler for grammar, replied: 'No, I was hit over the head *with* a chair *by* a demonstrator.' And after Iranian terrorists invaded the American embassy, killing some people, the excited interviewer's question, 'Ambassador, will you tell us just *exactly* what happened?' was calmly answered over a poor telephone line with, 'No. I can't tell you exactly what happened but I can tell you exactly what I saw.'

'Just' is in fact no more than an opening, a throat-clearing noise. I'm not an experienced interviewer, but used occasionally to catch myself doing double starts to questions: 'When did you – when did you compose your symphony?' This was not hesitancy: the first 'When did you' was merely a clearing of the throat, a substitute for the once fashionable BBC opener: 'Tell me . . .' – a device to get the vocal chords moving that figures prominently and frequently in archive interviews. But unlike 'just' it at least had a meaning. A modernised *Merchant of Venice* would probably have 'Bill Shakespeare, just where *is* fancie bred?' – for the opening 'just' always brings in its wake an equally overstressed verb later in the sentence.

I also like the almost impertinent keep-it-short injunction which interviewers build into a question: 'Very briefly, Reverend, just what *is* the implication of 2,000 years of Christianity on Western philosophy?'

And of course I end (or 'wind up') with the stock closing question: 'Where do you go from here?'

Perhaps it's a mistake to begin a programme with an illustration so thought-provoking that the listener spends the rest of the time thinking about it. I tuned in recently to *The Interview*, a brilliant Radio 4 feature. It dealt with the art of successful job interviews, and must have been of help to thousands. It opened with a prospective employer winding up an interview with 'Can I ask you one more question? What would you say is your greatest character defect?' And of course I spent much of the rest of the programme wondering what I would have said. An academic exercise: no-one is likely to offer me a job anyway; and besides, I would have been hopelessly thrown by the fact that he said '*dee*fect' instead of 'd'*fect*'. So I might have felt obliged to reply, 'My inability to change with the times, an irrational impatience with those who readily do, and a deep reluctance to unlearn what I learned many years ago.' And it would have been back to the Labour Exchange. Sorry, Job Centre.

Which is why I forgot I was supposed to be listening to the radio and became engrossed in the *Oxford English Dictionary* instead. 'Interview', it says, is recorded as far back as 1514 and comes from the French *entre vue*, 'a meeting of persons face to face . . .'; but 'interviewing' did not arrive until 1869, when it was 'confined to American journalism' (and wonderfully lampooned, by the way, in an essay by Mark Twain). But 'interviewee', according to the *OED*, is a BBC invention of 1959, attributed to Freddie Grisewood. Since then the art has come a long way, and its principal academy, *The World at One*, is twenty years old.

Political or investigative interviewers are usually journalists of distinction or former politicians themselves. These are the deep-sea anglers who play the slippery big fish, the fraudster or politician who has something to hide, whereas the chat-show hosts deal with the amiable tiddlers who merely come to sell something. For some reason, shiftiness and dishonesty are more easily exposed on the radio than when the culprit can be seen on television, wriggling in embarrassing discomfiture; and one is always amazed by the ability of Sir Robin Day or one of the other heavyweights to remain calm and polite when faced with an interviewee who tries to hide behind verbal aggression or downright rudeness.

The chat-show host who gently encourages guests to exchange pleasantries with him, or steers them towards carefully rehearsed or previously discussed jokes or anecdotes has less need to think on his feet, or rather, his seat. But you can always tell if things are not going well – say, if the interviewee forgets the pre-transmission chat and the host in desperation has to jog his memory ('And, er, wasn't there an amusing thing that happened to you when you were playing Hamlet in Copenhagen?'). This kind of interviewing is much more of a team effort than many listeners realise. I am always amazed how anyone can use the words '*My* next guest . . .' when he or she has been furnished with an entire library of cuttings, a clipboardful of facts, and perhaps questions written by the producer with the help of an army of researchers. There is also the failsafe of an earpiece through which the producer can drive an interviewer like one of those cable-controlled toy cars. Or did you think all TV personalities wore hearing-aids? (The art of using the earpiece appears to lie in not blurting out 'OK, Nigel, will do.')

The interviewer needs charm but the kind discernible only to the outsider, for as soon as he knows he's got it (like Wogan), it can become an excess of self-esteem, and he's lost it. But above all he needs what Bishop Henson called 'the fatal facility for continuous utterance' – which is why non-political interviewing and disc-jockeying may go hand-in-hand – and why there are so few great masters, like John Dunn and Brian Matthew on Radio 2. Jimmy Young is rare in that he has a foot in both camps but it is fair to say that he probably considers himself less of an interrogator than a kind of sound-board off which a politician can bounce his opinions at the listener. But although he, too, has his supporting troops, he is often obliged to discard the prepared questions and do some quick thinking. Nothing shows the power of the media better than a news bulletin opening with 'The Prime Minister, speaking on the Jimmy Young Show, has revealed that . . .' Whenever I hear that historic recording of Neville Chamberlain's speech on 3 September 1939 ('Eh em speaking to you from the cabinet room . . .'), I wonder if World War III will open with the words, 'Well, Jimmy . . .'

'In addition to expert knowledge, the sporting commentator must also obviously have a good voice and great fluency . . .' said an anonymous writer in the *BBC Handbook* of 1928 – and thereby coined a new word. The above passage is quoted by the *OED* as the earliest instance of 'commentator'. But we've come a long way since *Radio Times* carried a grid diagram of the football pitch for each commentary game and commentators called out numbers like map references to describe the position of play for the listener at home. The modern commentator has turned his job into a fine art, does a lot of homework, performs minor miracles of instant analysis and player recognition, and endlessly researches complicated statistics. But if you listen critically you will find that the considerable art and admirable science of 'comment-ating' (first recorded, according to the *OED*, in the *Radio Daily*, 1939) are embedded in thick layers of solid cliché matter: a few grains of nourishment in a great bulk of preformed plastic pudder emerging as ready-made phrases. To start with, radio commentators to a man think we still have our grids before us and never fail to tell us that 'Everton (or whoever) are playing from right to left', or 'United are defending the goal away to our right'; which isn't much use when they don't tell us where they're sitting. And nothing is ever merely 'to our right': it is always '*away* to our right'. In football you can paradoxically 'get back in front'; shoot 'narrowly wide'; or 'leave yourself open at the back' while remaining perfectly decent. Managers are said to hope for 'a result', which means a favourable one; or to 'get on terms', meaning equal terms (or 'even stevens').

The trick seems to be to extrude verbiage on automatic pilot so as to gain thinking-time, and to pad out even the clichés. Shots are therefore not just 'high' or 'wide' but 'high, wide and not very handsome'. Adjectives are freely attached as appropriate (the 'gangly forward', the 'hapless goalkeeper', the 'disconsolate red-haired defender', etc). It's this split-second ability to adapt old clichés to the ever-changing kaleidoscope of play that is the real art of keeping talking. Should there be a goal, the crowd always 'erupts'. Goals come in various sorts from 'soft' and 'scrambled' to 'world-class' ('*What* a goal!'). Even when the commentator is working on television he will thus relentlessly describe what every viewer can see for himself. John Motson, who is extremely good at his job, once said, 'For those of you who are watching in black-and-white, Norwich are playing in yellow . . .' – which makes more sense than might at first appear.

Smaller clubs are 'minnows', and when they beat one of the big clubs in non-league fixtures they become 'giant-killers'. For 'the Cup', like death, is in each season described afresh as 'the great leveller'. For penalties the referee 'had no hesitation in pointing to the spot', and the player who takes the kick invariably 'steps up'. When you hear that a player who scored a goal 'had time to pick his spot' it means he was able unhindered to set up his shot, not that he had a bad dose of acne.

Do not be alarmed if you hear staccato bursts like 'Moran . . . Jones . . . taken short . . . Smith . . .' They are passing the ball, not water. 'The ball breaks for England' spells no breakage; nor does 'it breaks off the head of an Arsenal player'. You may think balls are round but they can also be square, long, short or wide ('he lofted a square ball into the area'); also through balls, chipped balls, fifty-fifty balls, intelligent, loose – and dead. A dead ball specialist is not a deceased footballer but one who is good at playing from 'dead ball situations', that is, free-kicks and the like, kicking a ball that is at rest. Balls bear little more than the maker's name, but they provide important reading-matter: 'He read that ball well.' In commentators' parlance the football field is 'the park', and the ground 'the floor'. Goals are never merely kicked but stabbed, latched, knocked, nodded, hammered or slotted home; or tucked away, scrambled, screwed or glanced in; not only 'pushed' or 'slotted' in but also 'pulled back'.

out. His left-foot shot cannoned
off McIlroY to leave Rimmer
debating if he ought to take up
tiddlywinks. But Arsenal, who

Albion packed their penalty
area like they had heard there
was a sale on there. And despite another fruitless plunge by

The Blues left the field to a
richly deserved standing
ovation from a crowd
which was already dream-
ing of silverware.

With his departure a few minutes
later the urgency went out of
Leicester like the air out of a penny
whistle.

...aar was now suffering
...ne of his rushes of blood to the
head and for several minutes he
mishandled like a drunk juggler.

with a lovely pass that split the
Liverpool defence like a chisel
for Emmanuel to drive a fierce

header was so delicately placed
it would have gone through a
keyhole. Alas for Gray, though.

ceded in recent months - Taylor's legs were swept from under
him and Hoddle's penalty shot
smashed into the net like a
well-delivered custard pie.

Davies cavorted like a
circus-trained giraffe in the Chelsea
penalty-box

It was therefore appropriate that
the only goal after half an hour
should be scored when he was
nonceably off duty, like a sentry
sneaking a cigarette behind the
guard hut. Radford and ''

other end where Lloyd and Smith
idly flexed their muscles like
bouncers at a Darby and Joan club
dance.

fortunate to lose.
Liverpool erupted in this match
like a spring that has been coiled
too long. In the first minute.

SHATTERINGLY beaten by
Porto in midweek, and with a
sick list like someth... out of
the Crimean War, U ASTON VILLA came to the Den
like a sleek limousine finding
itself pitted against a production
saloon.

gradually diluted to less
theatrical tactics, like incessant
high crosses from the wings,
and they had about as much
success as a Scottish comic in
Chad.

functioning. The weakness
showed here, like a traffic light
as Hodgson struggles to get into liance.

West Ham were
already wearing the dazed look of
men who had been struck by
something unpleasant while
standing under scaffolding.

miskicked. Dalglish, darting in
was more collected,
like a dirk to stab the ball in
off the far post.

vective. Case measured was
for Dalglish to run on to down
the right, which nine times ou.
of 10 would have been as precisely delivered as a letter
...ure hit
Clemence dropped it and
was left scrambling on hands
and knees like a man who has
lost one of his contact lenses

But the Kop's smiles, not to
mention their voices, froze like
snow in a fridge when Smith
pushed a careless ball to Gray-

Birmingham did most of the
attacking, but their moves looked
like old-fashioned steam trains
running slowly on disused and
rusty railway lines.

From the start the players
were inclined to give the ball
the kind of attention that a
pork chop might have expected
from a pack of ravenous dogs

moves. First, from a short
corner the England man thrust
a low ball, deadly as a stiletto.
into the goal area, only for

Highway skipping past his
erstwhile skipper, Hughes, with
all the confidence of a
millionaire And his cleavin...

Extra time was played out
while cramp-racked personnel
cluttered the pitch like the
departure lounge of Luton
airport during a strike

box, where Stoke's defenders
stood still as a petrified forest as
Leach ran in from the left to
head home as he pleased

But Dalglish was on hand and
he pounced on the ball around
the penalty spot like the
stockiest mongoose in the
business.

Piekering came along wit...
another shot which pissed outside, but at least Everton were
finding some answer to the
Arsenal pressure which was

once again totally vindicated. After
fighting with all the frenzy of a
food mixer to save the match, they
...me in with virtually the last kick

Glazier's second half was one of
almost religious stillness Coventry
had lost their initial enthusiasm.

"I think the defence is looking
a bit oldish," says Jimmy
Adamson, who has been to see
Brazil. "Chipped balls seem to
put them in a bit of trouble."

keeper's diving body hit the
ground. He had the glazed look of
a man struck by something which
had come out of the dark at him.

Gray's header
floated past Cooper with the
unstoppable majesty of a pas-
senger ferry coming into Dover.

Around him the Soviet
competitors were exploding in a
scintillating splashes. Bogachev
produced three triple somer-
saults with twist in his 20 sec-

Without Kennedy's influence
Liverpool were like a book
without its binding; much of
their play was loose leafed and
untidy, notable more for the

They ran about like the deranged heroes of a computer
game as they desperately attempted to prise open a very
sound defence.

blind alleys and for much
of the first hour the centre
of Everton's porous
defence had the look of
badly fitting double doors.

Kelly's sliced clearance on the
goal-line; Macari dashed across
the held like he was after the
last bus, shot and .. Rimmer

AYING in the shadow of the
Kop, with Liverpool swooning at
him out of the ramshu like a
squadron of Red Barons, Peter

His educated left foot was seen... impart few of its
£143,000 lessons as Liverpool, applying their science
powerfully, moved to the top of the First Division table
and sounded an ominous warning to their title rivals.

LIVERPOOL went skidding
out of the European Cup
in a Georgian downpour
last night. A storm of
three second half goals left
the English champions
shattered.

After an indifferent
opening spell, Everton
deservedly opened their
new season goal account
on seven minutes, after a
four-man bout of head
tennis.

WEMBLEY - BOUND Not-
tingham Forest redis...
covered their goal touch just
in time for Saturday's League
Cup final appearance, with
Kenny Burns and Trevor
Francis sounding a clear warning to Wolves with two goals
e'ch.

Villa hardly recovered from
their 2-0 defeat against
Penarol in Japan, were soon
three down to a Liverpool side
which swept over the frosted
...rfaces like professional ice-
...aters

field and Stein, as sinuous as a
signature, scored another by
beating three men at least

Parkes, Lampard and Martin,
whose long legs gathered in
the ball like garden rakes. But

not slow to demonstrate them
...either in midfield, where Law-
renson took the place of the
injured Souness, monopolising
the ball as if they had bought

67

Last-minute goals are 'snatched', possibly 'from the jaws of defeat' and often 'spare blushes'. Goalkeepers are fastidious fellows who set much store by spotless linen: 'He's had a clean sheet on each of the last four Saturdays.' There is also a good deal of shrugging off, as in 'Evans shrugged off the challenge of Brown' or even, 'Johnson got a broken nose but he shrugged it off.' Commentators either have an amazing sense of hearing, or are superb lip-readers, to a man; for they are always able to report what the referee or players are saying some sixty yards away in the midst of uproar: 'He shakes his head in disbelief and says how could I miss that' though spectators on television usually see nothing but a grimace and a lip-formation indicating some word beginning with 'f'. Or else it's, 'Ricky Thomas is claiming a penalty but Mr Taylor says to him oh no, laddie, I'm afraid you're not on.' And as the referee 'blows up' to signal the end of the game it's, 'And Mr Taylor says that'll do very nicely for the afternoon, thank you, gentlemen.' Purple football prose has been around far longer than commentators, and goes back to penny-a-line journalism, where you earned more by calling the goalkeeper the 'green-jerseyed custodian', the ball the 'leather' and the goals the 'white-painted woodwork' (Elgar wrote a little piece called 'He banged the leather for goal') and in print the clichés come even thicker and faster. A 'physical player' is one much given to fouling. Unprofessional conduct is called a 'professional foul'; but we are blithely reassured 'he *had* to do that' when one player hacks another down to prevent him from scoring. He had to do nothing of the kind, of course. He was merely thinking of his personal bonus that was at stake if his team lost, and so he was determined to go to any lengths to stop an opponent. (If the commentator is honest he will describe this kind of foul as 'cynical', not 'professional'.) If, as happens all too rarely, a player is sent off for such behaviour, he is said to 'take the long and lonely walk to the dressing-room for an early bath'. Even if he is only a couple of yards from the players' tunnel and is as lonely as a man can get with 50,000 baying spectators and the manager's consoling arm round his shoulder.

There is a special kind of football-writers' simile – again going back to the days of penny-a-line purple prose – which has to be seen to be believed. In the words of every manager: 'Wah Jimmy, that's what football is all about innit.'

———◆◆◆———

Eric Hammond of the moderate electricians' union EETPU took up the theme of an article of mine about the aggressive language of football-writers and condemned the vocabulary of violence and war indulged in by his more militant trades-unionist colleagues ('fight, smash, defeat, destroy, butchering this industry', etc.). If it isn't a 'winter of discontent' it will be a 'long hot summer', though I doubt whether either trades-union militants or the majority of the parrots reporting them care about the Shakespeare or William Faulkner they are quoting out of context.*

It is all part of the recognised language of confrontation (or confrontation *situations*). You don't have to be an educational psychologist to know that the teachers' foolish warcry, 'Disruptive Action', during their disputes of 1985/6, was sure to diminish sympathy for their no doubt excellent case. I mean, 'taking *disruptive* action'. The very words they themselves use to condemn the activities of unruly pupils! But this kind of crass stupidity is only what you would expect from the classroom kakistocracy common in English state-schools where often unkempt, ill-trained militants teach the scruffy, truculent ignorant. As dutiful affiliates to the TUC

* The lines *Now is the winter of our discontent/Made glorious summer by this son of York ...* come from Shakespeare's *Richard III*, 1,1, and have been appropriated only for the much quoted line, which has little or nothing to do with the way it is now over-used. *Long hot summer*: 'A threat of violence in Negro ghettos, when summer heat shortens tempers and crowds gather out of doors. The phrase began as the title of a 1958 movie based on a number of works by William Faulkner; a television series based on the characters, called *The Long Hot Summer*, ran on the ABC-TV network in 1965 and 1966.' (William Safire, *The New Language of Politics*, Collier Books, 1968, 1972.) John F. Kennedy, in 1961, after some particularly frigid talks with N. Khrushchev, made the impromptu, imaginative and ominously cryptic remark, 'It's going to be a cold winter.'

the teachers doubtless felt they had to mimic the recognised disputes jargon, in which words are turned into mantras made meaningless by reiteration; or have their meanings turned upside-down.

When British workers for one reason or another decide to stop work, take a day off and flop in front of the television surrounded by cans of beer, they call it a 'Day of *Action*'. When the steelworks were over-producing steel no-one wanted to buy and their closure was announced (a tragedy that destroyed whole communities) what did the unions do? They ordered 'Industrial Action', in other words, *in*action – a strike, so as to cripple the plant by stopping production. Which is, of course, exactly what the employers wanted in this particular case – a long stoppage if possible – in order that they may get breathing-space and sell their stockpiles without paying even lay-off money. But so ingrained is the belief that Strikes Hurt the Employer that the shop stewards* force their men to deepen their own misery.

The slogan 'Strike for the Right to Work' is so oxy-moronic it beggars belief. Industrial 'action' includes walk-outs, go-slows, sit-ins and work-to-rules (sic). Strikes range from protest to lightning, wildcat and guerrilla (that war vocabulary again). Take the protest strike: it is another tra-ditional exercise in hurting the wrong people. Say a bus conduc-tor is assaulted by a thug. Everybody out! And everybody is inconvenienced except the thug. On one memorable occasion a factory on militant Merseyside (where else?) was subjected to protest strikes because feral cats had got into the premises and left their smelly mark on the shop-floor. Neither the shop-stewards nor the papers, usually able to spot a weak news pun a mile off, had a moment's hesitation: it was just an ordinary 'wildcat' strike. 'Selective action' is much the

* Without wishing to be 'divisive' or 'provocative', I should mention that 'steward' comes from 'stye ward', a keeper of pigsties. I believe there still exists an ancient office of Keeper of the Royal Piggeries, which does not translate at all well into either German – *Schweinereien* – or French – *cochonneries*.

same as 'guerrilla', 'wildcat' or 'lightning', but the selection is a conscious act, not dependent on the finding of cats' excrement on the floor.

It is almost impossible for an employer in certain branches of British industry to invoke the law against employees for any but major crimes without also provoking some kind of industrial sanction. A man may be found smuggling out of the factory-gates whole motor-cars, which he assembles from stolen parts. If he is caught and sacked, the combined union assault-troops swing into action. The employer is accused of cruelly harassing the poor man: the operative word is 'victimisation'. The employer has the clear choice: drop proceedings or lose production. After the miners' strike of 1984/5 a total amnesty was demanded for those convicted of violent crimes, and further strikes threatened in efforts to get criminals released.

In the notoriously inefficient British newspaper industry, where the grossest abuses have long been rife, there is the famous 'Refusal to Handle'. This is an established euphemism for union censorship. It could be one of the print unions (or even the National Union of Journalists, nominally so concerned with freedom of expression) objecting to some opinion expressed by a writer. Many an editor has to deal, late at night, with a visit from a father of the chapel* bearing a proof ('The lads are not too happy about this'). And, of course, the editor must choose between capitulation and the loss of an issue. He usually capitulates. This happens on countless occasions but the public is usually unaware of any censorship having taken place unless the editor shows a modified form of courage and insists that the removed pass-age leaves a telltale blank space. 'Right of Reply', always

* Fathers of the Chapel are to the printing, newspaper and publishing unions what shop-stewards are to the rest of industry. This curiously ecclesiastical terminology, which appears to make a union official into a kind of high priest, is of some antiquity. Old engravings of printers at work often show their premises as distinctly ecclesiastical in aspect. Not only was much of the earliest printing done in the service of God but (just as 'clerks' were once clerics, men in religious orders who could write) a great deal of printing

went on in monasteries, many of whose fathers and brothers turned from being patient scribes into painstaking and accomplished compositors of type. Printing was gradually secularised but the ecclesiastical terminology remained. 'Every printing-house is termed a chappel,' says Randall Holme in 1688. In 1771 Benjamin Franklin, himself a printer, writes about 'reasonable alteration in . . . chapel laws'. The traditional purpose of a printers' chapel was that of a trade-guild which jealously guarded standards of learning and competence, whereas today's unions are concerned exclusively with wages, hours and working-conditions. Modern newspapers have large numbers of chapels (some as many as fifteen or sixteen), each with its FOC and now a good many Mothers of the Chapel too. Thus the terminology has come full-circle, as many newspaper proprietors, editors and publishers frequently find themselves obliged to make abject sacrifices at the altar of one chapel or another. Indeed, one of the print unions has a woman general-secretary, who is sometimes referred to as the Grandmother of the Chapel.

a contentious issue in newspapers, is sometimes offered but seldom accepted. The lads' demands for censorship are absolute.

'New' technology is, of course, another upside-down term. *The Times* for years had brand-new machinery rusting unused on its premises before the unions agreed to use it, though not until the paper had closed down for nearly a year. Even when such new technology (e.g. computer-typesetting) is admitted, its full effectiveness is hampered by a restrictive practice enshrined in another union buzz-word: 'double-keying'. This means that typesetting done by members of one union has to be done again by a member of another, thus doubling not only the 'keying' but the time, the wages, as well as the misprints, mis-spellings and other incompetences that disfigure the British newspaper industry.

Foul language on the f'kn shopfloor is the f'kn norm; but let the boss or a foreman from another union utter the same word to a worker and a f'kn walk-out is demanded.

'Norm', incidentally, is another British union word. Where Russia had Stakhanovites (named after one Stakhanov who was decorated for his prodigious productivity), post-war British industry has a 'norm': the lowest possible output obtainable in the maximum time taken and for the highest possible wages.

Union leaders have developed a vocabulary and style (and often pronunciation) all their own, often so grand as to sound stilted, using words and expressions their flat-capped-and-mufflered fathers would have gawped at: conditionality, guidelines, comparabilities, automaticity, har*ass*ment, diktat ('dick-tatt'), victimisatory, impasse ('imm-pess'), intimidatory, composite ('compo-site'), provocative, divisive ('divizz-ive'); and, of course, concepts like the social contract; or a predilection for convoluted expressions such as 'underpinning the wages infrastructure'. This kind of language has become almost mandatory (which has the stress on the 'date'). Union leaders speak not of 'our members' but '*my* members' (as in 'my members' aspirations') – which I would find insufferably patronising if it came from any boss of mine. 'The lads' are deemed to include the lasses. The more informal ups and downs of union speech demand that wages must be upped or tools may be downed. Tables figure large in negotiations. Either sporting ('we're bottom of the wages league table') or round, so that no-one is thought to be at the head. 'We must get round the table'; or simply 'we'll have to sit down', both indicate a willingness to negotiate, not to eat. If food is offered by the employers, the traditional fare is 'beer and sandwiches'; which has always struck me as an underestimation of trades unionists' tastes. As Pepys said, 'Strange to see how a good dinner and feasting reconciles everybody'; and unlike their flat-capped predecessors, today's union leaders live well and unashamedly rub shoulders with Tories in fashionably up-market, overpriced eating-places. One thing that does have to be on the table before they 'get round' it is cash: 'We must see money on the table.' This probably harks back to working-class card-schools, perhaps those of London East End garment workers who called money *oof*: ('Where's your oof?'), from German-Yiddish, 'Oof den Tisch' (on the table). Though when the militant firebrands of the TUC-affiliated National Union of Hebrew Teachers (173 members) get round the table they may prefer 'oof' to beer and sandwiches. In union negotiations 'deadlines' will come and go as meaninglessly as in hijackings or a Beirut cease-fire;

such deadlines are really lifelines. Working-conditions are described in quasi-historical or literary terms, 'Victorian', 'Medieval', 'Dickensian', or even 'ante-diluvian'; wages offers as either 'derisory', 'obscene', or just 'unacceptable'— a word made fashionable in many contexts by Edward Heath's coinage of the 'unacceptable face of capitalism'. Doors may be 'left open' or shut and there are constant attempts to 'find a formula', which is short for face-saving formula; this is usually 'hammered-out'. Talks may reach 'a temporary stalemate', which is absurd: in chess there is nothing temporary about a stalemate — it is the end of the game. Metaphors are mercilessly mixed, e.g. 'We demand a slice of the overall cake within the social guidelines right across the board,' or 'The door is still slightly ajar: I hope British Rail will sleep on it.' When a settlement is reached, one side or other invariably calls it 'a victory for common sense'.

As usual, Shakespeare has the neatest description of such eyeball to eyeball confrontations.*

There are interesting differences between the terminology of Labour/TUC on the one hand and Alliance/Tories on the other. Conservatives, for example, do not use the caucus (a favourite Labour device), have no smoke-filled rooms (smoking is rapidly becoming another self-inflicted working-class disadvantage) and make no demands 'on a no-strings basis'. They are less concerned with the niceties of rule books and constitution (I have never heard a Tory quote clause, sub-section or paragraph) and they do not call each other brother or comrade (which can in any case sound more than

* 'Eyeball to eyeball confrontation' is not only a foolish cliché but a tautological one. Confrontation comes from L. *frons*, forehead. One day perhaps, ACAS instead of inviting people to 'get round the table' will quote from the first scene of *Richard III*:

> Then call them to our
>   presence: face to face,
> And frowning brow to
>   brow, ourselves will hear
> The accuser and the
>   accused freely speak,
> High-stomach'd are they
>   and full of ire,
> In rage, deaf as the sea,
>   hasty as fire.

a little artificial when used in the context of some internecine, inter-union demarcation dispute). If delegates at a Tory conference called each other brother it could only mean consanguinity. Labour and the unions deny their conferences the definite article: 'Conference has resolved . . .'; and insist on a unisexual chairperson or a neutrally metonymous chair: 'We ask brothers to be silent while the chair is speaking.' Here 'the floor' is no longer the shopfloor but the body of the hall, where the ordinary delegates sit ('There was a most pungent motion from the floor . . .'). Voting seems to have far greater significance for Labour than the other parties – and one sometimes wonders whether Tories vote at all, or simply leave it to the old-boys' network. Labour has the famous card vote, by which union leaders hold up a piece of card that may be 'worth' several million votes. Not long ago there was a card vote fiasco of unprecedented magnitude when a delegate got confused and made millions of unsuspecting trades-unionists vote the 'wrong' way. Some said it was inadvertent, some claimed it was a calculated mischief, and others blamed the refreshments.

In an article in the *Sunday Times* Nicolas Mellersh made this extraordinary statement about British newspapers: 'We have in this country an overall standard of print journalism which, if it is not the envy of the world, is one of which we can be proud.'

I suppose 'print journalism' covers the women's and the glossy specialist magazines as well as the weeklies, which have not only sustained a long and honourable tradition but certainly improved on it in the last few years, with better paper and more colour (even the *New Statesman*, for years so down-at-heel, is beginning to look less like a cyclostyled university rag mag).

I don't know about Mr Mellersh but I'm not proud when I have to read a newspaper paragraph several times trying to make sense of it, or to scan the page for a missing line that has escaped into another news item. Does he take pleasure in the dreary, repetitive headline puns (and not just in the tabloids), the wearisome procession of misprints, the sheer lack of elementary technique among all branches of Fleet Street 'print workers'?

Can the print unions really be proud of photographs that come out as a murky, unrecognisable mess because members of one or more of the process workers' unions refuse to do their job properly, or worse, will not allow a modern process to be used? It must be even more disheartening to a photographer to see his work ruined than it is for a writer, because on the whole the standard of photography is going up, while simple literacy in the papers is now at an unbelievably low ebb. Press pictures are usually printed not to illustrate the news but so as to 'break up the text'. For example, day after wearisome day during the Liverpool crisis the same piggy eyes of the same little tinpot demagogue stared out at readers from the pages of the *Post* and the *Echo*.

I don't feel much pride when I ask the features editor of a newspaper 'Could we have this paragraph in italics?' and he replies 'We'll have to see if they're in a good mood downstairs' ('they' being the compositors). Once, when my typewriter went wrong and printed in single-spacing instead of double, 'they' were not in a good mood and sent the copy back to the sub-editor, who had to cut out each line with a pair of scissors and paste the strips on another sheet of paper in wider spacing. Then they deigned to 'handle' it.

We all make mistakes. But there is a limit to the incompetence the public should be asked to accept. If every radio broadcast or television show were as full of fluffs, malapropisms, grammatical howlers, mispronunciations, miseditings, bits of tape left out (or put in twice) – in other words the sort of thing you get in every copy of every English newspaper, from *The Times* to the meanest provincial tabloid, broadcasters would be laughed off the air. If every concert by the London Philharmonic Orchestra were not only peppered with wrong notes but you could never be certain if the members of the Bassoonists Union weren't going to be at loggerheads with Cymbal 82, and that members of the Cellists Federation might decide at the last minute not to show up, while the Piano Lid Lifters' Union insisted on holding a meeting on the platform during the concert . . . Or if a single cellist demanded (like some London comps) and got £1,000 for six hours' shoddy work . . . the mind boggles.

People used to say that whenever you read anything in the papers you knew about they always got something wrong. Now they're not even consistently wrong. You are likely to get the same name spelt three different ways in as many paragraphs. For contrast, take a look at the accuracy, the clean print, the neat typography and the rest, of the *Wall Street Journal*, *Le Monde*, the *Neue Zürcher Zeitung*, even the *Sligo Bugle* (or whatever it is called) and you will blush for Fleet Street.

I don't think the general public is aware how great a task the Maxwells, Murdochs and Shahs have set themselves as they try to break the unions' strangehold brought about by decades of weak management. The outcome is not in doubt, but my fear is that the result will not be a press that is appreciably better but simply a more profitable one for its owners.

'The workers' struggle . . .' You really do have to be word-deaf to take politics seriously. Joggle, waggle, boggle, goggle, wiggle, jiggle, giggle, snuggle . . . twee, facetious or comic-sounding words, all of them, and I suspect *struggle* joined them because it became a left-wing buzz-word after some early translator of Marx or Engels chose it for *Kampf* in preference to the more obvious but somehow less suitable 'fight'. (Even Hitler's *Mein Kampf* became *My Struggle* in the English version, not 'My Fight'.)

But the word 'struggle' always conjures up for me a picture of Edward VII, when on 9 February 1909 he arrived at Rathenow railway station and 'struggled to get into the uniform of a German Field-Marshal that was two sizes too small . . .' Now *that* perfectly describes a struggle. (He struggled so long that the welcoming German band was obliged to play 'God save the King' 17 times in succession till a purple-faced monarch finally emerged – which is why the incident is in the *Guinness Book of Records*.) The efforts of miners, workers, blacks, feminists and others who wish to improve their lot, need a more dignified word. The *OED* says *struggle* is 'a frequentative formation of obscure Middle

English origin' (which doesn't surprise me at all). But it could be worse. It's sheer chance that we don't now speak of 'the workers' pingle', as that word, which is Scottish in origin, is nearly as old as 'struggle', going back to at least 1513: 'Our folkis gan to pingill and strife . . .' and 'Now is the pingle, hand to hand . . .' Somehow, the famous 'But westward, look, the land is bright' poem by Arthur Hugh Clough which Winston Churchill so movingly quoted during the darkest days of the war would have been a non-starter if the opening line had been, 'Say not the pingle naught availeth.'

There is the not unrelated, purposely-ridiculous, American political coinage *boondoggle*, which surely seems to confirm that many foolish words end in -ggle or -gle. As boondoggle has been mis-defined on Radio 4 I give Safire's definitive explanation (in *The Language of Politics*), which says it means job-creation (perhaps related to the English word for an easy task, or 'doddle'?): 'A makework project . . . funds wasted through . . . political favouritism . . .' When the New York City Board of Aldermen was investigating relief payments in 1935, it was discovered that money was being spent for the teaching of tap dancing, manipulation of shadow puppets, and the geographical distribution of safety pins. One Robert Marshall told the Aldermen he was paid for teaching 'boon doggles'. Shades of the Greater London Council and Ken Livingstone's famous pingle on behalf of loony minority interests.

It is strange how some English words seem to congregate phonetically in groups of nastiness. All my examples below are from the S section of the *OED* (the only letter, incidentally, to get two volumes, whereas C has one and all the other volumes deal with two letters each). Can anyone explain why so many words beginning with sl- or sn- (fewer with sm-) seem to denote things or concepts considered by many to be unpleasant or unattractive? Could the reason lie in man's natural aggressiveness, and that s- words mimic the animal hiss? Slithering snakes, slimy snails, sly sneaks, slippery slush, slobbering slavering snarling sleuth-hounds, slaves, slaughter, slag, slander, sleazy slinky sloppily-dressed slatternly sluts (OK, they might be slender but against that there is the archaic slammakin for 'a slovenly woman'). A sloan (rangers please note) is a Scottish snub. Weavers call a snag in their yarn a slub; slops (and other still less attractive substances) are sloshed down sluices. *Chambers* give slurb for 'an area combining the appearances and qualities of a slum and a suburb'. The Scots call a smothered laugh a snirt, which must be related to sniffing snot up one's snitch — forgive me, this is getting out of hand. I quote selectively, of course, and would not wish to snub, cast snide, slighting slurs on, sniff or snigger at, beautiful words like sleep or slumber — and the less poetic but equally welcome snooze is not to be sneezed at, either.

I was reminded of all this by a reader from Preston who wrote to ask if I'd noticed that many words beginning with *sp-* are related to wetness, fluids, liquids, sphincters and orifices: spit, spate, splash, spray, spew, sp(l)atter, sp(l)utter, spill, spirt, spigot, spume, spring, sperm (and its dysphemism, spunk), spit, sputum, sprinkle, splish/splash/splosh. And spout: though she tactfully refrained from including my name in her list. Then another reader made a statistical analysis and found that the nasties outnumbered the nice, positive words by 31 to 6 (sl-), 12 to 1 (sm-), and 22 to 1 (sn-), working with *Chambers's Dictionary*.

The *Daily Telegraph* carried an alarming paragraph about Swiss Separatists, not in the Peter Simple column but on a news-page. Surely some mistake, I thought — just another boring old printing-error, like 'The Alban Berg Quartet of Vietnam' in the same paper (playing Chiu Bet, Mo Tsat and Hai Dun, not to mention Yo Han, the Vietnamese Waltz King?). But it was true. The age of protest has reached the peaceful cantons. Soon the Muesli Liberation Army will devilishly find a way into the impenetrable wrappers of processed cheese triangles and 'claim' responsibility (as the news always tells us: I would prefer 'admit') for the holes in the Gruyère. 'Swiss Separatists' sounds like the old riddle, 'Why is a Hoover like a Swiss Admiral?' Answer: 'Because it's a sucker that never fails.'

An adjacent column of the same paper had a story headed AUTONOMY THREAT BY ESKIMOS, which sounds almost as unlikely. Must be all those 'long cold winters' putting ideas into their heads. It is the fault of the news-creation industry, which has turned protest into a spectator-sport, giving ready exposure to every nutter wanting to liberate somebody or something, even hens (yes, there is a Chickens [sic] Lib), every crank who wishes to march, jog, rock, shout or just shake fists for or against anything.

'I had a row with me common-law wife' is sufficient excuse for anything from a vigil up a crane to a full-blown shotgun siege. Today's Saint Simon Stylites would expect a turn-out of fire-engines, priests, social workers, friends and relations to 'talk him down'. And television crews, of course: no wonder the crowd in a recent protest (in Brazil) egged on the demonstrator to jump, which he finally did – a rare thing – and the cameras joyfully zoomed in.

Prisoners in jails used to protest by banging on walls or generally making a din. They, too, have refined the art of protesting and devised the Roof Top Protest. This involves the dismantling of jail roofs and bombarding passers-by with slates, like zoo monkeys throwing nuts. No-one has ever explained how it is that prisons which manage to stop inmates walking out of the front-door allow them to stroll up to the attic and out through the nearest skylight with the greatest of ease. At the other extreme is the Dirty Protest – prisoners fouling their cells with their own excreta. The sympathetic say this must be a sign of the utmost desperation, others that prisoners are merely doing in an organised, protesting manner what they are accustomed to doing at home. Anniversaries of previous acts of protest are meticulously observed by further 'action', recorded and code-named in the press: Black Friday, Bloody Sunday (and for all I know Sodding Monday). Hunger strikes are purely media-exercises: ignore them and they will stop. And even if they do not, the martyrs are soon forgotten among the welter of other, worldwide mayhem on screen and page. Not long after one terrorist, Bobby Sands, had starved himself to death graffiti appeared in Belfast: 'We'll never forget you, Jimmy Sands.'

Demonstrations used to be a very un-English thing. Bernard Shaw said in one of his plays that there could never be a revolution in this country because the advancing mob, marching on Buckingham Palace, would disperse to buy the evening paper as soon as the newsboy offered the results of the three-thirty. The East End of London saw fascist and communist meetings and punch-ups before the war, but these were isolated affairs. There were even bomb outrages, usually carried out by 'anarchists' or 'fenians'. By modern standards of urban violence the Siege of Sydney Street, one of the landmarks of revolutionary behaviour, would barely rate the back pages. Today the slightest personal grievance may result in someone arming himself with knife or shotgun, holing himself up in his home, with or without an innocent hostage, and starting a siege, assured of full news coverage. (It must be said in fairness to the indigenous population that many of these sieges are started by immigrants from other countries.)

The slightest grievance warrants the calling of a Protest March and, should those with opposing views get wind of it, a Counter-protest March. The old English fascist chants ('Foive, six, sem, ite, who do we appreeshi-ite? Mosley!') sound almost genteel compared to the new guttural raucousness: 'OUT, OUT, OUT!' – which is, of course, a straight translation of the Nazis' cry, *Raus, raus, raus!*; and the raised, clenched fist (arm pumped up and down) the leftist equivalent of the flat-handed Hitler salute.

After the last war there was the Housewives' League, said by many to have been sponsored, certainly encouraged, by the Conservative Party to protest against fair-shares food rationing continued into peacetime by the Attlee government. It was a very vocal movement, but no-one would have called it strident: ladylike and proper, down to the last nicety of the plural possessive apostrophe. Today's housewives are more likely to be feminists ('Women Against something-or-other') who will sing tunelessly or scream and chant in approximate unison, wave ill-painted banners at the television cameras, and use innocent children as sandwich-boards ('Babies For Abortion On Demand'). At the drop of a nappy they will organise a Petition, or a Pram-Protest, blocking roads and impeding traffic. Occasionally a woman chains herself to railings (in imitation of her suffragette sisters who really did have something to complain about) or symbolically cuts a hole in a wire fence, but on the whole these events are more noisy than violent. The Sit Down Protest appears to be losing favour. Children learn militancy early, at school, where (encouraged by many a bearded teacher) they are urged to join the National Union of School *Students* (my italics), which prepares them for life at university, with its Lecture Boycotts and Rent Strikes. But much student and juvenile militancy goes in cycles of fashions, too. For the more serious protester handbooks are available, and formerly respectable journals like the *New Statesman* occasionally publish useful hints on how to make bombs, put burglar-alarms out of action and generally make disruption and protest into a serious hobby. But during the middle 1980s, when students had much to protest about, they confined themselves largely to mindlessly shouting down selected Conservative speakers. Shouting down is indeed one of the most favoured methods of protests, not least in the House of Commons.

Another variation on the protest theme is doing what you like doing, and would be doing anyway, but declaring that it is *for* or *against* something, such as Rock Against Racism, with its implication that if you abominate rock and its sweaty, gyrating junkies you must be a racist. The estimated number of protesters at a rally is always doubled by the organisers and halved by the police and the rest.

But I get carried away. What the Swiss Separatists did was to steal the Unspunnen Stone, a tourist attraction of Interlaken. This, of course, they learned from the Scottish brethren of a generation ago, who, in an early instance of militant protest, took the Coronation Stone, or Stone of Scone, from Westminster Abbey, where it had lain since the time of Edward I. And thereby hangs another of those BBC folk-tales. Announcers had been warned not to offend the Scots further but to pronounce 'Scone' with the authentic Scottish umlaut: neither rhyming with 'bone' nor like 'con' but (as it might be written in German) 'Scünn'. Thus a news-reader was heard to say, 'There is still no news of the whereabouts of the Stone of (slight pause) Scünn, stolen from Westminster Abbey, where it had lain since the time of Edward isst.' When the inevitable memorandum came he retorted angrily, 'How the hell did you expect *me* to know it should have been pronounced "Edward Iced"?'

<hr/>

'STEEL MENDS FENCES WITH SDP . . .' said the main headline in *The Times* at the start of the 1985 SDP conference. The intended meaning was that an alleged rift was being healed. But there are two sides to fence-mending, as has been pointed out by William Safire. As the proverb says, 'Good fences make good neighbours'; in other words, let's be friends but stay separate, and above all don't let your dogs chase my sheep. Safire traces the other kind of fence-mending, political repair-work in the constituency, to a Senator Sherman of Ohio, who, when he 'made a trip home in 1879, ostensibly to look after his farm but actually to see to his political interests . . . insisted to reporters that he was home "only to repair my fences".' A related political activity, the uncomfortable-sounding 'sitting on the fence', says Safire, goes back to 1828, when the 'don't-knows' were officially listed as 'on the fence'. He also quotes the *Georgia Journal* of 1840: 'Our advice to all politicians who have a hankering after the praise of all . . . is to take a position near the fence, on the fence, or above the fence.'

But it would be unwise to ascribe all picturesque political coinages to the Americans. The further they go back, the more likely they are to have been English exports to the New World in the first place, like the filibuster. However, the 'Right to Work' slogan was not only imported from the USA but was turned politically inside-out when it got here. In the 1950s it was an American management war-cry in closed-shop disputes, and referred to a worker's right not to be called out on strike when he wanted to work. The early Alliance promise to 'break the mould' proved to be less apt than Mr Roy Jenkins had imagined. He thought of the mould as a stereotype, and vowed (I think that's the correct journalese verb) that with the SDP things would be different. In fact it is a term used by sculptors, who break the mould so that no further cast can be made of their original and thus reassure the client that a copy of the statue he bought will not appear in his neighbour's drawing-room.

On the whole the SDP speeches seemed refreshingly free from the usual mind-numbing clichés of politics, judging from the few bits I heard – for when it comes to political utterances my boredom threshold is low. I become so fascinated by little verbal carbuncles that I clean forget to listen to what they are trying to tell me. Although they were hoping to offer a new outlook, the SDP speakers tended to steer clear of the 'I see . . .' construction, which Safire traces to one Robert G. Ingersoll (1876): a clever device because the speaker is relating his vision, not making a promise that can later be thrown in his teeth: 'I see our country filled with happy homes . . . I see a world at peace, a world where labor reaps its full reward . . . I see a world without the beggar's outstretched palm . . . the piteous wail of want.' And after a few 'I see's' (probably accompanied with a lowering of both pitch and volume) comes a slight variation: '. . . and, as I look . . .' This kind of thing never fails. (When Mr Enoch Powell saw the Tiber foaming with much blood he said it only once and was quoting from Virgil.)

The most important element in a rousing speech is repetition. Consider the memorable address (in which surely no gag-writer had a hand) given on 28 August 1963 by Martin Luther King. The clever thing was that he introduced the variation as a throwaway, quietly at the beginning, almost as a composer might hint at a later theme: 'I say to you today, my friends, that in spite of the difficulties and frustrations of the moment I still have a dream. It is a dream deeply rooted in the American Dream . . .' And only then did he embark on his slow crescendo-diminuendo dreams effect (for once 'carefully orchestrated' is not so far from the mark): 'I have a dream that one day on the red hills of Georgia the sons of former slaves and the sons of former slave-owners will be able to sit together at the table of brotherhood . . .', followed by shorter sentences, each beginning 'I have a dream . . .' After that the contents of each dream no longer mattered. The audience was his – though when you hear the speech now you may feel that he went a shade over the top, with just a couple of dreams too many.

But he certainly started something. Today, whenever I hear some would-be demagogue open a dozen successive sentences with 'Dis gummunt . . .', accompanied by the obligatory finger-stabbing and followed by a baying ovation (with the rhythmic chanting so familiar from old newsreels of Nuremberg rallies), I am tempted to reflect how the word comes perilously close to a happy misunderstanding: from L. *ovare*, to exult, or *ovum*, an egg (in the papers invariably 'rotten') as for throwing?

'Why do you always . . .?', like 'When are you going to . . .?', is not recommended as a conversation opener between husband and wife. Yet I am always grateful if a member of my family points out some irritating habit I have unthinkingly acquired. But I am not married to radio – only living with it, a compulsive listener; and, I admit, a hypercritical one. Though again, as an occasional broadcaster myself, I make any implied criticism with a nervous glance over the shoulder.

Working and listening at home I am probably more aware of radio trends and habits than producers are. They don't listen much, certainly during the day, for they are too busy producing their own programmes; and there is still a kind of old-fashioned gentlemanliness about the BBC. After all, you can tell a man his flies are open and he will thank you for sparing him embarrassment; but point out some personal quirk, habit or fault he was not aware of (especially one connected with speech or communication) and he'll never speak to you again.

Things are certainly not so delicately done in other fields of public performance. If in my last career I had been unable to play a smooth scale of C major and always slurred-in, say the intervening C sharp when going from C to D, the conductor would soon have taken me aside: 'Look here, Fritz, I think you ought to practise your scales or else we'll have to get someone who's mastered his elementary technique.'

Exactly the same applies to 'droring conclusions', 'the London to Australiarairace', and that shabby old lady of broadcasting, 'Laura Norder' – not to mention persistent mispronunciations and mis-stressings that turn many a statement into nonsense. Everyone has to learn and we all make mistakes. But we should not be allowed, for our own good, our own *pride*, to go on and on making them. Here again, Radio 3 in its relentless pursuit of musical excellence, employs a panel of listeners (usually retired professionals) who are asked to report on certain broadcasts. So far as I'm aware there is no equivalent check on speakers. There is a woman-reporter whom I recorded three years ago talking (repeatedly) about 'nuclear' as 'new-key-lar'. She is still doing it. Another reporter insists that 'molecular' rhymes with 'pole-ruler' (the stress on the first syllable). Some, in an interesting manner, reveal a degree of word-blindness, pronouncing words in the way they mistakenly spell them. One said 'he was adamnant', another that someone 'nearly went beresk'; we've had 'Roman mosiacs', 'restauranteurs', 'two years of torturous negotiations'; and (repeatedly on *You and Yours*) that distressing complaint 'arthuritis'. Many if not most younger radio speakers, innocent of elementary school Latin, think that 'and the rest' in that language is 'eck-settera' and that the second month is 'Feb-you-ary'. These are matters for frequent and grievous (not 'grievious') complaint, and you'd expect every producer who takes his job seriously to get speakers to re-record or, if live, take them aside later for notes, just as a theatre producer would do as a matter of course. No genuine performer has a right to be offended. On the contrary, the true artist welcomes every opportunity of improving his technique. When did you last hear a wrong note, a persistent mis-stressing of a familiar phrase, from the London Symphony Orchestra?

The stock reply to listeners who voice such complaints (and many do) is that they are making a fuss about trivia and that they are nit-picking pedants: 'You *know* what was *meant*!' We know what was meant, but (as in newspapers which – for a variety of different reasons – are incompetently thrown together) one could retort that carelessness over the small things calls into question the very accuracy of the facts. Analogy: I once felt a sharp twinge of fear in an airliner when I noticed that an ashtray had been refixed with two non-matching screws. Did they manage to find the right components for the engine?

Of course, many radio listeners, usually middle-aged and middle-class, complain for the wrong reason. They don't like *any* change and insist that the English of the 1980s must conform to what their grammar primers taught them in the 1930s. There are, for example, frequent complaints about that old stock introduction to news reports, 'This report from Joe Bloggs'. Sentences, they say, must have a verb. What rot. Feeling OK? What, you again? That may have been so when announcers allegedly wore dinner-jackets* and talked in a superior way, as if they had the Elgin marbles in their mouth. Radio today is more informal, but (one hopes) stops short of local-radio and Radio 1 mateyness. What irritates *me* about 'This report from Joe Bloggs' is that it is an unvarying cliché, that whoever keeps writing it into news-readers' scripts has not the time, or energy, or wit, or (worse) the verbal equipment to ring a few changes occasionally. This applies to much news on radio and television, because (as mentioned elsewhere in this book) many broadcasters received their earlier training in Fleet Street. There is a well-beaten path from London EC4 to Portland Place and Television Centre, and many a print-journalist enters Broadcasting House without wiping his prose.

* Did they ever? I suspect that this is one of those myths that have grown with repetition. What probably happened was that a single announcer turned up for work in the afternoon because he was going to a dinner-engagement.

Does *everything* that could be big, large, great, enormous, vast, giant (but please, not 'ginormous') *have* to be 'massive'? With synonyms like new, renewed, more, further, etc. do we have to have everything 'fresh'? Fresh talks, fresh initiatives, fresh storms, fresh fighting, and – in one memorable report, 'Three weeks after the earthquake fresh bodies have been discovered in the wreckage . . .' I expect any day to hear the preacher on the *Daily Service* announce a hymn from the BBC Hymn Book, or 'Fresh Every Morning'.

For a time every preview was a 'sneak preview', but that one got scotched. But still going strong is THE HAND-OVER THANKYOU. 'And now here's Frank Jones with the weather forecast.' And Frank comes in with a bright and breezy

'Thankyouverymuch.' Thank you for *what*? For mentioning his name? For being about to carry out the job he is paid to do? By all means let us be polite, and even thank him *after* he has done his bit. But mutual verbal back-slapping and thankyoudon'tmentionit bogus politeness tends to leave the listener feeling excluded.

Consider some of the conventions that have grown up in recent years. For example, the STILL LINK, used when two news items come from the same place: 'And still in Pisa, the leaning tower has shifted another two millimetres . . .' Good to know the leaning tower is still in Pisa.

The HOW WHY AND WHERE AND WE HEAR MENU. 'Why pig-farmers are angry at the Chancellor's latest plans . . . How a Durham housewife found herself on a privy that fell into the sea . . . Where you have to pay for beer in pre-decimal currency . . . and we hear how many people are dying in New York . . .' – the last one especially useful because it keeps listeners in ambiguous suspense: will the man *quantify* how many died or *specify* the manner of their death? I confess I'm unable to offer a better way, but someone must be able to think of alternatives, if only to surprise the listener.

The DRAMATIC PRESENT TENSE. For some reason the Radio 4 news-reader at 9 a.m. always has to pretend he is reading newspaper headlines: 'A Soviet airliner is hijacked in Siberia. Eggs are set (!) to go up this weekend and a British film wins an Oscar.' It is acceptable in newspapers, where it saves space. But in speech it sounds like a bogus dramatic narrative, like a panting messenger in Greek drama. To me this attempt at lending an artificial sense of immediacy to often distant or trivial events sounds ludicrous in spoken English; and it saves no time. If broadcasters are real people who give information to other real people they should surely speak like real people, not animated newspaper headlines. When the news-editor gets home his wife isn't going to tell him, 'The cat eats the budgie and is sick on the carpet.' The effect sometimes even manages to sound like some kind of Dramatic Prescient Future Tense: 'Also within this next half hour, one of the panda cubs born in Madrid dies.'

NEWS IS JUST COMING IN . . . A dangerous introduction to a late item. I know how it happens: the news-reader may already have started an earlier script, and is thus obliged to add a rider or even denial that is handed to him. So when he says, 'And we've just heard . . .' the knob-twiddling listener or viewer may already have heard or seen it on another channel half an hour earlier.

THE DEAD AND. The radio conjunction that joins nothing. People have been known to go into a cold studio and open their piece with a breezy, '*And* – hello there . . .' It is nothing more than one of those gargling noises we use so as to make sure the vocal cords work. Schools broadcasters use the AND IMPERATIVE: 'A-A-A-A-ND rest', which is related to the German '*Achtung!*' and the drill-sergeant's 'At-TEN----shun!' There's also the HEADLINE AND: 'Football-*and*-Liverpool are out of the cup . . . The weather-*and*-more frost is on the way . . .'

THE WITH . . . OPENER. 'With half an hour to go before the polls close . . .' and the

AS . . . OPENER. 'As the frost continues, many people . . .'

THE RADIO STANDFIRST. Newspaper news-stories often have an introductory paragraph, usually in slightly bigger type than the main body of the text. This summarises the news-item and, in theory at least, tries to give the reader-in-a-hurry a brief synopsis. In the papers this device is known as the standfirst. The skilled press sub-editor of earlier years used to be able to make the second appearance of the information slightly different. Repeating it word for word revealed him to be a man short of time, imagination or vocabulary: he would *pride* himself on his powers of elegant variation (and sometimes in his zeal indulge in florid prose). But alas, the only 'variation' modern newspapers can apparently manage is to pepper their columns with misprints and ascribe several different ages to the same person. The standfirst doesn't work on radio and television news bulletins, indeed it often sounds absurd. It goes like this. Newsreader: 'The raids are said to be in response to a whole series of violations of the cease-fire. This report from Joe Soap in Beirut.' And Joe's tape echoes exactly what we have just heard: '. . . the raids are said to be in response to a whole series of violations of the cease-fire.' But of course one has to remember that radio and television newsmen work under far greater pressure than those in Fleet

Street, and taped reports may be on the air within minutes of arriving in the news-room; and also that anyone who switches on after the standfirst may be grateful for the repetition. However, the late switcher-on is seldom considered. People who make programmes have an unshakable conviction that listeners at home have ears only for the programme to come. They keep looking at their watch (producers like to think) and saying 'Well, almost time to switch on for my favourite programme . . .' Reality is very different. Even the listener who *wants* to hear a programme sometimes forgets to switch on until after it has begun, or the telephone rings just as he does so; and he may miss vital information: the identity of the speaker(s), the name of the interviewer or interviewed, etc. There are no distractions in the studio, but in the home, normal domestic interruptions often supervene. I once heard an entire item on the *Today* programme (apart from the opening seconds) about a man who led a most interesting life, met Goering on the Orient Express and took part in some hair-raising adventures. But I never found out who he was, as there was no back-announcement; and after having presumably been initially identified (before I switched on) he was consistently referred to as 'he'.

THE FIRST-NAME FAMILIARITY. A speciality of radio chat-shows, on which guests are constantly addressed by their first names. The late switcher-on must wait to the end to know that 'Peter' was a famous theatrical producer and 'George' the Earl of Harewood.

THE NEWS POSSESSIVE. This is another newspaper time-saver which hacks pick up in Fleet Street and carry like a germ into broadcast English: 'Russia's Mr Gorbachov, Labour's Neil Kinnock, Solidarity's Lech Walesa . . .' Or, 'She beat Australia's Betty Wyndham in straight sets . . .' Even Radio 3 announcers sometimes succumb to this newspaper trick: 'Our concert comes from Manchester's Free Trade Hall . . .' (played by London's Philharmonic Orchestra? Conducted by Germany's Klaus Tennstedt?) though I know that lapses of this kind are carefully monitored and tactfully pointed out from within the BBC, for Radio 3 cares passionately about such things. Again, we don't talk like that at home, do we? Yet every day on radio and television we

hear (these are actual examples) 'Tennis's Davis Cup . . .'
and (this must have positively drenched the microphone)
'Simpson's of Piccadilly's Mrs Hedy Simpson . . .'; not only
'London's Heathrow Airport', which is merely superfluous,
but also 'Paris's Orly Airport . . .' which is both superfluous
and hard to say. Everybody knows where 'London Heathrow'
is; and what do these people *do* with the micro-seconds they
save by not saying 'Orly Airport near Paris'?

As people keep saying, the language *is* constantly changing,
and so is the style of radio, the style of news both printed
and spoken, and the very way in which we talk to each other.
Anyone who tries to fossilise English is sure to end up
sounding like an old fossil himself. But it depends who carries
out the process. When ordinary people have changed English
in the past they have usually done so gradually, or adopted
the usage of Chaucer, Shakespeare, Milton and Gibbon. Their
changes have always enriched English, whereas breathless
news formulae invariably impoverish it.

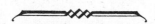

Radio drama is one of the cornerstones of Radio 4. Almost
as soon as the BBC went on the air, the wondrous possibilities
of inviting the listener to paint his own scenery were understood by the pioneers of the medium.

So it is hardly surprising that over the years a set of
conventions has been established which nothing can shift,
not even the latest technological developments such as stereo
or binaural sound; and many of them have been transferred
to television without undergoing the adaptation one might
have expected.

The opening announcements of a radio play always seems
to follow the custom that (however short the cast-list or
subtitle) the title must be repeated at the end of the introduction, rather like a child announcing the poem it is about to
recite. '"Great Dispensations", by Geoffrey Tinnisberg, with
Judi Blanch. Great (tiny pause) Dispensations."' Changes of
time or place are indicated by a slight fading-down of one
scene and fading-up of the next: a simple and effective device.
Less convincing is the Running Commentary, designed to
conjure up for the listener what he cannot see.

What's those lights coming up the lane? —
It's a car . . . it's going towards the house.
He's getting out —
He's got a gun . . . he's putting it to his shoulder.
He's going to shoot.
Look out!
(sound effect: 'bang').

All of which, apart from the shouted warning at the end, would have been absurd on television. Adapters of books into radio plays have lately taken to writing a part for the author so as to avoid such clumsy dialogue; but the Archers can always be relied on for good running commentaries:

He's down.
He's got up.
Look, Nigel, he's fallen over again!

Ambridge punch-lines at the end of each instalment usually come in duplicate so that no random household noise can obliterate it and disturb the wait-for-the-next-thrilling-instalment tension (especially on Friday nights, when it has to be sustained over the weekend):

'*What* are you going to do, Nelson? What *are* you going to *do*?'

Drama cliché lines are so predictable that at home we seldom fail to slip in the appropriate one before the actors can do so. A policeman comes to the door.

Wife: 'You better come in.'

In plays, every interview, even a cordial one, may be terminated with the stock line,

'And now if you'll excuse me I've got work to do.'

Real people are never able to get rid of a caller in such a clumsy manner, but instead go through all manner of contrived excuses, or start fussing over some task to show how busy they are.

When the caller finally takes the hint, he always says,

'I'll see *myself* out.'

The sense behind this (and other) time-saving clichés is that it permits the action to continue in the proper place. You would hardly want the pair to be heard trudging down the hall; and still less (in television plays) the camera to follow them.

People in plays, both radio and television, always seem to introduce themselves by giving their surname twice, just to make sure everybody gets it: 'My name is Jones. *Bill* Jones.'

No car door is ever locked in television drama. You just slam it and walk away. Apprehended criminals always say,

'I dunno what you're talking about!'

Middle-class persons when arrested are always politely informed, 'We won't detain you longer than is necessary, sir.'

The standard answer is, 'But there must be some mistake, officer.'

A criminal, on being relieved of a fire-arm or other weapon, is told,

'I guess we won't need this.'

There is an abduction or kidnapping-scene? As soon as the party gets into the car, the miscreant says,

'OK. Less go.'

And the victim whimpers:

'Where you taking me?'

American films are even more cliché-ridden, from 'My boy is a good boy' (the Italian-American mother of a mafia boss caught with a smoking gun in his hand) to 'I'm gonna hade myself for this in the morning', and, of course, the all-purpose 'Leave it to me, I'll hann'l this.'

The dreaded understains of American (or pseudo-American) drama are never far away:

'Bud I doan' understained.'

Have you ever tried adding 'And make it snappy!' to your order for drinks at your local public-house and watching the bar-maid's reaction?

Husband-and-wife or lovers' quarrels usually contain the line, 'Oh don't be so damn reasonable, Charles!'

. . . or whatever the partner's name is. Sex has come a long way since 2LO started broadcasting drama, and has, of course, gone all the way on television. Sexual intercourse is fully explicit on radio (where it can afford to be), with much heavy breathing and mind-blowing orgasms. On television this is trickier, especially as certain conventions have to be observed. Naked female breasts may not be shown before

9.00 p.m. (unless they belong to negro women in their native habitat), full sexual activity not generally before 10 p.m. Love scenes showing couples in bed usually start with both of them sitting up, the woman keeping the top sheet (seldom a duvet, for obvious reasons) firmly clamped under her armpits so as to hide her breasts (though these are more than likely to be revealed later). Things get going suddenly, without foreplay or any other pleasant formalities demanded by sexual good manners: the man rolls over and on top of the woman (even when brutishness is not indicated) and the action begins, though it is not necessarily shown. Often the camera cuts away to other things, and before long we are back to the sitting-up-in-bed bit. (This used to be the signal for the customary post-coital cigarette but smoking on television is now frowned upon even more than sex is by some.) But whatever happens, and however little or much is shown, it happens very quickly, giving those young who have stayed up beyond the 9.00 or 10.00 bedtime deadline a completely false impression of how grown-ups behave in bed. They may well grow up wondering where the fun lies in a few seconds of humping. It should be added that sex scenes and nudity are great stimulators of the ratings charts and are therefore almost obligatory in every television drama serial. Without naked flesh Channel Four would have to close down.

Working-class heroes apparently always go to bed in their vests, but almost all male television actors keep underpants on. Full-frontal male nudity is seldom seen, and then only in long shot or soft focus. Female nudity, however, is lovingly developed, so much so that many actresses feel themselves to be under pressure, fearful that they may not get a role if they refuse to take their clothes off. They are usually able, however, to keep their pubic hair private, thanks to all kinds of contrived shots which just happen to put objects between it and the camera.

But here, too, the saving of time is paramount (unless the intention is pornography – or pornophony?) so that everything is achieved after a short bout of heavy breathing.

The telephone rings. It always rings two double rings, by the way, in features as well as drama – 'ring-ring, ring-ring' – before it is answered. But before someone answers it in drama, someone is sure to say, 'I'll get it.' The unheard voice at the other end of the line may announce some disaster; and we are told the worst with the stock threefold burst of unfinished prose:

'Oh no. You don't mean. He isn't.'

Making a phone call on television is easy: two or three digits are dialled (the push-button has been slow to enter drama), these are immediately followed by a pair of ring-rings – and you're through. Dialling a full, ten-digit British number would, of course, take too long. Never is one able to achieve such rapid connection in real life. In television plays, whenever the call is interrupted and the caller cut off, or when someone at the other end hangs up, the frustrated caller will turn the hand-set towards him/herself and glower at it. This is invariable, standard television drama practice, and for all I know is taught at drama-school. Yet I have never given my phone a dirty look, have you?

When there is a corpse, even the hoary old 'Not a pretty sight!' is still sometimes heard. And when things get really harrowing one character is bound to tell another,

'You better try and get some sleep.' But not before a beverage is solicitously offered: 'Drink this, it'll do you good.'

Girls hotly pursued across open country always, but always, manage to fall over. When they reach safety they slam the door, lock it and then, panting and heaving, head thrown back, press themselves against it backwards, arms outstretched: a particularly foolish thing to do if the pursuers have a gun.

Every crime series or film has the obligatory high-speed car-chase, often with disastrous or even fatal results in real life, as impressionable, delinquency-prone teenagers feel inspired to go out and do likewise. Police officers have long drawn attention to the rise in car-chases immediately after dramatised ones are seen on television. Fist fights, too, are frighteningly and inspiringly realistic – though with one important exception: actors who have apparently taken a great deal of punishment, been felled violently and repeatedly, never seem to be much marked, apart from perhaps a mild nose-bleed. Goodies and baddies like to chase each other along long corridors (to give the camera plenty of room to move) or on high gantries. Falling, or being knocked, through windows is a favourite effect in the catalogue of gratuitous violence presented to us, which, too, has led to injuries to youthful imitators unaware that television glass is made to shatter spectacularly while not causing any injuries.

As for drama table manners, these are perfectly disgusting – curiously enough more so on radio when they are merely heard but not seen. Actors always make a point of taking a mouthful, speed up the chomping-rate, and only then splutter out their lines while at the same time chewing furiously. This is followed by a gulp of wine to wash down the half-chewed soggy mess, which is often fully visible in camera close-up. Do they have eating-classes at RADA? If a trendsetting precedent were to be sought it would probably be found in the chicken-eating scene of the film *Tom Jones*, in which a couple engages in what can only be described as oral sex, with the aid of chicken-legs.

It is easy to mock, harder to write a good script. Perhaps I should apologise to radio and television playwrights and producers for the foregoing. If I say, 'You hurt?' they must surely answer, 'It's nothing.'

Clichés are not confined to drama on radio and television but are an important part of ordinary, everyday radio programme-making. They are an aid in what is often a last-minute, high-pressure rush to get a programme on the air, and also help to cushion regular listeners (viewers seem to be less vulnerable) against the shock of the unfamiliar. For whenever *anything* is changed on radio, especially on Radio 4, whether it is the day, time or presenter of a programme, someone is sure to be upset. So any familiar quirks, habits and stock openings may be a comfort to many listeners. Others get irritated by what are heard as needlessly recurring stock ingredients (like Point Music and News Formulae – see pages 101 and 87). There are, for example, Standard Openers. Some broadcasters have their own 'Hello again', or 'Hello there' (where?), or even 'Greetings!', while some are content to wish listeners a pleasant time of day, as applicable: 'Good morning (afternoon or evening)'. Other gambits include:

The GOOD TO BE BACK opener. This is common round about September or at the end of a holiday season, when presenters return after a lay-off. One must surely ask oneself – did everybody really notice I was away?

The NO THIS IS NOT opener. As when starting an item with the 'wrong' signature tune or a purposely-misleading sound effect ('No, this is *not Desert Island Discs*'); related to

The UNLIKELY PLACE opener. 'A small semi on the outskirts of Swindon seems an unlikely place to find . . .'

The RADIO LOOK. When one considers that radio is a sound-only medium one is struck by the amount of looking that goes on: A Cool Look, a Sideways Look, a Lighthearted Look . . . such Looks may also be Quizzical, Not Too Serious, Irreverent – the list is long.

The SECOND CHANCE. 'There'll be a second chance to hear . . .' Few can listen to the radio all day and every day. Programme repeats are therefore a good thing from every point of view (though again, those who *do* listen to everything complain when some things *are* repeated). But some listeners seem to feel that to be given a 'second chance' sounds a little patronising, when 'a second opportunity' may not.

JOB SHARING. In the 1970s the BBC decided that if something was worth doing, it was worth paying two men to do it, a device copied from the affluent, advertising-financed American radio and television stations (whose pace is so fast and breathless that it probably needs two men so that one can take breath). It can relieve pressure in a live programme, permit hurried conferences away from the microphone and, of course, it makes *Today* what it is, with its pleasantly civilised, lighthearted backchat. But it also brought

The HANDOVER FIRST NAME CLICHÉ – tagging to the end of one's last word the co-presenter's name without punctuation or change of inflexion: '. . . but so far the Russians have shown no sign of letting up Peter.' This means 'I've come to the end of my bit of script and now it's your turn, Peter.' For some reason *Financial Report* on Radio 4 always needs two reporters taking it in turns to present the market trends and prices.

The FROM . . . TO . . . link. Probably as old as broadcasting itself but still heard surprisingly often. 'And from

Valiant Radio Fan. "CHEERIO EVERYBODY. THIS IS ROBERT CHARLES TAKING HIS MEDICINE."

Early radio mannerisms noticed in Punch, *1938*

sheep-farming in Patagonia to watch-repairing in Whitechapel . . .' This is related to

The BIG STEP BUT link. 'From symphony concerts to coal-mining may be a big step but . . .'

The TEASING MENU opener. A contents list is as useful in a programme as it is in a book. But whereas the reader can choose whether to consult the appropriate page or not, to read from start to finish or dip into its pages, the listener, it is felt, has to be wooed with come-ons, teasing and appetisers. Sometimes it sounds like a desperate attempt to stop the listener switching off. 'My guests today include a one-legged First Division footballer, a 78-year-old grandmother who is tomorrow pushing a pea up Snowdon, I mean the mountain of course, a Chinese vegetarian who has written a book in praise of abattoirs, and a man who makes *this* curious noise with an unlikely part of his anatomy . . .' Related to

The PLUS EFFECT. 'Plus we bring you . . .' And no menu is complete unless it ends with the magic words, 'But first . . .', without which radio as we know it would probably come to a standstill. There is also

The BREATH INTAKE EFFECT. A smack of the lips combined with a short, sharp intake of breath such as phoneticists might call a labial implosion. Lord Clark was an early master of it, and once one became aware of his punctuating lip-smacks (how was it his producer never did?) one became unable to listen to the wonderful things he was saying, waiting for the next implosion. In interviews and discussion programmes a sharp, audible intake of breath is also used as a signal of intended interruption, a polite message saying 'Will you shut up for a while because *I* want to get a word in?'

The MAYBE IT'S BECAUSE I'M A LONDONER syndrome. Those who suffer from it refuse to believe in 'Radio 4, Serving the United Kingdom', or perhaps fail to realise that we yokels in the provinces also sometimes tune in. Hence the frequency with which shows '. . . opening at the Palladium next Tues-day' or '. . . a new exhibition just opened at the Tate' are given publicity. An extreme example from Radio 3: 'Our lunchtime concert from St John's, Smith Square [i.e. in Westminster] begins in half-an-hour, so if you hurry you still have a chance of joining us there . . .' Not if you're listening in Solihull or the Shetland Islands. It is also a common assumption that if the weather is foul in London it must be worse elsewhere. 'Hello on this dank and dismal day . . .' reached my ears as I looked out on a brilliant, mild and cloudless winter's morning two hundred miles north of where the broadcaster was sitting. Referring to the counties nearest to London as 'the Home Counties' comes into the same category. Home is where the heart is, and mine, for a start, is not in Surbiton or Bishop's Stortford.

The ENGAGEMENT DIARY opener. 'Since I last had the pleasure of talking to you I had the honour of presenting the awards at . . .' or '. . . of opening a fête in Buxton . . .' or '. . . of narrating *Lenny the Lion* at the Festival Hall'. This is broadcasters' code for 'In my spare time I'm available for hire: rotary clubs, masonics, bar-mitzvahs and ladies' luncheon-clubs a speciality'; and might as well be followed by his agent's name.

There's nothing like old broadcasts to remind one of the changing style of radio. A talk I recorded only a dozen or so years ago, which I happened to hear recently on a tape, sounds not very different from the way I would have done it today, except that I pronounced the word 'racial' in two-and-a-bit syllables and with an 's' sound, 'ray-see'all', not in one syllable, 'raysh'l', as most people say it today, and presumably how I, too, would say it – if only so as not to sound correcter-than-thou (something that is now considered the greatest sin of informal radio). At the end of my talk, the announcer introduces the next programme as 'Bairnd Stairnd', which is not how Radio 3 pronounces 'Band Stand' today. Go back further in the BBC Archives and you will find the speech sounding absurdly mannered, although one did not notice this in the 1950s and 60s. I still have a recording on paper tape, made on a domestic machine called a *Sound-mirror* – of the very first time I was allowed to speak into a BBC microphone. It was on *Music Magazine*, that inspired brainchild of Anna Instone and Julian Herbage. Although then barely out of my teens I hear myself sounding ridiculously like a querulous, high-pitched professor: I must have been trying to model myself on Professor Joad of the *Brains Trust*, and the most famous professorial voice on the air. But the producers accepted it because it was then nothing unusual, whereas nowadays one would be called to order: 'Come on, you're talking to *people*, not giving a lecture!'

In the old days of *Music Magazine*, no speaker could mention a piece of music, even in passing and however familiar, without having it illustrated by a few bars from it. I suppose the thinking was, 'the BBC has the finest gramophone library in the world, so let's use it.' *Music Weekly*, the programme's successor, has grown out of such predictabilities. Although the BBC now has an even bigger collection of records which grows by the hundreds every week, listeners get the benefit of the doubt and are expected to know that Beethoven's fifth starts 'rat-tat-tat *tum*'.

But outside music programmes the time-honoured need-to-illustrate cliché flourishes, and in different manifestations. One is 'Point Music'. *You and Yours, Kaleidoscope, Woman's Hour, Going Places, Breakaway*, the chat shows, the science, medical and other topical programmes – they all do it, and the *Food Programme* does it most consistently, while *You and Yours*, broadcast on weekdays, does it most often. The regular Radio 4 listener will recognise the habit instantly. Think of a subject, and it is introduced with the first musical landmark that rises up on the producer's (sometimes limited) musical horizon. A useful and informative item (perhaps on *Woman's Hour*) about retirement? Out comes *Will you still need/feed me when I'm sixty-four?* Boats? We hear the strains of *Messing about on the River*. Love and Marriage? Well, what goes better together than that ditty about a horse and carriage? Fashion? Without fail, we get the song whose idiotic refrain tells us that Beau Brummel was *A Dedicated Follower of Fashion*. Poverty in America? *Buddy* will be there to spare a dime. Riches in the City? *Money Makes the World Go Round* or *Who Wants to be a Millionaire*? Glasgow in the news? Sir Harry Lauder is wheeled out to proclaim in his alcoholic manner that 'Glasgie belongs tae mee'. (The same goes for *London Pride* but not to anything like as great an extent.) Let sweet-eating and its effect on dental caries be discussed, as it often is on *You and Yours*, and out comes a song called *Sweets for my Sweet*. An item about pronunciation? *You say tomato and I say tomayto*. The only tune makers of programmes about gardens, or country-houses and their gardens, seem to know is – yes – *Country Gardens*, and always in a version as far removed as possible from the innocent old English folk-dance collected by Percy Grainger. I need hardly continue, but it must be added that Vivaldi's *Four Seasons* are the hardiest of perennials for spring, summer, autumn and winter programmes.

Certain pieces of music become for ever associated with certain subjects, e.g. space travel with the first few bars of Richard Strauss's *Also sprach Zarathustra*; or athletics with the signature-tune of a popular British film. Producers are conditioned to this one like Pavlov's dogs. Mention the words 'running', or 'race-track', or 'Olympics' – and someone immediately starts lamming away at those tin cans whose metallic clangour heralds the evocative but somewhat minimal four-note theme from *Chariots of Fire*.

Point music gets even worse when pop music is invoked, as some young producers are under the (surely wrong?) impression that all Radio 4 listeners are as knowledgeable about pop and rock records as he/she is; and here the grown-up listener is further hampered by being seldom able to discern the yowled-out words.

Whatever food is mentioned on the *Food Programme*, from aubergines to zabaglione, they are ready to garnish it with some unsavoury gobbet of introductory pop music: not because it's good music but because it's there. This programme goes so far as to employ a special musical researcher, unaware that some listeners are at least as hostile to junk music as they are to junk food. But I wouldn't put it past the *Food Programme* using a couple of bars from Parry's *Jerusalem* for an item about artichokes.

You also get International Point Music, music employed to transport the listener to a certain country. Over to Paris – and the obligatory squeeze-boxes start wheezing. (I am sure it is all because the signature-tune of *Maigret* used accordions in the 1960s, for I have never heard an accordion in France.) Dateline Vienna? Anton Karas is sure to twang out a couple of bars of the theme from *The Third Man*; Athens – the same goes for old *Zorba* on the bazouki. Switzerland and alpine Austria, however, have to share the oom-pah music to which yodelling, *Lederhosen*-clad peasants perform their bottom-slapping dances. Everything must be spelt out in a few well-flogged bars of stock atmosphere, and must be done in the most obvious way possible. Subtleties are not encouraged: for example the clever piano piece *Manhattan Skyline* by Heitor Villa-Lobos whose melodic line is meant to follow the ups-and-downs of the New York skyscraper silhouette.

Back home again, and you will find that no news or features item actually starts with speech. 'This report from Joe Bloggs on the picket lines' opens with a few seconds of anonymous and meaningless shouting and jeering, before Joe himself is heard. If Bloggs reports from a picket line or a union meeting, out comes the same four seconds' worth of stock baying. A report from Beirut or any other trouble-spot invariably starts on the all-too-familiar chatter of machine-gun fire that could just as well be Nicaragua, El Salvador, or No.EC2A1(s) in the *BBC Sound Effects Catalogue*. This kind of thing is called 'Actuality', and so ingrained is the apparent need for it that its perpetrators no longer notice how ludicrous the effect can be. The announcer says, 'And now another programme in the series, *A Small Country Living*. Here's Janine McMullen.' And in the next sounds Janine apparently treats us to some comic animal impressions: 'Quaa-quaa-quaa-quaa-quaa-quaaaa . . .' – until we realise it is a tape to let us know she's going to talk about her experiences with ducks. Or else '. . . and now here's Sheridan Morley with tonight's edition of *Kaleidoscope*.' But he is not. What we hear is some as yet unexplained *noise*. It could be a minute of Scottish mouth music, Richard Burton in *Hamlet*, a raving, drug-crazed pop group or the entire Royal Philharmonic Orchestra. Whatever is about to be discussed is heralded by some kind of introductory puzzle-sound. But we can be certain it won't be S. Morley that enters on what appeared to be his cue. This sort of cliché is kept up throughout *Kaleidoscope*. The programme dispenses with back-announcements (so important for late switchers-on) to let the listener know what he has been listening to. All that happens is that the presenter suddenly stops talking – you don't know whether he's finished with the subject or not – and up starts, without explanation or identification, another *noise*: whether relevant to what went before or what comes after, we do not know. It is the silliest way of turning a corner or changing gear, but this excellent arts programme has made it its special hallmark. The trick somehow manages to turn the entire programme into a sort of feeble guessing game, an over-used kneejerk effect like those teasing tabloid headline clichés.

Many broadcasters receive their early training in newspaper offices, and so it would indeed be surprising if they did not apply some of the characteristic tics and tricks of the trade to the spoken word. The *You and Yours* programme, mentioned earlier, is highly topical and heavily consumer-orientated, takes much of its material from the daily papers; and does so at the shortest notice, hot with the latest news. It is therefore the prime example of tabloid prose unthinkingly transferred to speech. Listeners are given the full sub-elementary-school 'humorous' headline treatment of the *Star* and *Mirror*. So, on *You and Yours*, judges get a wigging, painters have a brush with authority, dentists get hard facts to chew on, musicians hit a low note . . . and grown-up men and women who think they have escaped Fleet Street idiocies by *not* buying a paper are treated to the very same journalistic bilge over the air. No wonder many of them seek refuge with Radio Three.

It is night. We know it is, because the BBC's Resident Owl is wheeled out. No-one *ever* goes to prison on the radio (whether in fact or fiction) without the final, echoing slam of that tired old cell door. I heard a fascinating, *Checkpoint*-type, feature programme about the dangers British holiday-makers can encounter when travelling on the continent of Europe. It was a true story, carefully and rivetingly retold on Radio 4, in which the victim of a French hotel disaster recounted her harrowing experiences. For the recording she was sitting in the comfort of her own home in England, talking to an interviewer about her plight two years earlier. As she says, 'there was a fire', we get a few moments of crackling flames superimposed on her voice. Just to remind us what flames sound like, you know. 'I was rushed to hospital,' she says; and of course we hear the sounds of an ambulance going 'hee-haw, hee-haw, hee-haw' (an English one at that!).

No-one can embark on a radio train journey without our being reminded what a choo-choo sounds like, and the producers will go to endless trouble to make sure we get the right kind of engine from among no fewer than 500 railway items in the *Sound Effects Catalogue*. If they don't choose the right one, the letters start coming in. A little feature about the apple crop? As sure as eggs is eggs it will open with a crunching, munching sound in revolting close-up of someone taking a great bite, followed by my pet aversion: a broadcaster talking with his mouth full (which, incidentally, is another favourite *Food Programme* trick). As the conductor Ernest Ansermet said to a persistent joker at rehearsal, 'Vonce is funny, tvice is funny. But always by God never!'

The 18th century was the age of the harpsichord, the 19th and half the 20th the age of the piano. Now a third era is in full swing, as you can hear whenever you turn on the radio and television, by the pop music, the jingles and the signature tunes. As anyone with half a musical ear will confirm, the age of Strum and Twang has arrived, and seems likely to stay. But those who have *two* ears should try to keep the monster within bounds – at least on Radio 4, the world's last civilised radio speech-and-a-little-music channel. Here, too, Strum and Twang is making inroads. Gresham's Law applies not only to money and speech but also to music: the bad is driving out the good everywhere, the ready-programmed, synthesised 'noise' ousting the musical sound produced by a real, live craftsman-musician. Even if a musician is employed, the do-it-yourself guitarist is usually favoured to those who can really play, just as the crooner is preferred to the singer.

It is nearly always a tuneless non-song intoned by a toneless non-singer to a self-strummed guitar accompaniment that opens or figures in radio chat shows – the ill-tuned guitar being an instrument regrettably so portable you can take it everywhere (and with it a box of tricks to make it louder). Any entertainer can learn the three-chord trick in about half an hour – usually the wrong three chords. That's the Strum. The Twang is electronically synthesised. This revolution in noise-generation has come about in the last couple of decades, when someone discovered that electronics could be made to produce the weirdest, strangest whooping, plopping and peeping noises, synthetic crashes, clashes and splashes of sound, whoopings and whinings – at the turn of a knob. And it's cheap, too. A little electrical aptitude and a do-it-yourself instruction manual will teach you, too, to make what a listener to *Feedback* described as 'twanging bed-spring noises'. No previous experience or musical training required. You can also throw away your drum-kits. 'Tracks' can be laid down containing the regular, machine-like drumming noises that are the first essential of today's popular music, a reiterated pulse without which the musical yobbo is unable to contemplate listening to music. Contemporary pop 'singing' is, of course, wholly based on electronic artifice. Engineers can cleverly turn any non-singer, a footballer or Linda McCartney, into something that approximates to the popular idea of singing.

Yes, I know about junk music, because I, too, have occasionally helped to create some: nothing more than jingles, though we referred to them by the politer name of Radio 4 Identification Signals. Their function (like that of a signature tune) was a positive one. Among all the proliferating bands and channels, pop, local, pirate, police and foreign radio, the identification signals are the bugle calls in the hubbub of battle, signals that can be heard and understood where a spoken command – or announcement – is not. This is, of course, also the prime function of a signature-tune, the sound that tells you that your favourite programme is about to begin. Even the Greenwich Time Signal performs that function. I may be listening to music on Radio 3 in one room, but I can hear the six pips coming from a set in the next room, and by the time they get to the elongated peep, I can be by the other radio to catch the news headlines.

Our first lot of Radio 4 jingles was a set of neutral variations on a simple folk-song, done mostly in horn harmonies; and the music was played by real people on real instruments, not robots, synthesisers or electric strummers. These jingles were followed by another set, considered by many listeners 'too Radio 3' or – even 'medieval' ('Here is the News read by

Henry VIII'). They were all eventually howled off the air by adverse opinion, for the BBC does take notice. Though the strange thing is that listeners get used to even the most irritating noises (as they might get used to a wart on the nose of a loved one) and eventually the complaining letters get fewer and fewer. The long-running signature tune of the *PM* programme is a case in point. Thousands of listeners are obliged to turn down the set so as to stop this noise from assaulting their ears. When it first appeared it created an almost unprecedented outcry, but more than a decade later it is still here, and no less offensive: an electronic abomination which starts with someone apparently knocking hell out of the exposed strings of a broken old upright piano, followed by a sort of synthesised burbling – a radiophonic representation of someone breaking wind under water? And if this were not enough, there is another noise during the programme itself, when the presenter says, 'And here are the news headlines': on comes a perfunctory three seconds of whooping on a two-note alternation like someone hawking up a load of phlegm. As a final insult, the tune appears again at the *end* of the programme – which, if a signature tune is intended as a signal, can only mean 'we're finishing now, so it's safe to listen'.

The *Today* programme made a brave attempt at introducing a sig tune (as well as interjectory jingles) but this too produced a flood of protest letters and telephone calls. The tune was good, composed by John Dankworth, and played by him on a saxophone, an unadulterated musical sound free from radiophonic interference. But the programme editors did not realise, as listeners instinctively did, that it was a night-club sound: what Indian musicians would call an evening *raag*, and totally unsuitable to the time of day. The saxophone at the best of times, and however well played, has acquired a pleasant sort of sleaziness which was simply unsuited to the brisk brightness of the programme. Furthermore, the occasional unaccompanied interjections (intended to keep two different subjects apart, to force a change of mood) merely gave the impression that Brian Redhead himself punctuated his sentences by picking up a sax, blowing an eight-bar riff and putting it down again. And at the end of the programme, the saxophone went up and up and up in a sequential figure, to a strained high note (I could almost hear the news editors conferring in Fleet Street journalese, 'Let's end the programme on a high note . . .'); which, of course, Dankworth hit triumphantly each time. But the whole point of virtuosity is that it should sound like a one-off *tour de force*, and contain an audible element of risk. To hear it being accomplished daily at the appointed moment was reminiscent of another experiment, when, to introduce the *Up to the Hour* programme, we were invited to admire James Galway's breathtaking double-tonguing in Gossec's *Tambourin* every single day at 6.30 a.m. It was like going to watch the same circus trapeze act every day. After the tenth time even perfection becomes a yawn.

Sleazy saxophones also featured (to my mind inappropriately for a supposedly bright morning programme) in the up-and-down tune devised for the experimental *Rollercoaster* on Radio 4. And if the Canadian/American radio meaning of 'rollercoaster' had been taken into account the music itself would have been different, too; for on the other side of the Atlantic they use the word 'rollercoaster' for an early-morning programme that provides a continuous ride for different kinds of listeners who join it as they rise, get ready for work, possibly continue listening on their car radio, and then leave it again to be superseded by another type of listener. Different intellectual heights of brow are supposed to be taken into account – from early-rising manual workers to later-rising business executives and, presumably, house-coated middle-aged housewives with middle brows doing the dusting later still. But it never worked. You cannot classify listeners as broadly as that, neither in America nor here.

I yield to no-one in my admiration for the work of the BBC Radiophonic Workshop. Their concoction of a sig tune for the do-it-yourself brains trust, *Home-ing In*, for example, is a delightfully imaginative montage of musical sawing, hammering and screwing sounds that accompany the cheerful whistling of a handyman. But unfortunately this nest of electromusical geniuses has been overtaken by commercial developments. Not only are electronic noise generators cheaply available but every calculator, every space invader or

digital alarm-clock and most home computers are now programmed to make radiophonic sounds. The noises of moogs
and synthesisers can be heard wherever there is a microchip.
Local radio programmes squirt out a Strum and Twang jingle
every time they lack something interesting to say, which is most
of the time, so the slotting-in of a jingle cassette has become a
substitute for thought. Unfortunately, 'real' radio is in constant
danger of following the local radio trend.

Most jingles and sig tunes take no account of the content
of the programme they introduce. Radio 4 has always been
the Network of Pleasant Surprises. Its programmes have a
way of taking the listener by the ears. The network never
talks down at one except, sometimes, *You and Yours*, which
is really a kind of national local radio; and here, too, the
matter (though seldom, alas, the manner) is often totally
absorbing. (In its anxiety to be topical, to produce follow-up
investigations of newspaper news, it can also forget itself
occasionally. Dealing with the 'morning-after' pill, it brought
on some dreary woman intent on telling listeners – who might
have been having their lunch – what happened 'when the
sheath came off'.) So the *You and Yours* sig tune merely
matches the vulgarity (in the true sense of the word) of its
contents, and so do some of its voices: straight out of the
sharing-caring, equal opportunities social-worker's advice
cubicle. It is an ear-shattering, up-and-down-shaped, electronic twanging noise, and sheer aural torture. At the start
of the programme, as soon as the 'menu' has been announced,
the tune catches you again, with a totally unnecessary 'sting',
a sort of electronic full-stop, to punctuate the end of the
menu. And a recent change has been for the worse, if that
was possible. Most broadcasters can indicate by means of
inflexion when they have got to the end of a sentence, but
not on (national) local radio.

The signature music on Radio 4 always seems to aim low,
as if to invite the populace to come into, say, an art exhibition,
with the 'Roll up, roll up!' tricks of the showground barker.
Before the adult listener can get involved in a programme he
must all too often brave weeny-bopping music. *Your Move
or Mine*, *Science Now* and *Medicine Now* are presumably
intended to appeal to grown-ups. Yet they start like rock

shows. Other listeners with whom I compare notes confirm that they, too, are forced to turn down the sound for the throbbing and thumping, and up again for the programme proper. Of course, one then misses the menu. This is another favourite radio trick – making speech fight against background noise by having people talk against music, giving the programme contents over insufficiently faded-down jingle-jangle. It may sound fine in the studio, under perfect listening-conditions with good equipment and trained ears. The possibly elderly listener at home, with failing hearing and a cheap portable (or the travelling listener on a car-radio driving in the 'shadow' of a mountain) can seldom hear speech and music simultaneously. *Going Places* pollutes its music (I'm sorry I must use the term) with superimposed traffic noises, and *then* gives its menu *on top of that*, between bursts of roaring jets and vrroom-vrooming motorbikes. As if there were not enough noise in real life! Do we need to be reminded weekly what music sounds like when drowned by traffic? One gets the feeling that if they were able to pump exhaust gases out of the radio into our living-room *Going Places* would do it. *Breakaway* refreshingly has a 1930's record, of a tune so named.

Every producer who originates some wonderful new programme thinks he knows exactly what he wants as a signature tune for it. But few seem to take into account that the BBC has the greatest concentration of musical expertise (not excluding jazz and pop) willing to give advice. *Bookshelf* until recently shared a twanging sig tune with a travel programme on television, so it has now changed it to another strumming twanger, radiophonically-distorted pseudo-guitars playing crypto-Bach. Why not (for a programme that caters for intelligent listeners) *real* Bach, played straight? It is an insult to suggest that most Radio 4 listeners are unable to take it. Ditto *Round Britain Quiz*, which also recently abandoned the old strum for a new one. The *Medicine Now* jingle used to start with something that was intended to remind us for a moment of a heart-beat. Fair enough. But what was the meaning of the great, shattering, echoing crash, not unlike that old BBC cell-door, with which it ended? No-one ever told us; and when that horror was scrapped, it was replaced by another one equally puerile. And *that* is the great objection from many Radio 4 listeners. The programme *contents* credit them with being intelligent grown-ups, yet the music is fit only for raving teenagers.

The *Moneybox* programme has a sig tune which takes literally the *OED* definition of jingle – 'the affected repetition of the same sounds, or of a similar series of sounds . . . without regard to the sense'. The sense is there all right – in the form of a witty verse or two from 'Instant Sunshine' telling what you should do 'If you have moneytospend . . .' But who wants to hear the same financial advice, even when wittily rhymed, four times, i.e. both before and after the programme, which is repeated? The group is a prime example of modern instant, live Strum and Twang, though redeemed by comic words (usually audible, too) in the best tradition of *Punch*. But their music consists of about three all-purpose tunes that are belted out on the three-chord-trick principle, to a relentless perpetuum mobile of twanging. *Stop the Week* is another programme whose music often goes slumming by comparison to its thought-provoking verbal stimulus. Its sig tune seems to come out of the *Moneybox* stable but is unique in one respect. Listen out for the third voice entry in that cumulative final chord: it skids around desperately in search of the right note – and only just gets there, just as the chord stops. You can't miss it: the lyrics go 'piddle-di-daah'.

Woman's Hour has yet to find a satisfactory successor to the 'Merry Wives' theme of decades ago. For a long time someone in the office had a fixation for flutes (I hate to mention this, but Plato said it was an instrument fit only for whores, inducing female lasciviousness). Until recently a breathy flute figured in both the sig tune and the letters noise: 'And now for your letters . . .' followed by an inane four-bar tootle-tootle. At present *Woman's Hour* has the best opening signature tune of all. It's called silence. After all, the programme follows within a couple of minutes of the 2 p.m. news, which has the GTS pips to act as muezzin to summon the faithful. But the letters slot is topped and tailed by a delicious, jokey radiophonic jingle ending in a half-suppressed little fart (of the type we used at school to give the onomatopoeic name 'threep'): a mystery noise until Sue

McGregor explained it was the sound of a piece of paper being wrenched out of a typewriter. Ah so! There's nothing like a joke that has to be explained – especially one repeated ten times a week. On the other hand, the ladies always chose their serial signature tunes with skill and taste to suit the atmosphere of the stories. I especially remember a threatening number – full of low, growling brass instruments. However, it sounded rather less low and ominous at the proper speed after someone pointed out that they'd been playing a 45 disc at 33 rpm.

Unfortunately radio and television have a propensity not only for junk music but also for turning good music into junk, or, at best, into sounds deprived of meaning by too frequent repetition. *Brain of Britain* for many years was introduced by a jazzed-up version of the last movement of Mozart's *Eine kleine Nachtmusik*, K.525, perpetrated by Waldo de los Rios – who also brought you the Symphony No. 40 in G minor enlivened by disco-drumming, the *Horse of the Year* sig tune similarly adapted from Mozart's K.522 (which does, however, possess a last movement with a certain galloping quality) and who later died by his own hand. Nothing, it appeared, could shift the harebrained arrangement from such an intelligent programme – until, at last, Radio 4 relented, and gave us Mozart neat and unadulterated. But unfortunately even good music, heard in the wrong place and too often repeated, loses its magic as well as its meaning (have you ever tried chanting the 'To be or not to be' speech to yourself all day long?); though the non-musical may accidentally benefit by becoming aware of good music they might otherwise never have heard, and find themselves inspired to hear some more.

There seems no end to the gullibility of the general public where commercial popular music is concerned, no end to people's willingness to rush into the shops and buy anything the industry's PRs and the pop journalists tell them is good. *Radio Times* recently extolled Frank Sinatra's wonderful breath-control, telling us that he made a point of listening to the playing of Heifetz so as to learn phrasing. That was news to me, but then my ignorance in the pop-music field is profound. I always thought crooners had their songs written to suit their particular style, and particularly their often limited range and powers of phrasing. The general lack of breath-control prevailing among many of the greatest entertainers is surely shown by the manner in which some of their best-known songs have to be divided up into bite-sized chunks. For example that jolly English folk-tune *Country Gardens* has the word '*ga*-arden' on the first three beats of the fourth bar: dotted crotchet followed by quaver and crotchet. It means singers have to sing three-and-three-quarter bars in one phrase. But crooners and other untrained voices cannot make their wind last that long. So they sing '. . . in an English country (crotchet-rest and big gasp) ga-arden'. The last word is scrambled out as three quick descending quavers.

It is significant that one seldom now hears the word 'crooning' – which, the *OED 1972 Supplement* says, means 'to sing popular sentimental songs in a low, smooth voice, especially into a close-held microphone . . .' It was soon established that every entertainer should be able to dance a little and croon a little, and some do or did both very nicely, like Frankie Vaughan, Ken Dodd, etc. Today every one who can breathe into a microphone is ludicrously described as a 'singer', though no-one would describe, say, the gyrating George Melly as a *dancer*. My analogy is that if Frank Sinatra and, to take a random example from the other end of the vocalists' spectrum, Robert Tear, are both described as 'good singers', then Sir John Gielgud and our neighbour's budgie are both 'good talkers'. And incidentally, notice how today's 'singers' spurn the latest technology of the almost invisible radio microphone. They could stand up there just like Tear if they wished, and sing; and if they wanted to gesture or do a little dance they would be able to do it far better unencumbered by all the equipment. But no. They *need* the customary choreography: one elbow-up, fist clenched holding the old phallic object close to their lips (changing hands now and again), while their gyrations are geared to the need for whipping the microphone cable round their legs like a skipping-rope and prancing over it.

Surely we should again distinguish between a crooner and

a singer. There's room for both, but let us not confuse the two. Both may be able to sing in tune and bring an expressive quality to the songs they utter. Both may have the power to move us. But a singer *sings*, has something called 'range', in vertical terms of the musical scale, and the power to project his voice. And a crooner *croons* (often very beautifully) and relies on amplification and other artifice for being heard. Without this his range may be about two foot six inches with a following wind. Or even with it: *I'm* (breath) *dreaming* (breath) *of a white* (gasp) *Christmas* ... or else, *And now* (breath) *the end is near* (breath) *and so I face* (gasp) *the final curtain*.

Incidentally I seem to be in a minority in believing that *My Way* must be the worst song in the history of music, at least since Josquin's *Hélas! qu'elle est à mon gré*, which he wrote for the 16th-century King Ludwig XII, who had no vertical range at all, for he could manage to hit only *one* note; but that song at least had interesting accompaniments. *Down your Way*, I'm told, has to operate a quota system, otherwise everyone would choose *My Way*, which just proves once again that the taste of the masses is unerringly bad.

Firms take great trouble to give their premises attractively designed reception areas, with magazines and publicity material disposed on low tables, and risk the wrath of feminists and equal-opportunity freaks by employing only glamorous female receptionists. But do they ever ring themselves to find out what sort of reception their telephonists give callers, whose first impression of their firm is often aural? I am usually rather shy and absurdly polite, rising from my seat when a daughter's boyfriend enters the room (though they usually don't when I enter). But when my voice is safely disembodied and I'm unseen, courage never fails me to shout at a rude or incompetent telephonist. A few are well trained (some so well you know they can't mean it: a certain hotel answers with the unvarying formula 'Grand-thank-you-for-calling' before you have said a word); but the rest range from the bored to the unintelligible, from the offhand to the audibly plain stupid or studiedly rude.

The same goes for over-protective secretaries who regard anyone wanting to speak to their boss as an unwelcome intruder. I don't mind 'Who's calling?' But when, *after* I tell them, I hear the sound of a hand being clapped over their mouthpiece (you can always tell), and am then told, 'I'm sorry he's out/unavailable/in a meeting', I immediately suspect he's lurking by her side, mouthing a negative and unavailable only to me. The tactful telephone person states the boss's absence first and only then adds, 'Can I say who called?'

Another stock question, 'Where you from?', based on the false assumption that we all work for some firm or other, only encourages me to act stupid ('Well, I'm from Liverpool, but I wasn't born there . . .'); but the infuriating 'What's it in connection with?' immediately rouses an anger I would probably control if face to face with some dumb 20-year-old who is as pretty as she's thick. Here a studied insult is called for. Try 'I want to speak to the organ-grinder, not the monkey'; or, if you want to be more insulting, 'When I go to the doctor, I don't undress for the receptionist.'

There are other pests. Telephonists who simply don't respond to your utterance, for instance. Have they heard you, have they fallen asleep, or has the line gone dead? You just don't know. For them, even to say 'Putting you through' or 'One moment, please' is too much of an effort. And for me, 'Just a *minute*' is too long a wait, especially on a long-distance call or when I could be doing something else. And here's another thing. The well-trained operator says 'Trying to connect you' every 15 seconds or so, or offers to ring you back. Few do; and when you ask them to do so, out comes pat the most infuriating parrot-call of indolent British industry: 'It's not company policy.' Shun like the plague any firm so determined to be unhelpful as to train its employees to say that.

I would also ask message-givers to avoid the transatlantic confusion of 'Mr Jones *called*'. Female cats on heat and Americans who use the telephone may be said to 'call' (and dogs leave 'calling-cards'). But when an Englishman calls he appears at one's front door; otherwise he rings or (tele)-phones. The phone-in formula 'Thank you for calling' has probably helped to spread the practice. Does no one phone, ring, ring up or ring in any more? Let's have no 'call' girls, at least on Radio 4.

Another pest: busy telephonists who take off the receiver (or whatever their particular equipment demands) because the ringing annoys them, but say nothing until they find it convenient to do so (some treat you to a burst of recorded pop-music-while-u-wait). Sack them, I say. I'd rather wait my turn with the comforting ring-ring in my ears than hang on to a dead line, wondering if I've been cut off.

But we all have telephone mannerisms. In spite of the Telecom recommendation 'Announce your name or number', I just say 'Hallo' and let the caller identify himself first, in case it's the neighbourhood burglar checking up. Busy male executives have a way of barking an aggressive 'YES?' when they pick up the receiver; and show how busy they are by slamming it down at the end of even the friendliest conversation, leaving you to say a feeble 'Goodbye' to yourself.

At the opposite end are those who seem unable to terminate a call. British Telecom must make a fortune out of my family. When we have said all there is to say, we start tossing 'OK then' back and forth – only to think of yet another thing we meant to say. I also like the b'dummers. They have their own holding-signal which goes 'b'dum, b'dum, b'dum' and means 'No, we haven't been cut off – I'm thinking.'

Then there are those who waste your money or theirs by saying, 'Wait a minute while I find a pencil.' There should be no telephone without a writing-instrument nearby. If there isn't one handy, it's a sure sign of a chaotic household.

And incidentally, the BBC has a new telephone system, with holding and ring-back facilities – but it has missed a musical opportunity. When you dial on American systems, you get (as with some calculators) a melodious note for each number, right up the scale of C major, from *doh* for 1 to *re* a ninth higher for 9, and the lower leading-note *ti* for the nought. But the BBC phones play only three notes, one for each vertical bank. Thus American musicians can memorise numbers by singing them: mine in the USA is a reiterated interval of an upward seventh, an inverted hee-haw; but in the BBC my seven digits play 'Put an-oth-er nick-el in'. So what's my number?

It used to be very simple. A group of musicians was collectively known either as a band or, towards the end of the 19th century, an orchestra, even though that Greek word had originally more to do with dancing than playing music. When 'lovers of Harmony' banded together to form clubs they translated the term into Greek and thus founded Philharmonic societies, the first one in London in 1715 (the Philarmonica Club) and later the London Philharmonic Society. In Vienna they preferred friends to lovers, and the more cumbersome German *Gesellschaft der Musikfreunde* (Society of Friends of Music) to the Greek-based 'philharmonic', though they eventually borrowed *Philharmonie* from their English counterparts.

In older times small groups were called waits or minstrels; and there was the delightful collective noun 'noyse': 'Oh that we had a noyse of musitions to play . . . as we goe' (Chapman, 1598); Ben Jonson in *The Silent Woman* (1609) mentions 'a noyse of fidlers', and when Falstaff (in *Henry IV part I*) wants music to entertain him and Doll Tearsheet he engages 'Sneak's noise'.

The string quartet for which Beethoven wrote many of his works was led by Ignaz Schuppanzigh and therefore known as a matter of course as the Schuppanzigh Quartet, just as other bands were named after their leader. And so things remained for well over a century, producing the Léner, Busch and Griller quartets. (Occasionally there were, however, slight difficulties. David Martin, of the Martin String Quartet, sometimes received letters addressed to 'Martin String, Esq.') But when Norbert Brainin and his colleagues in 1947 chose one of Mozart's middle-names for their string quartet they started a new trend. The trend became a flood and now, with so many gifted young musicians entering the profession, string quartets and other groups are finding it increasingly difficult to think of names. Soon they were followed by others named after composers, whether these wrote string quartets or not – Allegri, Gabrieli, Alberni, Arriaga, etc. Thus you may hear the Glinka Quartet playing a Borodin quartet, the Alban Berg Quartet playing Schubert and the Schubert playing Janacek; while Janacek plays Kodály, Borodin and others; and all are merrily playing Haydn. On radio it is absurdly confusing and can sound more like a list of sporting fixtures than a concert. More recently quartets started to call themselves after famous violin makers: Gagliano, Guarneri, Stradivarius, Amati, etc. whether they play on instruments by those makers or not – and at £100,000 or more a throw they usually don't (though the Amadeus have, or have the use of, one Amati and an entire quartet of Stradivaris).

An 'outside' name removes the leader's *droit de seigneur* over his colleagues and makes for easier changes in personnel. Previously they could hardly get rid of him and retain his name, but newer quartets are, so to speak, able to vote the chairman off the board. The day of the personality cult is in any case on the wane. I felt acutely embarrassed when Hugh Purcell, the producer of *Start the Week*, with a nod to the Swingles, called our resident singing-group the 'Spieglers'. Although the name has stuck and the group still exists (write to your nearest concert agent: *Advt.*) I still find it hard to utter the nonce-word. Yet one *should* be brazen about these things, for in the competitive world of music the meek inherit very little. Sir Thomas Beecham had no compunction about naming his orchestra the Beecham Symphony Orchestra and also formed the Beecham Opera Company; though as he used money earned by his father's famous Pills ('Worth a Guinea a Box') he was also publicising the sponsor's name. Later he even more brazenly adopted the 'Royal' prefix for one of his orchestras: a title which is in the gift of the Queen. But such is the British capacity for compromise that although muted indications of displeasure were released from Buckingham Palace he was eventually allowed to keep it. The bright young English conductor Richard Hickox, using private sponsorship, founded groups that used regularly to be announced on the radio as 'the Richard Hickox Singers, the Richard Hickox Orchestra, conductor Richard Hickox' (who else?) and often the announcer was obliged to iterate the name again and again – 'in a performing edition prepared by Richard Hickox, with Richard Hickox himself playing the harpsichord continuo . . .' I somehow can't imagine there could ever have been 'The Adrian Boult Orchestra' and indeed the Richard Hickox Orchestra now goes under the name of The City of London Sinfonia. But well tried.

Pop music set a fashion for snappy but meaningless single-word names – probably dreamed up while someone was under the influence of 'certain substances' – Police, Queen, Cream, Wham, etc., which are echoed in the field of 'real' music by Counterpoint, Dreamtiger, Equinox, Pegasus, Lilliburlero, Resonance, Galant, etc. The group calling itself Lontano is presumably best heard from a long way off; and one can only suppose the Quodlibet players make up random music as they go along. But the Rondom Ensemble appears to be (as Churchill said of Alfred Bossom, MP) 'neither one thing nor the other'. What the Lotus Harmonic Jesus Orchestra plays, apart from silly tricks with trendy titles, I do not know. And a new group directed by the distinguished composer Paul Patterson which specialises in contemporary chamber music would go down like a lead balloon in the United States billed under its name (which none of its members bears) – the Manson Ensemble. How about 'The Yorkshire Ripper Players'?

Old confusions prevail or are compounded. The London Saxophone Quartet consists of four saxophones, the London Horn Quartet of four horns, as you might expect; and the London Serpent Trio of three serpents – but the London Horn Trio of Violin, Horn and Piano, as you might not expect – unless you are familiar with the professional jargon that calls Brahms's op. 40 for that combination his 'Horn Trio'. This group once turned up at a music-club to play the Brahms only to find that no piano had been hired. Lucky it wasn't the Trout Quintet, or the performers might have found a fishmonger's slab on the platform. Perhaps one day a string quartet will take its name from Beethoven's op. 74 in E flat, known as the 'Harp Quartet' because of some pizzicato effects. The 'Beethoven Clarinet Trio', incidentally, is for clarinet, cello and piano.

Naming groups after the greatest work for that combination in the repertoire is a newish trick. The group which calls itself the Archduke Trio cannot but suggest that it has some kind of private lien on Beethoven's op. 97 (unless they really are three genuine archdukes). Serve them right for having on one occasion been described in the papers as 'the arch "Duke Trio"'. (But then the press always gets it wrong

– from the *Allergy Quartet* and the *King's Sisters* to 'the chilling *Girian Quartet*'.)

There was a Virtuoso String Quartet even before the war and a Virtuoso Ensemble after it, but the name has an un-English ring about it. If anyone were innocently to ask a great English violin virtuoso 'Do you play the fiddle?' he may admit, 'Well, yes a little' and enjoy an inward smile. A continental would draw himself up to his full height and make it clear: 'I am X, the well-known violin *virtuoso*.' Did the members of the newish (and excellent) Paragon Ensemble bother to look up the word in a dictionary? 'Paragon – a model of perfection or supreme excellence.' Such descriptions are better applied by the listener, not the performer himself. A self-styled virtuoso or paragon is sure to have an off-day and invite derogatory comment, where the more modest might get away with it.

There is now a certain fashion for 'ye olde' group-names with quaintly archaic spellings: the Canterbury Clerkes or the Consort of Musicke; or tweely Englysshe, like the Parley of Instruments, and the English Concert. (I thought a concert was what one played *in*, not what performs it; or can't they spell consort?) But here, too, confusion has been confounded during the last few decades. It started with the Philharmonia Pocket Scores, published by Alfred Kalmus between the wars in Vienna and later in London. From these, Walter Legge got the idea for naming his Philharmonia Orchestra. This led to Sinfonias, as well as chamber orchestras called Sinfonietta – probably American inspired, for in the USA a symphony is both the work and the orchestra that plays it; just as their Chorales – formerly sung compositions like those Bach wrote – denote groups of singers that would until recently have been called choruses. When *The Archers* (of the long-running BBC series) decided it was time to form a soap-operatic chorus they naturally reflected real-life trends by naming it the 'Ambridge Chorale'. All this has inexorably led to absurdities like the Serenata of London – and it can be only a matter of time before two sonata players call themselves 'The Sonatina of Tunbridge Wells', or wherever. Thirty-odd combinations in the latest directory of British musicians have the prefix 'London' (or Londinium!) which is often hurriedly modified by addition of 'New' when it is discovered that there is (or was) a previous group with the same name; which presumably accounts for the existence of a foursome in London called the New London Bassoon Quartet. Or there is the distinguishing suffix '. . . of London' – or wherever. The Northern Sinfonia not long ago felt impelled to add the cumbersome '. . . of England' to its name, perhaps to make it clear they were not based within the Arctic circle. But on the radio they usually also get an unbargained-for intrusive r – the Northern Sinfoniar of England.

The groups named Zephyr, Borean, and Favourable Winds, respectively, blow things, as you might expect – fanning, who knows, the Fires of London. (Who in heaven's name thought that one up, and why?) But Horns of Plenty is an aptly-named group consisting of plenty of horns. I was hoping that Just Slides was a magic-lantern peepshow but it turned out to be a trombone quartet. The prefix 'Academy of . . .' was pioneered by the Academy of St Martin-in-the-Fields, which is as clumsy as their playing is deft. 'Baroque' is now a word to conjure with, used by a great number of performers claiming to have a direct line to the composer and to perform old music with absolute authenticity. Musical heretics who prefer old music played in tune on modern instruments using modern techniques will be delighted to hear that it comes from the Hispanic words *barrocco/barrucco*, meaning 'rough, grotesque, imperfect, whimsical'. Like 'Rococo' it was taken from architecture, where they denote an excess of ornamentation. Why, incidentally, is there no ensemble called Piano Nobile?

Many ensemble names are risibly macaronic, like the Harmonie Wind Ensemble, the Kleine Kammermusik Ensemble or the Forellen Ensemble, all of them mixing English, German and French. Many that claim to be Pro Arte or Pro Musica (they'd hardly be anti, would they?), for although Latin has died an untimely death in schools, dog Latin is very much alive among founders of musical groups. Cameratas are two a penny, the word (which does not appear in my Latin dictionary) cunningly combining suggestions of 'chamber' with 'camaraderie'. 'Musica' gets every kind of polyglot treatment, or has words (genuine or made-up) tacked on to

it, like Intima, da Camera, Antiqua, Nova (or Nuova –
Italian and Latin are often considered interchangeable). In my
ignorance I thought that Musica Reservata had something to
do with the price of tickets but apparently it has a nice
16th-century meaning. We also have the Modus Vetus Duo,
the Cantamus Bach Orchestra (do they sing?); and for all I
know the Accademia Nuova pro Musica di Kingston-on-
Thames. Capella is popular abroad, where the old German
Kapelle, as in *Dresdener Staatskapelle*, still serves; but when
Latinised, the Capella Coloniensis, for one, sounds more like
a painful complaint than a musical body. One group of lutes,
viols and sackbuts unaccountably harks back to the Greek:
Orkistra, thus quaintly spelt.

The Philomusica Orchestra also set a trend when it was
formed in the 1950s by members of the eponymous Boyd
Neel Orchestra. One hoped they were 'lovers of music', as
the title implies, not musophobics. Among classical/mythical
figures or concepts which have been pressed into service by
English groups are Amphion, Apollo, Minerva, Cosmos,
Aquarius, etc., though we are not usually told why. Gemini
'consists of various instruments', says the *Music Year Book*.
In pairs? Played by sets of twins? The Arion Ensemble might
have been named either after the 'semi-mythical poet and
musician of Lesbos . . . who was thrown overboard by
sailors', or else after Adrastus's horse, 'famed for its swift-
ness'. We are not told. But some years ago there was a
mother-and-son sonata partnership which was informally
known (behind their backs, needless to say) as the Oedipus
Duo. The Camerista of London presumably chose their name
because they thought it meant 'chamber-music players'. If it
does, none of my dictionaries say so. But they do reveal that
a *camerista* in Italian is a chambermaid, or lady-in-waiting.
Are these *cameristi* players perhaps all female? Sheba Sound
and the Portia Ensemble (like the Portia Trust dealing with
female offenders) certainly are, at least nominally, though
they appear occasionally to admit the odd honorary male. Is
everything peaceful with the Vesuvius Ensemble at rehearsal,
or do they occasionally erupt? The Proteus Ensemble
would be cleverly named if it did not contain just two
performers – countertenor and lute, for the dictionaries

define protean as 'readily assuming different shapes'. The players of the Janus Ensemble, for all I know, sit back to back when performing. Or perhaps the group plays music both old and new. When the William Byrd Singers are announced on the radio it sounds like the dawn-chorus; and fortunately the Kensington Gore Singers are not as bloody as they sound: Kensington Gore is a London street, between the Royal Albert Hall and the Royal College of Music.

There is a burning desire (nay, a need) to be different at all costs, but it often goes beyond what is reasonable for a tradename. Wherever the Baccholian Singers got theirs from it cannot have been a dictionary. What are they? Melan*choly* votaries of *Bacch*us? Are the four players of the Medici Quartet doctors? Or the Oktavian transvestites? It is said that an early Amici Quartet was at one time known for having almighty rows at rehearsals; and every Camerata runs the risk that comrades may one day fall out. Ultimately it does not matter what one calls one's baby. When he grows up he will lend his own special meaning to the name.

———⟨⟩———

By the sound of it, Broadwater Farm Estate, the scene of the 1985 Tottenham riots, might be an English rural retreat where yokels respectfully pull their forelocks to the passing squire or exchange pleasantries with the village bobby. In reality it is one of those cynical euphemisms favoured by the planners and architects since the 1950s for their award-winning utopian piggeries. That at any rate is the socio-modish view, which never fails to add that the high-rise planners and architects themselves always preferred to live low-rise, in the garden suburbs, or in a country-house if they had built enough high-rise blocks to be able to afford to buy one. But unfortunately neither the planners nor the architects could have foreseen what TV-blinded pigs were to inhabit their towers, sub-humans (usually white, it must be stressed) who drop their ordure where they walk, in lifts and on staircases, and drive out the decent folk of all races. After all, tower-blocks work well enough in other countries, and even in some British city areas, e.g. much-maligned Toxteth,* where Belem Towers, on the edge of Prince's Park, could win prizes any day simply because care was taken to fill it with decent folk. Which (sorry comrades) is another way of saying that the rents are on the steep side.

There was doubtless once a Broadwater Farm in Tottenham, long demolished. We have 'farm' developments in Liverpool, too, where planners and councillors took a delight in pulling down historic buildings like Jericho Farm and Cantril Farm, replacing them with overspill piggeries — and adding insult to injury by keeping the old rural names, with the addition of 'Estate'. Now, when someone says he is 'living on an estate' you have to check his social group. Does he mean rolling acres of countryside or the new concrete slums? The Broadwater residents themselves (many of whom have never seen a chicken except on the table or television), say they 'live on the farm'.

The namers of 'estates' built on what was formerly farmland even sometimes consult old maps and call their grey new streets 'heys', after the original fields, such as Grassy

---

* 'Toxteth' is a largely imaginary Liverpool place created by the media parrots, who fell upon this old word because it must have suggested to them something unpleasant — a cross between toxic and a tocsin; and broadcasters like Sir Robin Day always seem specially to relish uttering its threatening, hissing sound. Toxteth is indeed the name of a parliamentary constituency, but before 1981 Liverpool people never used the word, except possibly when there was a parliamentary election. The 1981 riots in fact started just *outside* the Toxteth boundary, and moved to its northern-most edge, usually known as Granby. At the place to which they spread, the flames of the burning Rialto (a fine art deco picture palace) and of the 18th-century Racquets Club lit up a road-sign saying 'Toxteth 1¼m'. To say 'the Toxteth riots' therefore sounds to most locals as absurd as it would be to speak of the 'City of Westminster Carnival' when meaning Notting Hill. The confusion arose partly because Liverpool council employees, trying to find something to do to justify their wages during the 1970s, erected 'Toxteth' signs without having any clear idea of where to put them.

This ignorance has spread to the journalists on the local papers, the *Liverpool Daily Post* and *Liverpool Echo*, and reporters on the two local-radio stations who, like their fellow-parrots nationwide, are always saying 'Toxteth' when they mean 'a deprived urban area in South Liverpool'. The *Guardian* has variously described Toxteth as 'a largely black area' and 'a black ghetto'; and between them the parrots have placed 'in Toxteth' any tumble-down street three miles away. Conversely they are unaware that parts of the more prosperous areas of South Liverpool, parts of Queen's Drive, Otterspool and Smithdown Road, Prince's Park, Sefton Park and Fulwood Park, *are* all in Toxteth. Much of Toxteth (it was geographically always Toxteth Park) is still covered by acres of grass and trees, or tree-lined, quiet, middle-class streets, for it was originally King John's deer-park, later belonging to the Earls of Sefton; and it spreads over about half the area of present-day Liverpool. The name – Stochestede in the Domesday Book and Tokesteath in 1212 – has been variously interpreted, from 'Toki's landing-place' to 'wooded shore'. Early in the 19th century, as Liverpool expanded because of its fast-growing commercial prosperity, an 'overspill' town was planned in the park, to be known as the Township of Toxteth, together with another, the Township of Harrington. The latter failed almost completely, and the former was limited to piecemeal development, with splendid merchant-palaces in extensive grounds, many of which survive.

Hey, Lower Hey or Marled (i.e. gravelly) Hey – and thus discredit yet another old word. Occasionally one of these monsters of the old urban utopia is rehabilitated by a developer and (fortified behind high walls, bricked-up ground-floor windows, with entry-phones and 24-hour security-guards) made fit for civilised people again. But of course it has to be renamed, like a company re-emerging after bankruptcy, or else no-one will have anything to do with it. One ex-slum has been renamed 'Flambards' (the power of TV again!), another, 'Minster Court'; and here's another socially mobile word, 'court', which has moved from a royal residence down to the notorious 19th-century slums known as 'court-dwellings'; and up again, from the 1920s, to blocks of desirable flats. These are often also called 'mansions', a late Victorian and early Edwardian genteel-ism that spread well into the 20th century. The blocks of dwellings endowed for the poor by the American banker George Peabody became Pea-body *Buildings*. Other phil-anthropists followed and duly had their munificence comme-morated with their name – and thus to live in 'buildings' for a

'Townships', incidentally, have entirely disappeared from the English scene and chiefly denote shanty-towns occupied by South African negroes; and 'inner city' is a sociologists' shibboleth meaning 'deprived area' – as 'inner city' as the suburban areas of Tottenham and Handsworth.

long time denoted charity-aided but respectable poverty. 'Tenements' had a chequered reputation, from the Latin for a holding to the ordinary word for what is now a flat or apartment, but later synonymous with a pre-war slum. London built tower blocks called 'Points', like the ill-fated Ronan Point, part of which collapsed and discredited an entire method of building in one dramatic accident. Liverpool favoured 'Heights' for their tower blocks, and successive administrations in the ding-dong of local 'toytown' politics gave them such names as 'Entwistle Heights', after a Tory council leader; or, with consummate irony, 'Gardens' like 'Myrtle Gardens', where not a blade of grass was allowed to grow except in the cracks between the concrete; or 'The Braddocks' for two ugly giants, after John and Bessie, the revolutionary Labour firebrands of the post-war years (by present standards about as revolutionary as the Davids Owen and Steel): both are about to be demolished. Perhaps the Liverpool liking for 'Heights' was a subconscious reaction to the notorious 'cellar dwellings' that infested the city for many years after the 1840s, largely inhabited by the poorest Irish immigrants. The cellar dwellings problem was solved with typically brutal 19th-century thoroughness: the cellars were filled in with sand. After that, the local authorities took things in hand, and there followed much splendid Bylaw Housing – street after terraced street of often ugly but always well-built houses for 'artisans', many giving good service to this day.

Americans have long appreciated collective security on their estates, guarded by barriers and gate-keepers and called 'condominiums' (from con + dominium, joint ownership, not what you think). Mrs Thatcher has bought a 'unit' in an English one, but when they become general in this increasingly robber-infested country they might be called 'conviviums', a much jollier word. At present many new upmarket urban developments masquerade as 'villages': nostalgia again, and once more I cite my home town. Just below the Anglican cathedral there used to be a conglomeration of Georgian houses, neat and pretty, with street-names such as Nile Street indicating their date. Of course the council pulled them down, leaving the site derelict for years. Now they are building – guess what – imitation Georgian houses, and the development is at present grandly named a Piazza, which would have been more suitable, if anywhere in this country, outside the Roman Catholic cathedral nearby. 'Close', the traditional name for the area surrounding a cathedral, was presumably not posh enough. And just to consolidate the desirable foreign atmosphere, a group of newly-built 'Georgian' houses has changed from St James's Road to St James's Plaza.

A glance at estate agents' literature will show that no more 'streets' or 'roads' are being built. Modern man prefers to live in a *drive*, a *walk*, a *view* or a *green*. *Close* and *crescent* are almost as outmoded as *street*, *road* and *avenue*. And no more tea-parties in the back garden. This area, paved, is now the 'low-jah' or 'patty-oh', reserved for sun-loungers and barbecues.

Liverpool has copied the banana-republic practice of naming tower blocks, schools and colleges after living politicians and planners. Once again, a time-honoured British custom has gone by the board – perhaps more a rule than a custom – not to commemorate in bronze men whose feet might yet prove to be of clay. As some English councils and all banana-republics know, this can lead to hurried renamings if the subjects so honoured blot their copybooks: just as in South America and Africa where avenues change their names with each deposed ruler and, usually, the date of the most recent revolution ('Avenue of the 29th February'). I mean, can you imagine the 'T. John Smith School of Moral Philosophy' – with T. John Smith sitting in prison for accepting bribes from property-developers? (But then you now have to check whether someone claiming to have enjoyed residence 'in the Albany' means an exclusive set of London rooms in Piccadilly or an inclusive one, behind bars, on the Isle of Wight.) The Militant Loonies of Liverpool excelled themselves by (among other idiocies) erecting a commemorative plaque in the Town Hall to a bunch of convicted criminals. And the late Greater London Council provided some wondrous examples of revolutionary, commemorative renaming-mania. The GLC leader and his wild-eyed committees stopped at nothing in their zany lunacies; and when they ran out of terrorists to erect statues to or rename streets after they started on their remaining dray-horses. One pair, previously called Samson and Delilah is now (unless the new order has re-named them) called 'Peace and Friendship'. Someone should commemorate the demise of the GLC by calling the back-yard of County Hall 'Piazza of the First of April'.

The most curious place-names are undoubtedly found in the United States, where people from so many different countries settled and brought their languages with them. Places in Britain and other countries with a long and ancient history grew slowly and gradually, have village, town and city names whose meanings are rooted in the distant past. American immigrants, on the other hand, were usually obliged to start by building on open country, so that they could begin from scratch and invent what they considered a suitable name for the place in which they were about to settle.

If they were of English origin they might have chosen names that reminded them of home. There are no fewer than 22 *Londons* in the USA, some 18 *Bostons* (all named after the town in Lincolnshire), and even more *Bristols*; and nearly 30 *Newports* (which is why Americans almost automatically add the country to the place-name: 'I'm going to *Paris, France* . . '). But they did not always retain the idiosyncratic English pronunciations, like 'Gloster' or 'Wooster', but give to both their *Gloucester* and *Worcester* (to name but two) the full three syllables.

They also have to specify, if they mention these places in Europe, *Rome, Italy*; *Utica, Sparta, Thebes, Syracuse, Ithaca* or *Athens, Greece*; for there was during the 19th century a fashion for naming American places after those of European classical antiquity. *Philadelphia* is the City of Brotherly Love: from *philein* + *delphos*. Spanish settlers, often those who came north from Mexico, are responsible for naming *Los Angeles, San Francisco, Santa Margarita, Las Palomas*, etc.;

Dutch ones named *Harlem* (the original place in Holland is *Haarlem*), *Flushing* from *Vlissingen*; *Nassau*, *Yonkers*, and *Bowery* (from *bouwerei*, a farm). New York was previously New Amsterdam, but long before that it had the Indian name *Manhattan*, now applied only to the island but from earliest times the name for the whole area.

The French-speakers and Creoles in the South produced *New Orleans*, *Louisiana*, etc. There are *Stockholms*, *Belgrades*, *Florences*, *Christianias*, *Venices* and *Bremens*, where Scandinavians, Slavs, Italians or Germans founded settlements. In spite of recent American-Russian tensions there is (or at any rate was until recently) a *Moscow* in Idaho (though constant agitation from certain residents for a change will eventually prevail, if it has not already done so): *Berlin*, Alabama was during the last war changed to Sardis, in deference to anti-German feeling.

Countless places are named after people, both American and European, like *Jackson*, *Washington*, *Bismarck*, *Roosevelt*, *Lafayette*, *Taylor* or *Randolph*; even the showman P. T. *Barnum* has no fewer than six towns to his name. The suffixes -town, -ville or -burg(h) produced *Johnstown*, *Jonesville*, *Pittsburgh*, and many others. *Dallas* is so called after an early American Vice President. Some town names were inspired by women: perhaps English queens, princesses, or merely the wives or mistresses of the settlers and founders, like *Charlotte*, *Augusta*, *Ada*, *Alma*, *Marion* and *Elvira*.

Biblical and religious influences caused places to be named after those in the holy land or the Bible: *Jordan*, *Sharon* or *Canaan*; *Aaron*, *Abraham* and *Moses*; and – surprisingly – several *Sodoms*, too, appear in American gazetteers. There are places called *Trinity*, or those named after great religious figures such as Charles Wesley: about half a dozen *Wesleys* or *Wesleyvilles*; and twelve *Luthers*. *Concepcions* and *Sacramentos* abound in Spanish-Catholic places, where *Trinity* becomes *Trinidad*, as do numerous ones named after saints, e.g. *Santa Barbara*.

But not all Americans were immigrants. The Indians had been there for thousands of years, and evolved their own place-names of either factual or obscure origin; and many survive to this day, proudly borne in full (though a few

130

inevitably get abbreviated in everyday use)— *Kajakanika-mak*, *Kakekekwaki*, *Hoolethloces*, *Chattanooga*, *Chemqua-sabamticook* and, of course, *Arkansas*, *Milwaukee*, *Tallahassee*, *Chicago* and *Kalamazoo* – all now taken for 'real' American names but in fact Indian for centuries before there was a United States of America. Or indeed a Canada, for there, too many hundreds of Indian names survive: e.g. *Manitoba* and *Quebec*; and there, as one would expect, the French colonisation is also strongly reflected. Some historic Indian locations in North America almost rival that enormous Welsh place name, although *Quohquinapassakessamanag-nog* is now *Beaver*, and Lake *Chargoggagaugmanchauga-goggchaubunagungamaugg* is known to the local inhabitants as *Webster* for short.

Some places were given the names of mineral treasure that was found (or sometimes merely sought) there; so that there are now towns called *Bromide*, *Chrome*, *Chloride*, *Cement*, *Leadville* and *Coal Run* – but no Asbestos: if there were, health campaigners would doubtless press for a change.

In both east and west the settlers' often rather grim sense of humour is apparent, as in *Tombstone*, *Arizona*, reflecting the wild days of the West, and also *Horsethief Trail*, Color-ado, and many other examples familiar from the wildly over-glamorised Hollywood films. H. L. Mencken also lists *Burning Bear*, Colorado; *Sleepy Eye*, and *Pig Eye Lake*, both Minnesota; *Gizzard*, Tennessee; *Hot Coffee*, Missouri; *Rough-and-Ready*, California. The state of West Virginia alone has more or less attractively named places called *Affi-nity*, *Bias*, *Big Chimney*, *Bulltown*, *Cinderella*, *Cowhide*, *Jingo*, *Raven Eye*, *Skull Run*, *War Eagle* and *Stump Town*.

Were the first citizens of Maryland students of Rabelais and his early English translators, with their fondness for fanciful erotic euphemisms? For in that state are to be found *Bald Friar*, *Dame's Quarter*, *My Lady's Manor* and *Soldier's Delight* – and also, perhaps inevitably, *Issue*. California has a *French Lick*.

In *Lancaster County* (itself derived from *Lancashire, Eng-land*) in the State of Pennsylvania (which is named after the 17th-century English settler, William Penn – *sylvania* is a made-up, Latin-based word meaning 'wooded land'), the town of *Intercourse* has become a tourist attraction on the strength of its name alone: thousands of visitors flock there to have their letters franked at the Post Office. Not far away are *Paradise*, *Mount Joy* (the American equivalent of the German *Venusberg* made famous by Wagner?), *Bird in Hand*, and *Blue Ball*; also *Bareville* – a pioneering nudist colony?

The American attitude to *Intercourse* (the town, that is) is in marked contrast to the characteristically toffee-nosed attitude of English officialdom. In the early 1980s someone discovered the village of *Lover* in Wiltshire and took his Valentine cards there to be posted. His friends in time copied him, the news spread, and others began to send their ready-stamped Valentines to the village post office with a covering letter asking the post-mistress to frank and forward them. But as soon as the post office authorities got to hear of it, they ordered the kind and helpful Mrs Southorn, who looked after *Lover*'s sub post office, to 'discontinue the practice'. This received a lot of adverse publicity, so the decision may later have been rescinded. But thanks to the new mania for 'rationalisation' (which means reducing the service while increasing the charges), most village post offices are now obliged to send letters for franking to the nearest central post office, so that lovers' letters posted in *Lover* would probably in any case now bear a Salisbury post-mark.

You need only browse in a gazetteer at the end of a book of road-maps to see that English place-names are sheer poetry, though they are not always what they seem: anyone working audibly for the BBC would be well advised to consult the *BBC Pronouncing Dictionary of British Names* (edited by G. M. Miller and published by Oxford University Press) for idiosyncrasies and anomalies of pronunciation. I have heard announcers say 'ta, poorly', as if replying to a question about the health, for Tarporley in Cheshire (see below); and 'mee-oles' for both Meols in Cheshire and Meols in Lancashire, but apparently it's wrong for both: the first is 'mells' and the second 'meelz'; while East and West Meon are 'mee-on'. Often the local vernacular conflicts with the 'standard' pronunciation preferred by outside speakers. People who live in Shrewsbury say 'shroosbury', but the upmarket way seems to be 'Shroesbury'. No-one in Coventry says anything but 'Coventry', it seems, but upper crust folk (and a few news-readers) say 'Cuvventry' (as in a witches' coven). There is probably a basis of tradition in the various ways; but when in doubt the BBC, I'm told, rings the local vicar or post office to ascertain current practice. Cirencester is now as written, but I certainly remember being firmly taught to say 'sisster'; also 'toester' for Towcester.

Many anomalies occur when the pronunciation of place-names and of the families which also bear them has parted company; or when different branches of the same clan disagree among themselves, like the Pepys family, who are variously 'peeps', 'pep'pis' or 'pips'. Tra*fal*gar Square always has the stress on the second syllable, but the earlier Earls Nelson said '*traff*'l-gar'.

Go through a telephone dialling-code book for, say, Wiltshire (part of it temporarily disguised as the synthetic county of 'Avon') and you will fall in love with places called Maiden Bradley, be smitten by the village of Bitton and charmed by Charmy Down, Chew Magna, All Cannings, Godney, Peasemore, Peasedown St John, Pucklechurch, Upton Noble and Wyke Chamflower. Some places, like Easton in Gordano or Compton Dando, have a romantic Italianate or Spanish ring to them while remaining perfectly English, and many, like Chew Magna, add such Latin qualifications as Magna, Parva or Ambo. Piddlehinton is no piddling little place but takes its name from the (salubrious) river Piddle. Of course, inhabitants of quaintly-named English places get so used to their place-names that, unlike the foreigner from twenty-five miles away, they see nothing comic in them. Local newspapers cheerfully bring headlines like DOWAGER'S BOTTOM TO GET FACELIFT, BARKING SCHOOL-CHILDREN TO BE PSYCHOANALYSED, or LADY SEEKS COMPANION IN BATH. In North Wales a local paper reported that the village church at Hope was looking for a new organist – under the headline HOPE ORGANIST RETIRES; and in Cheshire, news of an accident was brought with the seemingly deprecatory headline MERE MOTOR CYCLIST INJURED. There was (perhaps still is) a male-voice choir from the Yorkshire village of Idle which used to figure in the pages of the *Musical Times* under the splendid name of 'The Idle Glee Singers'; and I once saw a reference in a place called Failing to The Failing Optical Company – maybe the result of years of shortsighted trading policy. However, the Women's Institute of a village in Essex reported (in a newspaper cutting I have somewhere) that it had been unanimously decided to change its name from 'The Ugley Women's Institute' to 'The Women's Institute of Ugley'.

There is not only poetry but also a fine rhythm about many English place-names. Whenever Sir Malcolm Sargent was rehearsing the first movement of Beethoven's seventh symphony and someone found difficulty in articulating the all-pervading, insistent six-eight rhythm, he would say, 'Think of "Birmingham, Birmingham, Birmingham" and you'll get it right!' Beethoven would have found little inspiration in German place-names: Saarbrücken, Mönchen-Gladbach or Garmisch Partenkirchen are hardly the most musically inspiring sounds. But look at any signpost in Cheshire and you can sing right through the first movement of Beethoven's seventh: Timperley, Tarporley, Alderley, Mobberley, etc. and many of the two-syllable places within about twenty miles of Liverpool and Manchester can be made to sound at least as good as some of the lyrics Wagner set to music:

Ashley, Byley, Irby,
Shrigley, Birley, Kirby;
Caldy, Saltney, Arley,
Stanney, Stapeley, Darley;
Helsby, Pensby, Abley,
Plumley, Kirkby, Tabley.

But around Liverpool the places seem to have a more machine-like industrial clatter about them:

Aston, Bidston, Clutton, Dutton,
Eton, Huyton, Sutton, Hutton;
Hotton, Rowton, Neston, Storeton,
Beeston, Whiston, Weston, Moreton;
Upton, Cronton, Hatton, Halton,
Norton, Warton, Tatton, Walton;
Duddon, Cronton, Clotton, Barton,
Ditton, Elton, Shotton, Marton.

When did you last hear anyone say 'I must go and spend a penny'? Inflation and decimalisation have put paid to the expression. One is tempted to believe that the abolition of £sd in favour of decimal money was a carefully considered, cynical confidence trick. Everyone knew it would have been simpler and cheaper to make the shilling ten pence, keeping the florin and abolishing the halfcrown. Many eminent and clever people advocated it and indeed the florin was introduced as early as 1849 to prepare for such a system. But it would have been harder to hoodwink the populace into paying 8s. for a sliced loaf, 3s.6d. to post a letter, and five bob for *The Times*. Yes, I do find it easier with decimal money to count my change at a glance (i.e. without appearing to do so) and we no longer need the dear old ready reckoner for percentages; but all in all the decimal system was a fraud against which there was no defence. The old 'tuppence' and 'thruppence' have made way for the (e)uro-coinage two pee and three pee (we never said 'two dee'!) and so has the plural penny: people now speak of 'one pence'. And a sports commentator excitedly cried, 'He's cleared seven feet one inches!'

The weather men are trying hard to mess us up. Don't let them win. Discuss the temperature with your child every day in Fahrenheit. For one thing they are confused themselves, having recently started to say 'Celsius' in place of Centigrade. For all I care they can change to Reaumur (as on the continent) next week – but my body *knows* when it's 100° and needs a couple of aspirins, while 37.8°C means nothing. In summer I can tell the difference between 78 and 80 degrees Fahrenheit, but Centigrade, with its larger units, doesn't tell me a thing. (Which is why the headlines will never scream at us '41.4! PHEW WHAT A SCORCHER'). People simply refuse to think decimally, just as they will go on buying cars with a good mpg and walk a hundred yards, not metres, to the pub for a couple of pints, not half-litres.

Police will go on asking for (and getting) the height of suspects in feet and inches – 'five-foot-eleven', not the equivalent centimetres – but some manufacturers have halfheartedly mock-decimalised: I recently ordered some bookshelves described as 8,289 mm × 457 mm which, when translated, came out at 6 ft. × 1 ft. 6 in. Others have kept feet and inches but give fractions of inches in decimals. One small consolation: 'a unit of brightness in the metre-kilogram-seconds system' is called a 'nit'.

THE DECIMAL SYSTEM.

Brown (entering Pork-butcher's Shop in France, and seizing a large Sausage done up in silver paper). " KESKERSAYKERSAH ! "
Fair Charcutière. " C'EST DU SAUCISSON DE LYONS, MONSIEUR."
Brown (who always confuses measures of weight with measures of distance). " ALORS VOULEZ-VOUS ME DONNAY OON KILOMAYTER DE SOBISSONG DE LYONG ! "
Fair Charcutière (who is never surprised at English eccentricity). " UN KILOMÈTRE, MONSIEUR ? CERTAINEMENT ; MAIS IL FAUDRA NOUS DONNER UN PEU DE TEMPS ! "

The 24-hour clock has also failed to catch on. People have a choice, and stick to real time (which is as well, as my watch only goes up to twelve). So do radio and TV. British Railways uses the 24-hour timetable, but enquiry operators still say 'three', not 'fifteen hundred hours' (which is a lot of hours!). Dammit, everybody *knows* there are no trains at three a.m.

Postal codes were badly thought out, too. Instead of going for all-numeral zip-codes they mix letters and numbers, with the inevitable confusion between handwritten S and 5, G and 9, etc.; whereas everyone learns to write numerals clearly – there's money at stake. (My post-code is L8 3SB, but L8 35B also reaches me, provided you put the address as well). Telephone numbers, on the other hand, have been more difficult to remember since they went all-numeral; and besides, give you no indication of where people live, unlike PADdington, BAYswater or VICtoria. In America, alphabetic dialling is coming back: just as the English county names will assuredly return – the SDP is already committed to their cause. You would hardly credit that it was a *Conservative* government, on the advice of an Oxford academic, which sanctioned this monstrous idiocy, abolishing at a stroke the thousand-year-old Ridings in favour of non-places which announcers can't even pronounce, like 'Weshorksha' and 'Sowshorksha'. There are crazy anomalies – places situated on the banks of the River Dee on the Wirral (*recte* Cheshire) having to be described as 'Merseyside' in the address; and endless confusions, as between Tameside and Thamesside unrelated to the Rivers Tame and Thames, respectively. And why did we have to lose quartos, octavos and duodecimos, foolscap, imperial and double elephant in book and paper measurement, when A3 and A4 are roads? True, the differences between troy, avoirdupois and apothecaries' weights (437½ grains = 1 fl. oz.) were troublesome, but chemists are now more likely to make much bigger, fatal, errors by moving or missing a decimal point than they were to confuse, say, drachms and minims.

Why didn't we put the national foot down and make the Euros change to furlongs and chains, bushels and pecks, or hogsheads, pipes, butts and tuns of wine; or (serve them right) force upon them the Scottish liquid measures (4 gills = 1 mutchkin, 2 mutchkins = 1 choppin = half a pint)? A couple of acres of garden is meaningless in hectares (on the BBC pronounced like Hector's); and Shakespeare would hardly have written 'Full 182.9 centimetres five thy father lies . . .' I maintain that they would never have bothered to fight the Wars of the Roses if all that was at stake had been the New Counties:

How dost thou fare, good cousin South East Humberside?
Thy extramunicipal cares sit heavy on thy brow!
Alas, I bring thee news of plund'ring militants from Merseyside
Advancing redfaced through the County Metropolitan
Of Greater Manchester. Nay worse, our brother, Duke of Rutland
(Or Leicester East I trow he's now) hath broken with my liege
The District Council Chairman; and Kevin, Earl of Yorkshire
Tyne and Tees, is hast'ning to his aid with Uncle Gwent,
Our trusty Chief Executive . . . etc.

Like many other ex-smokers I've become a fanatical cigarette-hater, barely able to remain civil when smoked at, in other words a typical example of the intolerant convert. A couple of years ago, at a rather grand dinner, I sacrificed half a glassful of the host's splendid wine by pouring it into the ash-tray where a fellow-guest (the boyfriend of a renowned playwright but I drop no names) had parked his acrid cigarette between courses and between us. He made quite a little scene and – verbally – slapped my wrist. But I was not ashamed. His bad manners greatly outstank mine. Smoking is now rapidly becoming yet another self-inflicted disadvantage of what I daringly call the working classes. Walk down an inter-city train and mentally classify the occupants of smoking and non-smoking carriages into the sociologists' ABCD categories. It's in the smoking areas that you will find the tattooed arms, the dirty shoes on seats, ale-guts bursting out of teeshirts, tabloid newspapers, empty beer-cans and, of course, cigarette smoke in the air and fag-ends on the floor. (This observation is not difficult to make as British Rail designate open carriages half smokers, half non-smokers, in the hope that the fumes will refrain from crossing the dividing line. They don't.) Now, I too can make bad smells. These are not harmful to health and don't linger in people's hair and clothes. But I restrain myself (though I've often thought of marketing a synethetic near-equivalent, in suitably labelled spray-cans which could be carried in self-defence). But twenty years ago it did not occur to me, as it still doesn't occur to smokers, that my cigarettes might have affronted my fellow men, or worse, harmed my children; though I would never have taken a blaring radio into a public place and assaulted the ears of others. I think we have all become more sensitive to smells and generally cleaner. Time was when a filthy, grimy mac was standard issue for the English male and not confined to flashers or browsers in dirty-book shops. You could always tell a foreign visitor by his clean, light-coloured raincoat. It was a time when men's jackets and trousers were dry-cleaned once or twice a year (whether they needed it or not). I maintain that without the advent of deodorants and washable, non-iron clothes the Beatles could not have prospered, at least in the Cavern, where condensed sweat used to drip off the low ceiling back on to the dancers who had generated it, like a miniature rain cycle. The pervading smell was hot but clean. By the early 1960s the Odo-Ro-No stick had become acceptable even among men. Women were always cleaner and took to deodorants immediately. And with only a tap in the back kitchen, working-class girls were well turned out and sweet-scented, if only of Palmolive. They used to say among British colonists that even in the African bush an English gentlewoman could keep herself fragrant on one saucerful of water a day (which is probably why no English gentleman drinks his tea out of a saucer).

In the first act of Mozart's *Don Giovanni* the hero suddenly exclaims *Zitto! mi pare sentir odor di femmina . . .*', upon which Leporello compliments him on his sense of smell: *Cospetto! che odorato perfetto!* This *odor di femmina* is not a nasty one, but neither is it pleasant; and only men perceive it. If you are a man you'll sense it instantly in big stores like C & A and Marks & Spencer, but not in your DIY store, which brings me to another kind of assault. Perfume, originally used by women to mask hormonal and other smells, does nothing of the sort – it only creates a mixture. It also assaults the nose, can make you feel queasy in a crowded train and put you off your food in a restaurant; and you need only brush against a heavily perfumed woman to come under suspicion when you get home in the evening. In my view one who splashes it on before noon is no lady (and ditto for too much lipstick that smears cutlery and glasses, cheeks and collars). On the other hand there's no smell more blissful than a newly soap-washed girl in a freshly-ironed cotton dress on a summer evening, if possible with a bonfire not far away. If scent-manufacturers could produce a synthetic version of *that* they would do a great trade. But you can tell what their game is by the very names they choose for their wildly overpriced wares – the actual scent in a £45 bottle costs no more than a few pence, the rest is duty, packing, and 95 per cent advertising – forbidden names like *Poison*, *Opium*, *Coco* (actually from Chanel, but we're doubtless supposed to think of cocaine); more surprisingly *Tramp* (why not 'Vagrant' or 'Grime'?); and, unbelievably, *Je reviens*, which takes us straight back to *Don Giovanni*. Surely the perfumier M. Worth can't have been innocent of the curious amatory predilections of one of the Kings Louis (or was it Napoleon?) who used to send messages to his mistresses, *Je revien. Ne lavez pas.**

* Because of its pronunciation ('you lay') the cosmetic Oil of Ulay is labelled Oil of Olay in the United States, to avoid any kind of misunderstanding. (See also p. 168.)

The Times' headlines are in a different class altogether from those of other newspapers. This is exemplified perhaps by 'Lord Denning Bowls Wide' (over a leading-article disagreeing with a judgment of his). But its fondness for old-fashioned sporting metaphor could also confuse the foreigner. I mean, would a Frenchman understand, '*Lord Denning joue une balle passée*', which is what they call a bye (*Harrap's Standard French Dictionary*)? Perhaps, but for a German visitor this would have to be translated as *Lord Denning wirft einen Ball, der nicht vom Schlagmann geschlagen wurde* (*Collins's*). It opens up a translator's paradise. The French for lbw is not, as you might expect, *jambe-avant-guichet* but *mis hors jeu à pied obstructif*; for which the German umpire is, as usual, obliged to call out a short story: *aus sein, weil des Schlagmannes Beine von einem Wurf getroffen wurden*. But then, what can you expect from a language that turns a batsman into a 'hit-man'? (A slip-fielder, by the way, is *ein Eckmann*, called in French, *chasseur posté à droite du garde-guichet*.) Warming to my researches I find that an over is *sechs aufeinanderfolgende Würfe* (presumably *Jungfernwürfe* if maiden). The French for a maiden over? *Série de six balles où aucun point n'a été*. A googly is given as *ein Wurf, bei dem der Spieler dem Ball einen Drall gibt*; for which the French have *balle qui a de l'effet à droite du batteur*. The German reader could probably cope with 'caught behind' – *hinten gefangen*? But not with silly mid-on: *Dummkopf im Mittelpunkt*?

A stump in German is *Stab*; and to make a duck, *ohne Punktgewinn aus sein*. For this the French have a neater expression, *faire chou blanc*, to make a white cabbage. A fielder in French is elevated to a hunter, *chasseur*, which sounds far more energetic than someone who just stands there for most of the game if nothing happens to come his way. Mid-off: *chasseur en avant et à droite du batteur*, and mid-on, *chasseur en avant et à gauche du batteur*. This in German is the ludicrous *Vorne und etwas zur linken Seite eines rechtshändigen Schlagmannes*. Cover point: *joueur qui double celui qui est posté à droite du guichet*.

Leg: *le terrain à gauche du joueur qui est au guichet*, and square leg, *chasseur à gauche du batteur dans le prolongement du guichet*. Leg-bye: *point obtenu par jambe touchée*;

and leg-drive: *coup arrière à gauche*. Short-leg: *position à gauche et un peu en avant du joueur qui est au guichet*.

The difference between a French boundary and a German one is: *envoyer la balle jusqu'aux limites du terrain*; and *Vier oder sechs Punkte für einen Schlag über die Spielfeldgrenze erzielen*.

Bye: *Lauf bei Bällen, die nicht vom Schlagmann geschlagen worden sind*. Or should it be *Auf Wiedersehen*?

NEW CRICKETING DRESSES, TO PROTECT ALL ENGLAND AGAINST THE PRESENT SWIFT BOWLING.

Early Victorian protection against fast bowlers (Punch 1854), *or Kricketschnellwerferpanzerschutzkleidung, as the Germans would call it*

It was Mark Twain who said, 'Some German words are so long they have a perspective.' For in German you can make up new words simply by stringing old ones together, adapting them with case-endings, making adjectival nouns, turning verbs into nouns and adverbs into adjectives. In this way you can express any idea without borrowing from other languages, and although the resulting word will certainly be long, no-one could call it beautiful.

If you were to go into any German class-room at secondary-school level and chalked on the blackboard the word *Hottentottenpotentatentantenattentat* – a single word of thirty-six letters – every ten-year-old of normal intelligence will tell you what it means (and without consulting a dictionary) even though he or she had never seen this monstrous collection of syllables before. All that is needed is a quick dismantling of the word into its component parts, starting at the end: a kind of verbal stripping-down that comes quite naturally to the German-speaker. The German reader is used to keeping long word-sequences in his head. Many sentences are extremely long, and it is not until he gets to the end that the meaning is revealed by the verb, which in turn is qualified by its ending, its tense and whether there is a negative in front of it. In exactly the same manner the longest of words can be stripped down, backwards. *Hottentottenpotentatentantenattentat*. *Attentat*: An attempt on the life. *Tantenattentat*: An attempt on the life of an aunt. *Potentatentantenattentat*: An attempt on the life of the aunt of a potentate. Yes, but what kind of potentate? A Hottentot potentate, of course. So there you have it. Half a yard of what looks like gibberish is turned into a word pregnant with meaning: an attempt on the life of the aunt of a Hottentot potentate. I am sure such a foul deed isn't carried out very often, even in the restlessly backward – sorry, *emergent* – states of Africa; but when it does happen the Germans will have a word for it, whereas the English must resort to circumlocution, or else a mixture of Anglo-Saxon, Old French, Latin and Greek.

And anent dismantling things: every handyman will know what I was asking for when I recently went into a shop to buy a set of Allen Keys. I don't know who Mr Allen was who invented that useful implement, a sort of positive spanner that goes inside a six-sided hole in a nut or screw rather than gripping them round their faceted circumference. The dictionaries don't help: even the latest *OED* Supplement goes straight from *alleluia*s to *allemandes* and *allergies*. But again, a German would not even have to consult a dictionary. The set of Allen Keys I bought happened to have been made in Germany and therefore had its native title on it. Over there you go into a shop and ask for a *Innensechskantenschlüsselsatz*. Working from the back once more: *Satz*: set; *Schlüssel*: key; *Kanten*: corners or sides; *sechs*; six; and *innen*: inside. So for those who still don't know what Allen Keys are, they're sets of six-sided keys to fit inside nuts with a hollow, hexagonal head. A dozen short words having a delightfully mixed ancestry in place of a single long one of impeccably teutonic descent.

Another example. 'Daddy, what are reparations?' 'Ah well, er . . . they're much the same as repairs – both repairs and reparations come from the Latin *reparare*, to make good – but at some time in the past the two words began to be used in different ways. You make repairs to a building; and make reparations to people or countries, usually by giving them money (which usually makes almost everything better).' But no German child would even have to ask, or look in a dictionary. In fact, there is no German equivalent of that glorious monument to the language, the great, umpteen-volume *Oxford English Dictionary*. For the German word for reparations is *Wiedergutmachung*: making-things-good-again; and in German there's hardly any difference between paying out money to countries after a war and kissing-it-better when a child has had a tumble. Which is why German is so functional, matter-of-fact and (to me) unlovable; whereas English is infinitely more flexible and lends itself to the minutely adjustable subtleties – and of course to puns and other jokes. That does not mean the Germans cannot write beautiful poetry. On the contrary. There have been some truly great translations of Shakespeare, which can even in German give one those marvellous shivers-down-the-spine as only great music and great poetry can. But it is a different kind of pleasure from that derived from English, and certainly a different kind of beauty.

One of the first things the Nazis did when they came to power was to start purging the language of all foreign influences. They abolished the *Kasserolle* and insisted on the German *Schmorgefäss* (or 'braising-utensil'); and the national need for economising was exemplified by much propaganda for the *Eintopfgericht* ('one-pot-cookery'), in which everything was to be cooked in the one vessel to save fuel. Lovers were no longer allowed *ein Rendezvous*. It had to be a 'stand-there-and-wait', or *Stelldichein*. Time-serving German composers (and there were plenty who enthusiastically supported the Nazi state – with the result that their later biographies often contain mysterious gaps in the lists of opus numbers) began to call the sonata a *Klangstück* ('sounding-piece') and themselves *Tondichter* ('tone-poets') instead of *Komponisten*. The Official String Quartet of the SS (honestly, there was one) indulged in *Streichervierspiel* ('string four-play') of Mozart's 'Stroking-pieces-for-four'. (*Streicher* is the standard German word for strings but happened also to be the surname of the odious editor of *Der Stürmer*.) This Germanisation fad was, however, not a new bee in some crazy storm-trooper's bonnet but had been first proposed at the end of the 18th century by a Professor Heinrich Campe, who had noticed how the German language was being eroded by the then fashionable Frenchification. The courts in every German-speaking country either spoke French (because it was the elegant thing to do) or added German endings to French words. For example, someone with a certain coldness of manner would be described as '*ein wenig frappiert*' (from *frappé*). Even Beethoven (encouraged by his nephew, who was studying philology) briefly followed Campe's teaching — long enough to give us the *Hammerklavier* sonata; and for a time he even called the trumpet a *Schmetterrohr* ('blasting-tube'). He soon forgot about it, of course, and went back to Italian-based musical markings, but other composers, notably Schumann, also took it up. Elgar, for a time, asked his printers to use English instrument-names, like Hautboy and Clarionet; and Percy Grainger (who had an obsession about everything Germanic-nordic) actually tried to speak in what he called 'blue-eyed' English: 'louden lots' and 'short-toned' for the internationally understood *crescendo* and *staccato*. His quartets were, more engagingly, 'foursomes', played by 'fiddles, middle-fiddle and bass fiddle'. When he felt depressed he declared himself 'mood-slumped'.

In spite of (or should I have put *pace*?) the foregoing I wish we could try a little harder on British radio to stick to English words. 'A *coup* in Peru' is no improvement on a revolt or uprising; and *Putsch* is worse (especially to those who know it means 'phut!' in German). Every arms-find on the news is now a *cache*, when it could just as easily be a hoard. Is wreckage not preferable to 'day-bree' (all the more when it comes in the American, phoney-French, stressing 'd'bree'); a stalemate or deadlock to an 'omm-pahss'; and a sofa to 'chaise-long' (or worse, 'londge')? If you have to pronounce *genre* 'john-rah', it is surely better to stick to the simple English word 'kind'. I felt a twinge of *Schadenfreude* (here's one for which the English are to be congratulated on having no equivalent) when an interviewer asked Bob Hope how he felt about appearing again at the Palladium (or wherever) after all those years. He teased her much as an angler might play a fish. 'A day-jar voo? What sort of a jar is that, young lady?' A sense of 'having been here before' is surely better, even if a little longer.

It is strange that English speakers who cope perfectly well with the German *ü* cannot, or will not, use precisely the same sound when it comes as a *u* in French words. Not one among the broadcasters who paid tribute to the French film-producer Truffaut called him anything but 'True Foe'. (I don't know if there is such a word, but 'douchesse' for *duchesse* sounds as if it could be something rude.) Yet the same reluctant users of the French *u* happily turn Gluck into Glück, Furtwängler into Fürtwängler – because they think an extra *Umlaut* makes a word sound more German. Though Schütz sometimes comes uncomfortably close to 'Shits' on Radio 3.

On the other hand (*pace* again), one doesn't want to sound *too* foreign, especially if one is. I say 'Baak' for Bach, like all my colleagues, and 'Moat's art' for Mozart (and certainly do not rhyme him with 'Joe's art' or 'beaux arts', as Beecham and his generation used to – but then they also followed the French in saying *Malheur* for Mahler). We can be sure that when Dussek took up residence in this country he accepted the way his English neighbours would have addressed him; and those who insist on 'Doo *Czech*' have in any case got it wrong. Webern pronounced his name to rhyme with a sassenach Rayburn, not like 'vay *bairn*', which is a smarter-than-thou English pronunciation. Come to think of it, I much prefer to be called 'Speegl', which is how it appears in the *BBC Pronouncing Dictionary of British (sic) Names*. Anyone who religiously uses the correct 'shp' is suspected of calling me a Bloody Foreigner. When I once included in *Mainly for Pleasure* a piece played by the Danish accordionist Mogens Ellegard, the producer rang the BBC Pronunciation Unit, which recommended something like 'Möyens Ell-a-görd'; and I did my best with it. The very next day the artist gave an autobiographical recital on Radio 4, and began, breezily and in excellent English, 'Hello, my name is Moag-uns Elly-guard and I'm a Danish squeeze-box player.'

Words do get themselves anglicised, or else we would still be saying *couvre-feu* instead of curfew, *jeu parti* instead of jeopardy. People keep writing in to ask, why 'Ma-nahg-wa' but 'Nicker-rag-you-are?' I don't know what the BBC's reply is, but Nicaragua has long been anglicised, though not its capital. The country even appears in a post-Lear limerick about the young lady '. . . who went for a ride on a jaguar./ She dolefully cried/as she woke up inside/'What a nasty old meat-eating nag you are!' Conversely, it is acceptable to say Paris in the English way, but Nantes cannot rhyme with 'pants'. Although Sinai is pronounced 'sin-eye' in Israel, Englishmen have for centuries said 'sigh-nigh'. But what justification is there for the three-syllable 'sigh-knee-eye'? There's also the intentional, coward's mispronunciation, most notably of the philosopher Kant. I have heard him called 'Can't', 'Cawnt', or 'Kent' (as in Monsignor) on Radio 3. There is only one correct way, and it is printed, with some reluctance, on p. 214.

The German attitude is all very patriotic and not without a certain native charm, but ultimately there is no getting away from the fact that almost everything that is beautiful in Western language comes from Greek and Latin, the twin founts of modern civilisation. Take the helicopter, from the Greek *helios*, spiral, and *pteron*, wing. Together, anglicised, they make a neat and euphonious word. It embraces its definition perfectly, but if you want to find out how it came about you may have to look it up in a dictionary. The German word for a helicopter, too, defines itself – but about as elegantly as a duck struggling to take off from water, and you certainly do not need a dictionary: *Hubschraubenflugzeug* literally, 'a lifting, screwing, flying thing'. No wonder every German now understands – and probably prefers – *ein Helicopter*, or even the American *Chopper*.

A heavy lorry in German is, literally translated, 'a heavy-goods-carrying-thing': the word long, functional and accurately self-defining. But here, too, English scores a neat verbal bull's-eye. We call it 'juggernaut', which has an interesting, Hindi-based origin. *Jagar Nath* was 'the Lord of All Creation who rode on a giant waggon that crushed all who got in its way'. What could be more appropriate for one of the 40-ton monsters that infest modern roads? And what could be sillier than the German word for the front-end of an articulated lorry combination (*articularius*, relating to a joint): *Lastschlepper* literally a thing that drags (or 'shleps') a heavy load?

A FRIENDLY REBUKE.

"THANKS FOR A VERY PLEASANT EVENING, AND GOOD-NIGHT, HERR PROFESSOR. I'M SORRY TO HAVE TO LEAVE YOU SO EARLY!"

"ACH! FRÄULEIN, WHEN YOU COME TO SEE US, YOUR STAYS ARE ALWAYS SO SHORT!"

While Sir Frank Whittle was developing the jet fighter in this country, the Germans were working on a similar idea. They called it *Düsenjäger*, which literally means 'nipple-hunter'. Their fighter plane was always a 'hunter', so when the jet-powered form came into use they joined the word to *Düse*, which is their word for a nipple in engineering applications. When, however, Germans want to refer to those attractive pink, raised bits of flesh with which female mammals feed their young, they brutally call them *Brustwarzen* – 'breast warts' – hardly a word to whisper during a romantic encounter; though I can just about imagine Hitler barking it at Eva Brown in the privacy of their bunker.

In correct German a bra is a 'bustholder' ('breast-container'), just as the scrotum is for them a workmanlike 'testicle-bag' (*Hodensack*) and a vacuum-cleaner an equally functional 'dust-sucker' (*Staubsauger*). No wonder German youth is becoming more and more liberated from its teutonic language and internationalising its colloquialisms. It is true that these are somewhat 'pop-music-orientated' (*poporientiert*), but who can blame them for preferring *Liebe machen* or *Sex haben* (having sex) to the revolting *Beischlaf ausüben* ('sleeping-with exercise') as used in formal speech and the press; which makes love sound more like an army manoeuvre.

Most English people know what a placenta is (from the Latin word for a cake). The Germans call it *Mutterkuchen* – 'mother-cake', making it almost indistinguishable from 'a cake just like mother used to make'. And while on this subject, let us look at obstetrics, from the Latin *obstare*, to stand in front, via *obstetrix*, a midwife. In German, once again, you have the functional and self-defining *Geburtshelfe* – 'birth-help'. At least it is shorter than in many more far-flung languages. I pick the Swahili dictionary almost at random, which gives obstetrics as *utabibu unaohusu uzazi wa watoto* – starting with a word for medical treatment and ending with 'baby'.

TO A FRIEND STUDYING GERMAN.

Si liceret te amare
Ad Suevorum magnum mare
Sponsam te perducerem.
—*Tristicia Amorosa.* Frau Aventiure.
von J. V. Scheffel.

VILL'ST dou learn die Deutsche Sprache?
    Denn set it on your card,
Dat all the nouns have shenders,
    Und de shenders all are hard.
Dere ish also dings called pronoms,
    Vitch id's shoost ash vell to know;
Boot ach! de verbs or time-words—
    Dey'll work you bitter woe.

Will'st dou learn de Deutsche Sprache?
    Denn you allatag moost go
To sinfonies, sonatas,
    Or an oratorio.
Vhen you dinks you knows 'pout musik,
    More ash any other man,
Be sure de soul of Deutschland
    Into your soul ish ran.

Will'st dou learn de Deutsche Sprache?
    Dou moost eat apout a peck
A week, of stinging sauerkraut,*
    Und sefen pfoundts of speck.
Mit Gott knows vot in vinegar,
    Und deuce knows vot in rum:
Dis ish de only cerdain vay
    To make de accents coom.

Will'st dou learn de Deutsche Sprache?
    Brepare dein soul to shtand
Soosh sendences ash ne'er vas heardt
    In any oder land.
Till dou canst make parentheses
    Intwisted—ohne zahl—
Dann wirst du erst Deutschfertig seyn,†
    For a languashe ideál...

Breitmann Ballads by
Charles Leland (Trübner, 1890)

---

* *Stinging.* An amusing instance of "Breitmannism" was shown in the fact that an American German editor, in his ignorance of English, actually believed that the word stinging, as here given, meant *stinking*, and was accordingly indignant. It is needless to say that no such idea was intended to be conveyed.
† Then only you will be ready in German.

Some years ago I read in the papers that President Pompidou was suffering from 'a condition in the anal-rectal region which is intermittently hyperalgesic'. I felt for him, as I, too, often get that condition – the doctors also call it proctalgia – though thankfully I have it only in its figurative form. But how very different from a report in an old copy of *The Times*, which told its readers, 'Mr Gladstone is suffering from a smart attack of diarrhoea.' To us this looks brutally frank, but the meaning of diarrhoea was at that time known to fewer ordinary people than it is now: the paper simply paid its readers the compliment of using the proper medical term. Country folk might have said he had 'the shitters' (the familiar shorter version is more modern) or formulated an English circumlocution, not a medical one.

Only last week I 'suffered trauma' – because I cut my finger playing with a ring-pull can-opener. But of course it was a different kind of trauma from that felt by a smart young journalist who wrote, 'The Motherwell episode sticks with me like an insidious trauma that refuses to die.' I wouldn't call him a fool. It would be rude, and he might argue that *trauma*, the Greek word for a wound, now has a wider meaning. If I called him a 'moron' it would be not only rude but just as 'wrong' as his trauma. Although it comes from the Greek *moros*, fool, it is another precise medical term we now apply indiscriminately. It really means 'an adult person having a mental age of between eight and twelve' and was adopted in 1910 at a meeting of the American Association for the Study of the Feeble-minded. An 'idiot' is one with an IQ below 25.

Where are all the mad and the feeble-minded today? Like neurasthenia (weakness of the nerves) which many people apparently used to suffer from, you seldom if ever now hear 'feeble-minded' and, it seems, no-one gets neurasthenia any more (in any case many of its sufferers probably had syphilis and the doctors did not want to say so). Modern medical men know more about the mind and are able to define conditions more narrowly, but they also do so in more cabalistic terms. At least until the rest of us catch up with them and crack their code. Being simply 'mad' (which in America now only means angry) has almost disappeared altogether. A modern Polonius would say to Hamlet's mum, 'Your noble son is mentally disturbed . . .' but the psychiatrist might tell her 'Your noble son suffers from a psychoneurotic personality of oedipal origin with hallucinatory manifestations . . .' Spastic is increasingly heard and seen in non-medical applications, usually uttered by women (often in supposedly 'caring' women's pages) as a trendy synonym for 'clumsy' ('When it comes to screwdrivers I'm a bit spastic . . '). I get rather 'neurotic' (Freud, 1918, with earlier instances) about that sort of thing . . . I mean, it gets on my nerves though I wouldn't go so far as to say I had a 'complex' (term coined by C. G. Jung, 1907) about it. I am surprised that feminists haven't yet exploited the fact that *herpes* means 'creep' in Greek – unfortunately in the sense of stealthy movement, not as one of their favourite terms of abuse for a man. 'Crucify' for fierce criticism is a usage which I consider less than 'kosher': for some words have a special meaning for some people, and they should be allowed to cherish them. The trouble is that the layman keeps copying, or misrepresenting, the expert.

The word cancer (other than 'in the body politic') is superstitiously avoided by many as the great unmentionable. 'The Big C,' a friend said when I asked him what a mutual acquaintance had died of. As the public becomes more knowledgeable the doctors have to find new names even for the hospitals. Liverpool had a 'Hospital for Incurables', which then became the less brutal 'Cancer Hospital', and this in turn was softened into 'Radium Institute' – until people realised what radiation treatment was used for. When I last looked it had become the non-specific 'Liverpool Clinic'. Venereal (euphemism: 'Social') Diseases used to be treated at the 'Seamen's Dispensary', which is a slur on sailors, as they have been known to bring home diseases other than venereal ones. Strange that the word comes from the alleged pleasures of Venus, yet has no semantic connection with either venery (the chase) or venality (buying and selling) since a combination of these three Vs must have landed many a devotee in the 'Special Clinic', as it is now called.

I once read somewhere about an American hillbilly farmer and his wife who possessed only two books: one was the

Bible, the other a Home Doctor. So when they got tired of giving their children Biblical names they started searching for names in the other useful book, and called their daughters Hernia and Anaemia, etc. Had they had twins they could have chosen Irene and Urine (and described them with the old simile, 'as like as two peas'); and if they had been able to resort to a cookery-book or the grocery shelves, there would have been even more scope: Ambrosia, Margarine, Atora or Pastrola. I know a girl appetisingly called Finola, but it is the Irish form of Fenella and Penelope. The adhesive Araldite cries out to be rhymed with Aphrodite.

Candida has been a favourite girls' name among the English upper classes for a generation or so, which shows that the aristocracy, unlike hillbillies, does not go to the medical books for inspiration. Candida (also known, equally prettily, as Monilia) are unpleasant fungi that seek out the most private places of women (the non-medical name for the condition being a straight translation, 'the whites'). Annulus ('in anatomy, a circular opening') would make a fine name for a boy, and so would Hymen (the Greeks' god of marriage), and there could, indeed, be classico-medical couples called, not Daphnis and Chloe or Acis and Galatea, but Alexis and Alexia (the word-blind brother and sister) or Myositis and Megalomania, not to mention those perpetually frustrated lovers, Dyspareunia and Phimosis. Dysarthria and Eulalia are a set of mutually incompatible twins (and the former seems to be winning in the spoken media, especially local radio).

Variola was not unknown in the United States even before the disease it stood for, smallpox, was eradicated. And indeed many girls the world over are given the more fancy form of Emily, Amelia 'a hypocoristic form of an Old German name . . .' (*Oxford Dictionary of English Christian* [sic] *Names*) which in the medical books means the 'total absence of the arms or legs due to a developmental defect'. I also knew a girl called Kerena, which is a shortened form of the Hebrew name of one of the daughters of Job (the other two being Jemima and Keziah); it has recently become fashionable to spell it Carina: and why not? It means 'charming, delightful, pretty' in Italian, but in anatomical terms it is the bit where the trachea meets the bronchi. Amanita sounds pretty, too, but is a deadly genus of fungi. Malaria, from *mal aria*, 'bad air', is also nice; and not to be confused with Milaria, which is prickly heat ('small nodules resembling millet seeds'), demonstrating how important it is for doctors to be good spellers.

But even some of the wilder fantasies have occasionally come true. According to H. L. Mencken, American medical students in the early years of this century 'who deliver colored mothers in the vicinity of the Johns Hopkins Hospital in Baltimore sometimes induce the mothers to give their babies grandiose physiological and pathological names, but these are commonly expunged later on by watchful social workers.' A few who got away were a Placenta, a Granuloma and a Gonadia; and in Evanston, Illinois, there was (though doubtless not for long, poor boy) one Positive Wasserman Johnson.

Sir John Squire, in a lecture delivered 'over the wireless' in 1930 (one of the earliest, if not the first, radio talk about words) suggested, conversely, that the more homely English names for diseases would make poor names for persons, and he defended the use of Latin botanical names. Can you conceive (he wrote) an Arthurian tale with heroes and heroines called Measles and Mumps? Or a garden of flowers called Croup, Cramp, and Stomach-ache? Yet listen to this: a poem, in the Pre-Raphaelite manner (with a slight Shakespearian cross), in which the names of diseases were used for knights, ladies, and flowers . . .

So forth then rode Sir Erysipelas
From good Lord Goitre's castle, with the steed
Loose on the rein; and as he rode he mused
On knights and ladies dead: Sir Scrofula,
Sciatica, he of Glanders, and his friend
Stout Sir Colitis out of Aquitaine,
And Impetigo, proudest of them all,
Who lived, and died for blind Queen Cholera's sake;
Anthrax, who dwelt in the enchanted wood
With those princesses three, tall, pale and dumb,
And beautiful, whose names were music's self,
Anaemia, Influenza, Eczema . . .
And then once more the incredible dream came back,
How long ago upon the fabulous shores

Of far Lumbago, all a summer's day,
He and the maid Neuralgia, they twain,
Lay in a flower-crowned mead, and garlands wove,
Of gout and yellow hydrocephaly,
Dim palsies, pyorrhoea and the sweet
Myopia, bluer than the summer sky,
Agues both white and red, pied common cold,
Cirrhosis, and that wan, faint flower of love
The shepherds called dyspepsia. Gone, all gone:
There came a night he cried 'Neuralgia!'
And never a voice to answer. Only rang
O'er cliff and battlement and desolate mere
'Neuralgia!' in the echoes' mockery.

I used to know a charming Liverpool man, now alas dead, called Patrick Cohen. He was the product of an Irish mother and a Jewish father, and, in accordance with the promise priests extract before sanctioning a mixed marriage, was brought up in her religion. Like so many Celts, she might have had in her the 'blood' of some swarthy Pedro shipwrecked with the Armada in 1588, and her genes conspired with Mr Cohen's to make Patrick very dark, very short and very Jewish-looking. But he was probably as devout as Cardinal Heenan and certainly a noted pillar of the local Irish-Catholic establishment. (I'm afraid I used to call him 'Lepre-cohen', though not to his face.)

He was by no means unique in the city, which has been for so long a melting-pot for seafarers and immigrants of all races. There was, for example, a famous Victorian organist who might have been invented by Ken Dodd for his Jam Butty Mines at Knotty Ash. He was called Oliphant P. Chuckerbutty, originally perhaps from the Indian subcontinent, something like Chakhabathi. My most treasured cutting from the *Liverpool Echo* demonstrates how smooth is the assimilation from foreigner into *echt* Scouser (see opposite page).

Mr Yoshida spent the entire war in Liverpool but there were no reports that he suffered insult or inconvenience; though of course, those were more tolerant times. I'm not so sure what might happen to him under similar circumstances today,

Hirohito's city cousin dies, 78

A relative of the Emperor of Japan, Mr Kanso Yoshida, of Kent Gardens. Liverpool. has died at the age of 78.

Mr Yoshida came to Liverpool from Japan before the First World War. and became a naturalised British citizen when war broke out between Britain and Japan in 1941.

Although he was second cousin to the Emperor Hirohito, Mr Yoshida was known to nearly all his acquaintances as Paddy Murphy.

and the chilling news that Arab terrorists singled out 'hostages whose names sounded Jewish' only confirms that things everywhere have got worse, not better. The idea that a person's name is necessarily an indication of his ethnic group, let alone his religion, is absurd. (I once amused myself browsing in some American telephone directories and found, I think, a Martin Luther Goldstein and a Moishe Kelly.) So is the myth that the blood in one's veins is responsible for slit eyes, a fair skin or woolly hair. Nevertheless Hitler prohibited Jews from being blood donors. His odious *Reichsleiter* Alfred Rosenberg, being Aryan, would have qualified, yet the Arabs would doubtless have branded him a 'Zionist'.

American-Jewish immigrants have always been keen on

anglicising both their forenames and surnames: Israel to Irving, Moishe to Morris or Milton, Goldberg to Gould, Cohen to Coburn (to name only one of many), Levy to anything from Lee to Lewis, Friedmann to Freeman, Ginzberg to Gainsborough. But contrary to general belief, the -berg ending is not necessarily Jewish, as it also embraces ancient German place-names, hence the Nazi Rosenberg, the princes Starhemberg and, of course, the Battenbergs, changed to Mountbatten in 1917 to allay anti-German feeling. (The Windsors, incidentally, were previously Wettins, and the Tecks changed to Cambridge.) Anita Loos (of *Gentlemen Prefer Blondes* fame) has a delicious passage about a Mr Ginzburg: '. . . only his name is not Mr Ginzburg any more because a gentleman in London called Mr Battenburg [sic], who is some relation to some king, changed his name to Mountbatten, which Mr Ginzburg says really means the same thing after all. So Mr Ginzburg changed his name to Mr Mountginz, which he really thinks is more aristocratic.' The Lords Montagu (as in Douglas-Scott-Montagu) are used to being confused with the Jewish Montagus and Montagues (as in Burton). Both mean 'pointed hill' (Spitzberg).

H. L. Mencken* quotes a passage attributed to Pepys which has long attained old-joke status: 'Today in ye clinic a tale told of Dr Levy who hath had his named changed to Sullivan. A month after he cometh again to ye court, this time wishing to become Kilpatrick. On request for ye reason, he telleth ye court that ye patients continually ask of him, "What was your name before?" If granted ye change,

* In *The American Language* (1919), quoting an article in the *Journal of the American Medical Association*; but I think Mencken took as genuine what was doubtless a parody. I can find no reference to Levy, Sullivan or Kilpatrick in the new *Pepys*. And 'clinic' is in that sense surely a post-Pepys word.

he shall then tell them "Sullivan".' Which brings to mind the equally dubious story about Mr Schweissmann ('sweatman'), who when asked how he could live with such a name, replied 'You've no idea how much money and trouble it cost me just to buy that w!'

It is difficult to explain to foreigners that Mr Roland Rowland is always called 'Tiny' because he is very tall, and that very short men often get the nickname 'Lofty'; though they would understand why people called Miller have always been 'Dusty', and might guess why men called Smith may be addressed as 'Smudge' or 'Smidge' ('Smudger/Smidger'). If they know about the Irish potato connection they will understand about men called Murphy being addressed as 'Spud'. But why are Clarks called 'Nobby', Martins 'Pincher' and Robsons 'Pop'?

When I was at school it was considered bad form to speak of a fellow pupil by his nickname when talking to a master, and even if he knew perfectly well who was meant he would invariably bellow 'Who?' and make one repeat the boy's correct baptismal name. To let the master hear his own nickname was unthinkable. Things are now more informal. Some of the older pupils are on first-name, if not nickname, terms with their teachers. And on radio and television chat shows both first and nicknames seem to be taken for granted, however old or distinguished the guest, however young and foolish the host. When Mr and Mrs Orton, aged 103 and 102 respectively, celebrated their 79th wedding anniversary, they were interviewed by some whipper-snapper of a BBC news reporter. Mr Orton called his wife 'mother' and the young man 'sir' – not obsequiously, but with the courtesy he was taught in his youth. But the interviewer addressed them as 'John' and 'Harriet'. He would not have spoken to his grandparents like that, but the Ortons had been dragged into showbiz, where mateyness prevails.

The same goes for news nicknames. Fleet Street hacks apparently cannot do without them, but in formal news bulletins they grate on the ear. Their use lends to squalid criminals a romantic aura they do not deserve, and certainly encourages them in their exploits. In spite of the fact that the police actually put out an appeal to the media not to refer to a violent rapist as 'the Fox', the papers persist, and so does the BBC (though the qualification 'known as the Fox' is sometimes added). This strikes me as irresponsible, although words are in general more carefully used at the BBC than anywhere else in the media: witness the studiedly neutral 'PLO fighter', which, unlike 'guerrilla' or 'terrorist', takes no sides. But news habits are ingrained. Hence the way radio news appears often to compete with tabloid usage: 'Mr Kinnock and Mrs Thatcher *clashed* on television last night' (knights in armour?).

One news editor got his come-uppance at the time a murderer on the run became known as 'the Black Panther' (and gloried in it) when the newsreader inadvertently read 'Pink Panther'. I know, and every other reader and listener knows, who is meant by Carlos Ramirez (and we also know that when he is caught he will not look anything like the only picture the press has of him, a podgy, bespectacled Bunter); but every newsman in the land feels obliged to add 'the Jackal'. It must boost Frederick Forsyth's royalties no end.

The more skilled readers and presenters are able to isolate a nickname in implied quotation marks, but most don't bother, so sensible news editors will leave these catchpenny tricks to the papers. When a certain British mercenary-adventurer repeatedly figured in the news, his nickname was rattled off on the radio without so much as a pair of parentheses, so that listeners might have been under the impression that, 50 or so years ago, a parson splashed water on the head of Mr and Mrs Hoare's baby son and solemnly intoned, 'I name this child Mad Mike.' But, of course, it may well be that Colonel Hoare prefers to be called by his nickname rather than his real one. Johnston ('Jomo') Kamau certainly did, for he abandoned his real name for Kenyatta. Unlike Stalin's name ('Man of Steel'),* the word Kenyatta had nothing to do with politics or Kenya, but in Kikuyu means 'fancy belt', an accessory he affected in earlier years in the same manner as later his fly-whisk. Perhaps white Kenyans are right to persist in the old pronunciation of their country

*Leon Trotsky, originally Lev Davidovich Bronstein, chose his name from the German 'Trotz', meaning defiance. The Germans write 'Trotzkisten' for 'Trotskyites'.

(to rhyme with 'seen ya'), though they do it because it reminds them of the colonial days.

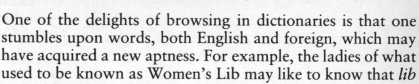

One of the delights of browsing in dictionaries is that one stumbles upon words, both English and foreign, which may have acquired a new aptness. For example, the ladies of what used to be known as Women's Lib may like to know that *lib* is an old English word meaning to castrate. When I mentioned that on the radio, I had a letter from a listener who confirmed that Scottish schoolboys called a desirably sharp pocket-knife a 'libber'. No wonder women now speak of themselves as feminists!

When a certain agile disco dancer came to temporary prominence a few years ago I happened to discover that *travolta* is Italian for upside-down. The name of another entertainer, Sedaka, is the Hebrew word for righteousness; and two of the Watergate villains were called 'Honest Man' (Ehrlichman) and 'Small Service' (Kleindienst), respectively. I would be surprised if none of the many German-speaking New York electors had made political capital out of the fact that Abzug (as in Bella) could be the exact translation of rip-off — if the Germans themselves did not now say '*ein Ripoff*'. A Polish friend tells me *Walesa* means idler, good-for-nothing: what we would call a slob — which in fact comes from the Polish/Russian *zhlob*. My habitual walesing-about in dictionaries reveals that a loafer comes from the German *Landläufer*, shortened and pronounced in the North German accent to sound just like the English word loafer. And the American bum (not to be confused with ours, which *they* equally confusingly call a fanny) comes from the German *bummeln*, the verb for such happy-go-lucky vagabond activities as Jerome K. Jerome's Three Men pursued.

After hearing my horse-loving daughter refer to a palomino, I wondered why a light-brown horse should be named after a little Spanish pigeon. I've forgotten again, for when I looked it up I found something much more remarkable. Several reputable Spanish dictionaries give, without comment, the secondary meaning, 'a small stain of excrement upon the tail of a shirt'. (*Bronco*, incidentally, is Spanish for a rough unbroken horse, which suggests another reason why that English brand of toilet-paper is unknown in Spain and South America.)

I always wondered why the English composer Francis Chagrin (1905–72) adopted that depressing, disappointed-sounding pseudonym when he was born Alexander Paucker, his real surname meaning kettle-drummer in the archaic spelling. The artistry of my favourite German tenor, Peter Schreier, belies the fact that his name means shouter in German. And Buxtehude is not just a German composer. It is also the name of the small place south of Hamburg where the family came from; and which German-speakers have always (and without reference to the composer) invoked in the same way the British use Timbuctoo: an outlandish God-forsaken, back-of-beyond kind of place ('They may compose stuff like that in Buxtehude, but here in Darmstadt . . .') Even Mozart referred to it in this sense, in the mock-Slavonic form 'Buxtihudri' favoured by Austrians.

This in turn reminds me of a story Stravinsky told. When he took up permanent residence in the United States, the immigration officer asked him his name. On being told it was Igor Stravinsky, he helpfully informed the elderly composer, 'You can change it, you know, if you want to.' At least Stravinksy wasn't peremptorily issued with one on arrival, as were so many other immigrants with difficult names. One German-speaking American answered to the very Scottish name of Sean Fergusson. When asked why he chose it, he replied that he didn't. The first immigration official had given him a new name which, by the time he got to the second desk, he had already forgotten. So when asked what it was he replied: 'I've already forgotten' in German, the only language he knew: 'schon vergessen'.

My name would mean mirror in German if it had the -el ending. But Austrians pronounce a final l with the rear part of the tongue instead of the tip, which gives rise to a common misspelling wished on us by some Austrian official. Maybe I should have adopted the upmarket, double-barrelled, anglicisation, Looking-Glass. In French, espièglerie means a prank, roguish trick or mischievous waggery. And in Italian, spigolatore is a gleaner. Perhaps of useless information.

During the Falklands war a new word, 'yomping', entered the language, but it never really caught on and seems already to be falling into disuse. There are two kinds of war words. Some, like 'yomping' or 'blighty', come from the slang of the British fighting man, others were looted from the enemy or 'liberated', as the euphemism had it at the end of the war ('I liberated this piccolo in Berlin from an SS bandsman'). Although the British (surely the *English*, in the wider historical context) always won their wars against foreign foes, they usually lost the battle of the words, trading-in their language and often getting a poor exchange. The very word 'battle' was a trophy: *bataille*, *battaglia*, etc., and in days of free spelling it mattered little whether the soldier (from *saudier*, Old French, from Latin, for 'one who is paid') brought back one *t* or two in his knapsack. Because the French have been the most frequent battle-partners most of the war words come from them. If the British private soldier rises through the ranks he does so almost entirely in French, from corporal or lance-bombardier to sergeant, colonel and all the way to brigadier and marshal of the regiment wearing symbols of their rank on their *epaulettes*. The army goes on *reconnaissance* over difficult *terrain*, camps in a *bivouac* behind a *stockade*, sounds *reveille*, catches *saboteurs* engaging in *espionage* (perhaps releasing them on *parole*). The populace may be *harangued* in a *communiqué* (issued by the *aide-de-camp*?) calculated to raise *morale*; or the soldiers *forage* for food, fire *fusillades*, send *dragoons* in *platoons* riding in *echelons* with mounted *bayonet* (from Bayonne, where someone decided to screw a *sabre* on a *rifle*). A *mêlée* could result in a wound requiring a *tourniquet*. They might make a *sortie*, and retire to the *depot* or *barracks*, to *carouse* and finally hit the straw (*paille*) on a *palliasse* (misspelt from French *pailliasse*). But many words were themselves looted, like the French *barraque*, which they captured from the Spanish *barraca* ('a souldier's tent or a booth, or such like thing . . .' 1617) and turned into a barrack; and *carouse* from the German *trink gar aus* ('drink right up').

The Royal Navy, as you might expect, remained more true

to English, with its able seamen and midshipmen, but adopted many Dutch words, like the scow (*schow*), caboose (*kabuse*), the taffrail (*tafereel*), and the *schooner* (apparently itself first borrowed by the Dutch from the English *scoon*, to skim over the water). For admiral, however, they went to the Arabs (*al emir*), as they did for azimuth (*as-sumut*). Even the cipher (*cifr*), magazine (*makazin* = storehouse) and arsenal (*dar accina'ah* = workshop) are Arabic in origin; and so is the drummer with his tambour, which the French stole from the Arabs (*tambur*). When British fighting men temporarily discarded their uniforms for informal dress they jocularly remembered the loose robes of the *mufti*, or priest. The dreaded assassins were the Arab *hashshashin* (literally 'eaters of hashish') who went on the rampage rather like the 'ganja gangs' who do much the same in East Africa.

During the first world war 'shell shock' were dreaded words on everyone's lips: men returned from the front physically intact but mentally broken by the horrors they had witnessed. By 1919 the Raphael Tuck range of coloured postcards included one showing two little chicks playing see-saw on an egg, from which a startled third chick emerges. The caption: SHELL SHOCK. Today's tabloids reserve it for headlines expressing dismay at a rise in the price of eggs; and speakers with a receptive ear for clichés usually profess to be 'shellshocked' instead of merely shocked. 'Over the top', the feared cry of trench warfare, has finished up on the stage, with actors and comedians who exaggerate their material. Blitz (from Hitler's threat of a *Blitzkrieg*, or 'lightning war') has also been demobbed ('I really must make a blitz on this untidy kitchen . . ') and the meaning of 'bomber' (formerly only the aeroplane) extended to include the man who plants a bomb. He may wear a 'bomber jacket', or, if a drug addict as well, use 'black bombers'. In some trades you can make a bomb legally: as a speaker said in a Radio 4 interview, 'My brother's moved to Belfast and started a glazier's shop, and now he's making a bomb.' Or 'XYZ dropped a bombshell' – which is an ancient form of ordnance, neither bomb nor shell, and now fired only by hacks. For them it is merely unexpected news. People are strafed (from WW1, when the hun invited God to punish – *strafen* – the

English: *Gott strafe England!*). They may have to take the flak (acronym of German for anti-aircraft gun, in both wars), sometimes wrongly written 'flack', which is American for a news hack. The Germans themselves coined *coventriert* after bombing the city of Coventry, but in this country 'coventrated' has fallen by the way. So has quisling, but ersatz is going strong. The Japs gave us little apart from kamikaze and the almost invariably misspelt hara kiri, not hari kari or any of half a dozen other inventions. The blockbuster, once dropped on cities from the air, is now a large, trashy novel that makes a bomb for publishers. I once had an idea for one but it was, as one now says, shot down in flames.

SHELL SHOCK.

It appears from what I glean about the Motor Show without actually studying it that the former Austin Motor Company (later BMC, British Leyland, B.L., etc.) once more used Austin as part of its *marque* — and things have come full-circle: when an industry gets into trouble you just change the name. But when many years have passed and old troubles are forgotten, nostalgia takes over. I suggest car makers go for a little more nostalgia when finding names for new models. Austin recently introduced the *Montego*, Honda the *Shuttle*. Spot the trend. The Japs choose an ancient English word for a dart or arrow, for something that goes tirelessly to and fro; the British choose *Montego*, a foreign word intended, no doubt, to suggest the beaches of Montego Bay.

The Japanese sell by the million cars with friendly English names like *Sunny* or *Cherry*, suggest elegance and grace with their *Bluebird*, high spirits with the *Colt* and urban solidity with the *Civic*. We, meanwhile, give cars pretentious, foreign-sounding names like *Marina*, *Solara*, *Chevette* or *Firenze* (the last one pronounced in the tourist's manner to rhyme with 'here ends'): desirable and exotic and exclusive places such as ordinary folk used only to dream about but which are now available on cheap package holidays ('Having a good time, wish you were here, went to the *Fiesta* at *Cortina*, *Toledo* and *Granada* . . .') and evoke cheap booze and tummy bugs. An Australian friend reports that one of the favourite imports there is the French car they call a 'Pew-gott'.

It has all been overdone. I used to know a *Fiesta* that was from delivery so unfestively sluggish it became known to its owner as a 'Siesta'*; and an *Allegro* which was decidedly *poco a poco ritardando*. The *Sierra*, incidentally, will not go down too well in Latin America, where it is the name of a chain of funeral-parlours: an association as desirable with a fast car as the famous Black Widow road-safety poster the Jaguar brigade so objected to. If we must have foreign names, how about the Ford *Fiasco*? I dare them.

* As policemen and traffic wardens in the West End of London know, Arab visitors motoring in the capital sometimes revert to Bedouin camel-drivers' talk when their car has broken down and refuses to start, saying, 'It is asleep.'

When Britain had a flourishing motor industry, cars were often known by their horsepower, like the Austin Seven or Morris Ten; by the number of cylinders; or else by simple English names. Hillman had the *Minx*, the *Hunter* or the *Husky*. There was the Sunbeam *Talbot*; the small Singer was the *Junior*, a bigger, faster version the *Gazelle*. Humber used the names of English birds – the *Hawk* and *Snipe*. Some cars had place-names – Oxford, Cambridge and Westminster – that spelt British engineering prestige (no, dammit, we used to say *English*) and Rolls-Royce chose names that reflected the company's pride in noiseless elegance: *Silver Ghost*, *Wraith* and *Phantom*. Could it be that the industry might sell more cars if it reverted to good old English names?

However, English names insufficiently researched can spell trouble abroad, too. Rolls-Royce now know why the name 'Silver Mist' met unexpected sales resistance in Germany. *Mist* is the German word for muck or rubbish. The *Camargue* (named after a district in France) went down well in that country, but Rolls-Royce evidently don't know they have once again come badly unstuck with the *Corniche*. The firm recently lent one to a team of motoring journalists who reported in a Sunday colour supplement, 'Everywhere we went in France we were met with wide smiles . . .' Now, although *corniche* means a coastline, a desirable seafront (French for 'Golden Mile'?), it is also a variant of *cornichon*, gherkin; and as French is almost as rich in double meanings as English . . . well, I need hardly elaborate, except to add that Rabelais euphemistically but lewdly speaks of 'jouer à la corniche'. No wonder there were wide smiles everywhere. In America there was some resistance to motorcars made by the old Standard Motor Company. It was found that this was because in the States they like things to be not 'standard' but superlative. And, of course, their small cars were not called small but 'compacts'. Until makers began to advertise 'the biggest compact on the market'. Nor did the Americans fare too well at first with the Oldsmobile. In a country where only the new was considered desirable, the name seemed to have its own, built-in obsolescence; but people got used to it when they found that the firm's founder was a Mr R. Eli Olds.

Nor have all the foreign imports into Britain been without linguistic snags. The Japanese, wanting a name for a larger version of the successful *Colt*, presumably asked themselves, 'What is more powerful, more fully-equipped, than a young horse?' A stallion, of course. Whether it was a misunderstanding of what Mr Datsun said at the meeting, or a conscious decision to alter the word so as to enable Japanese salesmen to pronounce it, I don't know. But Colt now sell a *Starion*.

Fiat a few years ago introduced its *Panda* to Britain. An odd choice of name, I thought, and a confusing one, as Britain already had panda cars belonging to the police, so named because the earliest were painted black-and-white (though in Liverpool they used to be white with a horizontal red stripe, and known as 'jam-butty cars'). Then I heard that *Panda* was a last-minute panic change from the original name, which was *Rustica* – a kind of Italian translation of the (nicely English) *Countryman*. Some Englishman with a keen ear must have pointed out that an enquiry such as 'Can I testdrive one of them, er, Rusty Cars?' could have been misunderstood.

I learn from the *Food Programme* on Radio 4 that there is a firm which engages poets, writers, crossword puzzlers and other word-smiths to meet in informal committee to exchange ideas for product names, including those of motor-cars with their many linguistic pitfalls. There is indeed a firm, Nova-mark International, whose entire corporate energies are devoted to the task of finding names, consulting word experts and linguists from all over the world. There can't have been many anagrammarians in attendance when someone gave a well-known and still much advertised soft drink the name VIMTO. I have long treasured the wrapper of a pork pie I bought in Melton Mowbray (a place as famous for its pies as for Stilton cheese) whose excellence belied its emetic trade name: VOM pies, an acronym of Vale of Mowbray. You'd have thought that trade names would by now be chosen by internationally linked-up computers. But no: in France, we heard in the programme, there's a drink called SICK, and you can get BUM crisps in Spain. I no longer double-take at the Dutch gin BOLS, because 'balls' has lost its shock value; but German hoardings still shock British tourists with another drink called PSCHITT (a second-cousin to Sch-h-h-you know who?). And I noticed, last time I was there, that the cough-sweets and vapour rub known here as VICK are sold in Germany packaged in the same familiar two-tone green-blue but with the spelling changed to WICK. This restores the

English v-sound to the pronunciation, for the Germans say v hard like f; and asking a shop girl for a 'fick' might (in one way or another) have surprising results. A different, not unrelated, four-letter word appears on many an Argentine wine label; and you can go into Fortnums and ask for an excellent French dry aperitif called LILLET; pronounce it 'lee-yay' and you may have to repeat it in English.

From Japan comes a drink called Pocari Sweat, and John Murphy of Novamark says there is a Finnish de-icer called Super Piss (which is not so far removed from reality: when on a particularly dirty day the windscreen-washer bottle ran dry on a motorway there was nothing for it but to use my ingenuity . . .)

The German coffee firm HAG (an acronym pronounced with a long a) existed long before it developed the decaffeinated kind sold in this country, where it has by now probably lost all association with coffee-induced hag-ridden dreams. But in Britain the makers of lager* have recently gone overboard in trying to find 'German' names so as to lend some 'authenticity' to beer that is brewed, bottled, fizzed and sold in England from English malt and English water. The genuinely German-brewed Löwenbräu ('lions' brew') clearly provided the pattern for a host of English *bräu* beers, backed by TV and newspaper advertising campaigns that lack nothing *echt* German except perhaps the swastika. What is particularly laughable is the proliferation of phoney dots spattered over these trade-names, when you consider what cavalier treatment real umlauts, accents and *diereses* receive at the hands of the British printer.

* Lager means 'store' in German, especially something that has been laid down, e.g. drink. Lagerbier in German is simply beer that has been aged.

I have always wondered, too, whether the firm of Block and Anderson, which used to supply me with litho plates and Banda office equipment, has exported much to Malawi since amalgamating with Nig Securities Ltd and changing its name to Nig Banda; and if so, what Dr Hastings Banda, until recently the country's leader, thinks about the name. Want gleaming, sparkling white teeth? If so, according to John

Murphy, you can buy a toothpaste called Darkie.

There has been a spate of lawsuits about the alleged passing-off of trade names, and shops called Harrodds and Sellfridges were duly seen off by injunctions, though no-one can stop Messrs Chip & Dale from selling furniture. Liverpool has for years had the Jurex Rubber Company, another arresting name that invites a second glance, though it sells things industrial rather than personal. I once wrote about this clever name in our local paper and had a letter from the managing director which fairly put me in my place. The boot (to mix a metaphor) was on the other foot, for Jurex existed long before the London Rubber Company and its most notable product came on the commercial scene. In this field, too, there's confusion in Australia, where Durex is nothing more intimate than what we call by the (now almost generic) trade-name Sellotape: like the American rubber/eraser confusion, only the other way round. And this is worse confounded by the fact that there is an American rubber contraceptive sheath brand-named Cello, unfortunately pronounced 'sello', not like the instrument, or there could be some appeals to the trades descriptions authorities. But so far as I know no-one has yet complained to the Gnome Photographic Equipment Company that its 'Gnome Enlarger' didn't do what its name implies.

Lymeswold was surely an unfortunate choice for a recently invented blue cheese. Although Britain has an ancient tradition of place-named cheeses there is no locality with that name (though there is a Wymeswold); and, of course, the second syllable immediately suffered popular corruption to '-mould': perhaps another instance of a committee's deliberations producing a camel instead of a horse.

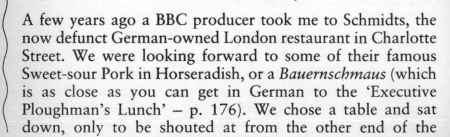

A few years ago a BBC producer took me to Schmidts, the now defunct German-owned London restaurant in Charlotte Street. We were looking forward to some of their famous Sweet-sour Pork in Horseradish, or a *Bauernschmaus* (which is as close as you can get in German to the 'Executive Ploughman's Lunch' – p. 176). We chose a table and sat down, only to be shouted at from the other end of the dining-room, where the waiters stood by the swing-door. One of them barked at us in a Gestapo accent, 'Who told you you could zit zere?' Meekly we moved to where it was convenient for them to serve us, which they did with bad grace. But then we'd known that Schmidts was famous for its rude German waiters, just as the London pub 'Dirty Dick's' prides itself on never removing dust or cobwebs. (The waiters must have been on good wages; I once left a penny tip, which speaks louder than no tip at all: after all, one Does Not Make a Fuss in Public.) On another occasion, staying in the Grand Hotel, Glasgow, a friend and I sat down in the Malmaison Restaurant at 10.20 p.m., expecting dinner. Too late for mine host. But instead of a quiet message of regret, there was a peremptory 'Can I *help* you?' (this time in a French accent) from across the room. Now, just as 'Aye-aye' in Scouse can, according to inflexion, mean anything from 'Yes' to 'What's going on here?' or 'Watch out or I'll hit you', so this was clearly not an offer of help but a way of saying, 'What the hell d'you think you're doing here?' We never had the chance to find out whether it really was a *mal maison*.

You often hear it said that people are friendlier in the north of England. They are. But the reason, dear reader, is that Englishmen still outnumber foreigners in these parts (some areas excepted); and I write this in the hope that my very name will preserve me from the wrath of the discrimination industry. Take a stroll in our park in Toxteth and (English) strangers will greet you and exchange a brief remark about the weather – provided it's early enough in the morning: it doesn't work later in the day. Try it in Hyde Park and you may get yourself arrested. In London the normal thing is to treat fellow-men with, at best, suspicion; or, at worst, with the wary hostility reserved for a potential enemy or shoplifter. Just like Beirut, Nairobi or Naples; because after all much of the London service industry is staffed by strangers. And the natives are learning fast, although in the courts foreign shoplifters still outnumber the locals by ten to one. 'Good morning' or 'goodbye' are seldom heard in shops. When you wait to be served the best you can expect is a sharp 'Next!', or simply the assistant's chin jutting interrogatively in your direction, a wordless 'What d'you want?' Service ranges from rudeness to bored indifference, and no regret is expressed if something is not in stock. In supermarkets (motto: 'Self Service with a Smile') you help yourself and words are unnecessary; though you may have to wait, apparently invisible, while check-out girls discuss last night's telly or their boyfriends across you. No 'please' or 'thank you'. A one-and-a-half hour wait for BBC material sent by the much-vaunted (but in fact dire) Red Star rail service provided a good opportunity to watch BR employees at work in London. No insolence, just indolence and total indifference. Moving at a snail's pace, they were clearly in the terminal stages of the English Disease, like sick men told that the slightest exertion could kill them. Some hard-working Asian shopkeepers, it should be said, still observe courtesies, including the bazaar address 'my friend', which means, 'my bargaining-partner'; and they have many friends.

I have recently tried the experiment of countering the mute, unsmiling, questioning look of London taxi drivers (a raised eyebrow means 'Where to?') with 'Good evening, could you take me to . . .?' So far I've not had a single greeting returned. One wouldn't expect or want the American 'Have a nice day' formula, and even less the Viennese shopkeepers' offer to females 'Kiss Your Hand, Gracious Lady' (*Küss' die Hand, gnädige Frau*). All one asks is politeness returned, and possibly even a smile. But all in vain. On London pavements you get jostled and shoved, just as you would in Paris or Rome. On the roads, too, there has lately been a distinct falling-off in traditional English courtesy; but at least you can usually foretell that the scruffy driver who fails to wear his seat-belt won't give any signals either. Oxford Street is closed to private cars. Spend ten minutes observing which drivers ignore the ban and you'll draw the same conclusions as mine. On public transport manners have almost disappeared. It is not the native Londoner but the immigrant or foreigner who feels he can do as he pleases. No seats are vacated for cripples or old ladies; dirty shoes rest on the upholstery; it is my observation that passengers who flout the smoking-ban are usually blacks or punks — in other words, people with grievances, real or imagined, for whom illicit smoking becomes almost a political act; one which combines flouting with flaunting.

Television doesn't help. Every play, every soap-opera seems based on people being rude to each other, indulging in smart repartee or general bitchiness, to gales of studio laughter. What an example to children *Grange Hill* is! People are afraid of being thought sissy. Offer a man a drink and rather than 'Yes, please' he'll say, 'Wooden mind'. Instead of 'Thanks' for a small service rendered you often get 'Cheers'.

It is all a great shame, for people are usually so nice to each other as soon as the initial suspicions are stilled. There are, alas, too many of us; and, like overcrowded rats, we bite each others' heads off.

On the way to Broadcasting House I pass a restaurant called *Garfunkels*, a name familiar as Simon's singing-partner of a generation ago. I never had much time for pop music (I mean that in the temporal sense, not dismissively: though 99 per cent of it is well worth dismissing) but I have remembered 'Simon-and-Garfunkel' for its easy-off-the-tongue rhythm, as one would remember any good trade name. So I am familiar with them without ever having (knowingly) enjoyed their music. But German tourists will not find the name appetising when they see it displayed over an eating-house; since *Karfunkel* in their language means a carbuncle.* Mr G.'s ancestor was probably one of those (see page 158) who could not afford to buy an attractive name of his choice (before spelling-reform G and K were often interchangeable) and perhaps he had one on his nose when the official issued the name.

* One has heard the word less in recent years, but the Prince of Wales helped to restore it when he called the proposed National Gallery extension 'a hideous carbuncle on the face of a much-loved friend'. My own simile was 'you don't restore a couple of missing bars in Mozart by inserting a bit of Stockhausen'.

One of the finest, certainly the most famous, restaurant serving Mexican food in London is called *La Cucaracha*. I am sure the kitchens are spotless, although I've never had the pleasure of eating there.

But I challenge the proprietors to anglicise the name of the establishment and display it over the entrance. Doubtless the allusion is to the popular Latin American hit song about the adventures of a cockroach, an insect which for all the poetic efforts of Archy and Mehitabel inspires little affection in people. 'Come and dine at the Cockroach!' The effect on diners would be like that of the 'Eat at Joe's' sign someone defaced with the addition '10,000 flies can't be wrong.' I am not a linguist, but sometimes I get bad vibrations about the way others use languages they know as little as I do, and I therefore feel the need to reach for a dictionary. Even when a translation is given for the benefit of customers the result can be less than helpful. *La Bussola*, a now defunct coffee house in Liverpool, kindly explained in a footnote that 'Cappucino Coffee derived its name from the coffee-coloured habits of Cappuccini monks.' Looking up *bussola* I find that it could be a ship's compass, a sedan chair, alms-box or revolving door, none of which were in evidence in that particular café. Perhaps the proprietor saw the word during a euphoric holiday abroad, liked it, and brought it home like a souvenir. That is what Lord Bernstein did when he called his cinema chain, and later the television company, Granada, to remind him of the pleasant time he had in Spain. Maybe one day someone will open a restaurant called *La Salmonella*: such a pretty name. (No worse, I suppose, than two adjacent entries in an old edition of *Mrs Beeton's Household Management*, which gave helpful hints on domestic ailments as well as aliments. In the index it says, 'Kidneys: braised', followed by 'Kidneys: inflamed'.) Ever since the Costa Brava and the Costa del Sol became popular with English package tourists journalists have found it an easy source for what they think are smart headlines. The development of golf courses for businessmen brought us many a headline 'Costa Golfa'; and the alarm-bells started sounding. Sure enough, the dictionaries reveal that *golfa* is a prostitute; so Costa Golfa, if it means anything, would be 'The Whoring Coast'. My Spanish friends tell me that the correct term would be 'Costa del Golf'. The news stories about English resorts being used for alleged social security swindles have produced the inevitable 'Costa del Dole'. The hacks accidentally came nearer the truth here

174

than they supposed. *Dolo* is a fraud, a swindle, in Spanish. Danish bacon offers Primal Cuts. 'Prime' wasn't impressive enough, so instead of suggesting 'first choice' they give the impression that Danish bacon is as old as time. Another marketing disaster occurred when a frozen-food company set up a trial sale of cod offcuts in batter, calling them 'Battered Cod Pieces'. The name was hurriedly changed to 'Cod Bites'.

I have never found the sign Pub Grub appetising (serve them right if some customer finds a grub in his lettuce); nor that other Ye Olde Englysshe fad, the Ploughman's Lunch,

"MARCH OF REFINEMENT," 1875.

Brown (behind the Age, but hungry). " GIVE ME THE BILL OF FARE, WAITER."
Head Waiter. " BEG PARDON, SIR?"   *Brown.* " THE BILL OF FARE."
Head Waiter. " THE WHAT, SIR? O!—AH!—YES!"—*(to Subordinate)—*
" CHAWLES, BRING THIS—THIS—A—GEN'LEMAN—THE *MENOO!!*"

which suggests it will be served in a grubby red, spotted handkerchief like farm labourers used to bring their sandwiches in. *Punch* once played on this when it published a cartoon of a man in gumboots, asking the barmaid for 'One Cattle Inseminator's Lunch, please.'

After the above appeared in *The Listener* Alan Protheroe reported that a restaurant had offered him an 'Executive Ploughman's Lunch'; and David Pollak that an establishment called 'Valmonella' had recently changed its name. But in Bristol there was an Italian-style restaurant called 'Stronzo's', which goes one better than carbuncles and cockroaches. *Stronzo* is Italian for a turd. *Bussola*, I am sternly informed by the lawyer representing a chain of 'units so named' is also the Italian word for a place of shelter – cabmen's or anybody's. Which in turn reminds me that outside the stage-door of the Royal Opera House, Covent Garden, there was for many years a tea-and-buns shelter labelled PULL-UP FOR CARMEN.

Excuses, excuses! I used to keep newspaper cuttings of what people said when apprehended for some minor dismeanour, but soon got bored with the same old lies or unprovable truths. A vicar, after he was arrested, explained that he was accosting prostitutes only so as to try to convert them. Vicarious pleasure? Mr Gladstone, too, spent much time in the company of 'fallen women', apparently to offer spiritual guidance. 'I only wanted to talk to them' figured frequently in proceedings arising from picket-line violence. Burglars caught in someone's backyard usually explain away their jemmy and gloves with the stock excuse, 'I was looking for my cat.' And you'd be surprised how many 'innocent bystanders' during the fashionable urban riots a few years ago carried half-bricks. They were all 'on me way to see me gerl-friend' – usually at 4 a.m.* Good excuses are found for speeding ('The canary was ill and I had to get him some medicine'), or even for drunken driving ('I thought it was water but they'd put vodka in my glass').

* One rioter deserves a footnote for inventiveness. Taken to hospital with severe cuts – which, it later turned out, he had received in a drunken fight – he said under oath in the subsequent court case against the police that officers had 'attacked him with a machete and slashed his penis to the bone'. Both the *Sunday Times* and *Observer* faithfully reported this as fact, without checking with their medical correspondent whether Liverpool men are really made of sterner stuff than the rest.

Conversely, when damages are at stake, plaintiffs (and their lawyers) try to exaggerate the effect of someone else's transgression. Once a favourable judgement or successful appeal is achieved, the victim may skip happily from court. I can almost hear the giggling from the privacy of many a bedroom when someone finds that the 'permanent loss of libido' (a favourite one, that) for which he or she was awarded damages has miraculously been cured. (I'm sure lie-detectors can be beaten, but have my doubts about a lust-detector, which, when you start to think about it, should be much easier to construct.) Dictators and their minions who travel abroad in order to consult with their cronies are always said to go for 'medical treatment'. On a lower level there is the footballer's face-saving 'thigh strain', usually a vague excuse from a manager who for reasons of tactics (or tact) decides not to field a certain player.

When the Duke of Edinburgh visited some African ruler many years ago, he was invited to go big-game hunting. This put him and his advisers in an invidious position. Speckled grouse are one thing, but taking pot-shots at the lovable leopard would even then have greatly upset the conservationists. It was therefore solemnly announced that HRH had developed 'a whitlow on his trigger finger'. This enabled him to attend the banquets and receptions but not the shooting-party. No one was deceived; and this little ruse probably helped the preservation of wildlife no end: few African rulers now shoot game (though their political opponents may enjoy no close season) and most safaris are photographic.

On the stage and concert platform, an artist may be 'indisposed' or 'overtired' for a variety of reasons (but never 'tired and emotional', an old press euphemism which has now been well and truly rumbled). They may include anything from the inability to learn a part to a subsequent engagement. However, an interesting new development occurred when a world-famous singer felt obliged recently to cancel a much advertised Covent Garden appearance because (his agent said) he had contracted 'stage-dust allergy'. This distressing complaint had never been named before and I have not heard of it since; but after the singer and his secretary took a holiday together it miraculously cleared up.

'Activities incompatible with diplomatic status' is the stock excuse for sending home a diplomat who gets caught doing precisely what he is here for, spying. 'Diplomat' suggests duplicity: Greek *diploos* means 'double', so he is by definition a double-dealer. And Sir Henry Wotton's famous definition of an ambassador (Latin *ambo* double) as 'an honest man sent to lie abroad for the good of his country' is itself a lie, for an ambassador who always remains honest and tells his hosts exactly what he thinks of them would be a poor diplomat. Does anyone really believe that a military attaché drills a squad of soldiers in the embassy gardens? Or a naval attaché sails paper boats in his bath? No, they are there to make contact with the right people and glean what information they can, with or without the help of a camera, bribery, letter-drops and the rest. Civilian spies from foreign countries masquerade as members of trade and 'friendship' organisations, and lately as airline ground staff. Import-export (remember 'Mr Greville Wynne, the British business-man'?) has always been a favourite cover. Most recently we have had the macabre joke 'commission agent' ('Mr Fixit' in the tabloids), a title given to one of Gaddafi's agents murdered in London for not carrying out his commission ruthlessly enough.

———————◇◇◇———————

Like almost every radio feature nowadays, an amusing programme about nudists and sun-worshippers on Radio 4 was punctuated by the obligatory occasional burst of point music (see page 102). And for any subject connected with the sun or sunshine, the first, the obvious and the inevitable choice is a catchy old ditty, *The Sun has got his Hat on*,* by Butler and Gay, from an old musical show popular in the 1930s. But you will never now hear the full version of the song. All performances omit

* I always used to think, as most of my contemporaries apparently do, that the opening words, 'The Sun has got his Hat on, he's comin' out today . . .' somehow referred to slightly overcast weather – i.e. the sun shining from a partly cloudy sky. But Professor Peter Fellgett points out that when the song was written nobody would consider himself properly dressed for going out unless wearing a hat.

He's been a-brownin' niggers down in Timbuctoo
And now he's comin' over here to do the same to you.

If they didn't the song would be branded as 'racist'. This is considered so even if the word is used in an historical sense. Dvořák's Quartet in F major was always known – by everyone, including the composer – as the 'Nigger Quartet', for it contains negro-based melodies. The BBC now insists that it must be called the 'American Quartet'. Delius's plantation opera *Koanga*, set in the West Indies among slaves, was refused an import permit by the United States because 'niggers' appears in it – used by the slaves themselves. In announcements of Debussy's *Children's Corner* suite I have heard a Radio 3 announcer say '. . . and the sixth and last movement is a Cakewalk.' Debussy's own title is in fact 'Golliwogg's Cakewalk', but some broadcasters feel they must bow to the pressures from the race relations watchdogs, who are trying to ban the traditional doll-like figure (created by F. Upton in *The Adventures of Two Dutch Dolls and a Golliwogg*, 1895), because of the allegedly offensive 'wog' element (whose origin, much debated, is, in any case, far from clear). The jam-manufacturers Robertson, who have used the Golliwog as a trade-mark for the greater part of this century, were deprived of a £40,000 contract by the Greater London Council because they refused to abandon their symbol, bravely continued to issue it as a badge.* On the other hand, the confectionery manufacturers Trebor Sharp, who have a successful line sold under the name of Black Jacks, have so far got off Scot-free (oops! mustn't say that or I'll get a caber tossed at me), in spite of the fact that the wrapper of every sweet also bears a golliwog (one g is now standard

* During the 1950s and 60s there was a fashion among promiscuous schoolgirls to wear one of the enamelled Golliwog badges (issued free by Robertsons) as a secret indication that they were no longer virgins. Boys used to say 'Are you a member of the Golliwog Club?'

spelling). As always the protesters are less than consistent in their choice of targets, and many of them are great lovers of the 'Black and White Minstrels' Show', which uses blacked-up pink performers and ignores the fact that many equally gifted black singers, dancers and actors remain unemployed.

During the war 'Choc'late Soldier from the USA' was a popular hit song, much recorded by Billy Cotton's and other famous bands. No-one thought it offensive, least of all the black GIs who got all the girls; and at the same time singers like Paul Robeson and Marian Anderson were universally adored, without condescension or patronage. They were, of course, called 'negro' or 'coloured' performers: had they been described as 'black' they would have been deeply offended. But when, a few years ago, the death was announced of an entertainer known as 'the Chocolate-Coloured Coon', the papers could hardly bring themselves to print his stage-name, even though most people had forgotten his real one.

We rightly object to another old hit, 'All Coons look alike to me', for such a song would be unthinkable today. But trendy librarians regularly rediscover Helen Bannerman's delightful tales from British colonial days about 'Little Black Sambo', and stage ritual bannings and book burnings reminiscent of the Nazi days.

Agatha Christie's play *Ten Little Niggers* has had to be changed by the publishers to *Ten Little Indians*; but not for long. Since the waves of Asian immigration during the last two decades a new version has made its appearance: *Ten Little Highlanders*. So far no word of protest has been heard from Scotland. In Vienna, however (where traditionalists still hold sway and the race relations watchdogs have little to bark, let alone bite, at) you can still go into any *Konditorei* or coffee-house and order a 'Nigger's Head – or *Mohrenkopf*; or else an *Indianerkrapfen* ('Indian's Doughnut') – both delicious, chocolate-covered spheres of *chou* pastry topped with whipped cream.

The music publishers Boosey & Hawkes, who had such difficulty in getting *Koanga* into the United States, also reveal that they had a formal request from the Race Relations Board to change the third line of the first verse of *Polly wolly doodle* to 'I jumped upon a *fellow*, for I thought he was a hoss.' Also

182

banned from songs is the word 'darkie' ('a patronising mode of reference to our black brethren . . .'), but the famous brass band from the North of England, *Black Dyke Mills Band*, is said to be enjoying a certain *succès de scandale* among black American lesbians who buy the record in the mistaken impression that the band is all-black and all-lesbian. Before the war polite English euphemisms for dark-coloured people included 'a touch of the tarbrush' or 'a lady of colour'; and Scousers still sometimes amicably call them 'smoked Irishmen', i.e. slightly darker-than-usual members of the large immigrant community of Liverpool. Supposedly polite old names sometimes managed to be offensive in an almost Mendelian manner ('One black and one white and two khaki . . .'): mulattoes, quadroons, octoroons, etc. in ascending order of whiteness. Indeed there is another old popular song called 'My Darling Octoroon'.

I was startled to read in a 1909 Ward Lock *Guide to Seaside Resorts* that Torquay in Devon prides itself on the fact that 'There are no niggers on the sands.' The bald statement made my indignation rise, but it quickly subsided again when I realised they meant not real blacks but blacked-up seaside 'minstrels'. Shop assistants report that people still often ask for articles or cloth in 'Nigger Brown', although that term has long been replaced in the colour charts by something called 'Scorched Earth'. Old habits die hard. As a recent Colonial Secretary found when he attended a former British colony's independence celebrations, which had been hurriedly but not terribly efficiently organised, and told his hosts: 'My word, you must have worked like blacks.'

Gresham's Law applies not only to money. Bad words, too, drive out the good. 'Bloody', for example, did not become a general swear-word until the nineteenth century, and was at first used only in the lowest criminal slang. But by the time the Revised English Bible appeared in the 1880s, its proper, sanguinary use already risked misunderstanding, and the translators felt obliged to change Zipporah's remonstrance in Exodus 4.25, 'Surely, a bloody husband art thou to me', to 'Surely a bridegroom of blood art thou to me'. The fuss over Shaw's 'bloody' in *Pygmalion* (which gave us the substitute, 'Not Pygmalion likely!') would be unthinkable today. But not so long ago a BBC directive firmly stated 'Blast, Hell, Damn, Bloody, Gorblimey, Ruddy, etc., should be deleted from scripts and innocuous expressions substituted.' Now the real meaning of the word 'bastard' has been all but abandoned, partly because its explosive beginning and hissing middle make it an effective expletive, and partly because social workers love polite euphemisms.

The euphemaniacs are at it even in the Isle of Man, that last refuge of a calmer way of life, where you can still leave front-doors unlocked and car thefts are almost unknown. But, the Manx papers reported, a Labour member of the upper house has just pushed through a measure to ensure that 'the word *illegitimate* will disappear from the statute books. Instead, children born out of wedlock will be known as *non-marital*.' During the same week new figures were released on the mainland telling us that every fifth child born in the UK is a bastard. But of course they did not put it like that. 'One in five babies is born to a single-parent mother.' Parthenogenesis presumably.

The English Bible has about forty references to 'concubines' – three of them translated from the Hebrew *lechenah*, a euphemism meaning 'singing damsel' (a likely story – like today's 'model', 'hostess' or even 'girl Friday'!) The others came from *pilgesh*, literally 'half wife', which is probably nearer the mark: a wife, yet not a wife. But the boy at our school who asserted that 'Solomon had 250 wives and 500 porcupines' would now have used the namby-pamby substitute, 'common law wives'. Not only sociologists: newspapers, the BBC and even judges now trendily speak of these mythical creatures. They are certainly a common phenomenon, but there is nothing lawful about their status and they are not wives; although the law quite properly gives them certain rights, and Scottish law does in fact recognise what it calls 'unions of habit and repute'. The *Liverpool Echo* has invented an interesting variation: '. . . the accused's common law son in law.'

The mistress ('something between a mister and a mattress' – why do I remember these schoolboy jokes?) has also changed her status. Until the end of the eighteenth century (often abbreviated to *Mrs*) it could be any woman, married or not. Then her status declined sharply and up to a couple of decades ago it would have been actionable for a newspaper so to describe someone's woman friend. They therefore invented all kinds of nervous circumlocutions, like 'permanent house guest', 'the woman in his life', 'constant companion', or 'live-in girl friend' — some of which have remained part of mediaspeak; and in the newspapers boys and girls can, of course, be of any age: 'Boy Friend, 92, Stabs Girl Friend, 84' is the oldest pair of tabloid lovers I have on record. A child born of a newsworthy irregular union is always a 'love child' and the place where it may have been conceived, a 'love nest', for the hack admits no love in marriage.

But there is no shortage of pseudo-sociologese words for unmarried partners, mostly American inventions: *mingles* (a portmanteau word from 'mixed singles'); *biological companions* (which is plain silly); *apartmate* (one who shares an apartment but not necessarily the bed); and the way-out *posselcue* (an approximate acronym made from 'person of the opposite sex sharing living-quarters'). There are *symbiotic mates*: and if you look that one up you will find it means 'two living beings that live off one another and suck each other dry'. In the North of England people are said to 'live over the brush', from the gipsy custom of declaring a couple 'married' who together step over a broom; not that the 'husband' is likely to do much sweeping.

Even today, liberated women who introduce their live-in sometimes get so embarrassed that they take leave of grammar or spelling: 'This is the man wot I live with', or simply 'my feller'. If it's posh words they are looking for here are a few suggestions: *colligates*, or *incatenates* ('two people bound, linked or chained together or mutually attached'); or *fere* ('a companion, comrade, mate, partner, whether male or female', *OED*). Even 'my bird' has an honourable lineage, from *birdsnie* or *birdsnye*; also *pyggesnie*: 'She was a prymerole, a piggesnye, ffor any Lorde to leggen in his bedde,' says Chaucer. Much better than any 'common law wife'.

News item from the *Daily Telegraph* (23.8.85): 'A man seen running naked through Ainsdale nature reserve, near Southport, Merseyside, just before a 34-year-old woman was raped, was being sought by detectives last night. The area is near a beach popular with naturists.' This report poses several questions. Does the *Daily Telegraph* know the difference between a naturalist ('one who is interested in, or makes a special study of, animals or plants', *OED*) and a 'naturist', the euphemism preferred by nudists; or did the man become confused and, running naked across Ainsdale sands, decide that a naturalist ought not to be wearing clothes, and in the process commit his monstrous crime against the woman? Or do Merseyside naturists and naturalists follow their different pursuits confusingly on the same site?

A London policewoman chases nude bathing boys along the banks of the Serpentine in Hyde Park, 1926

Newspapers observe strict conventions in their reports and descriptions of nakedness, usually preferring 'nude', for its more suggestive sound. Children are naked, sex- and guilt-ridden adults nude. To be naked is to be innocent, nude is

186

lewd. In the Bible according to Fleet Street the Lord would say (Genesis 3,11), 'Who told thee that thou wast nude?' Adam and Eve would have 'made themselves fig-leaves, strategically placed', for the human sex organs are known to the hacks as 'strategic places'; and garments or objects employed to hide them are always said to be placed accordingly.

The tabloids have only in recent years admitted pictures of naked women (now described, often inaccurately, as Page Three Girls), part of their relentless circulation-war. The accompanying paragraphs follow a set pattern of past achievements qualified by a 'but': 'Buxom Belinda began her career as a maths teacher but when it comes to vital statistics figures like hers . . .' etc. 'Curvaceous Carla used to be a female wrestler but since she's muscled in on the modelling world there's been no holding her . . .' Broadsheets seldom if ever resort to such idiocies, and when *The Times* once printed a full-page advertisement figuring a tastefully naked woman there was much outcry. The tabloids have progressed from pin-ups in armour-plated swimsuits via bikinis to full exposure of breasts. Nipples were at first avoided, and often clumsily painted out. Even bikini bottoms are now sometimes discarded, but only side or back views are shown: pubic hair is still taboo. However, there have been some delightful accidents due to 'show-through' on the poor-quality newsprint, when faint images from the other side of the page have accidentally supplied unwanted detail. At present the 'wet look', girls in clinging T-shirts, is much in vogue, as editors discover what normal men have known all along, namely that the half-hidden is more erotic than the fully-revealed. And in any case, those who want to look at pictures of naked women can get them in full glossy colour in the 'girlie' magazines, not in grey-on-grey newsprint.

The movement for going about naked started in Germany early this century, and its English adherents at first adopted the term *Spielplatz* (literally 'playing-place') which the Germans had coined for their wobbly outdoor sporting-pursuits. In further attempts to avoid specific mention of nakedness or nudity the Greek word *gymnosophist* was for a time pressed into service ('One of a sect of ancient Hindu philosophers of ascetic habits who wore little or no clothing, denied themselves flesh meat, and gave themselves up to mystical contemplation', *OED*). The magazine of the nudist movement, *Health and Efficiency*, enshrines a further two euphemisms, suggesting that those of us who go about fully dressed are likely to be less healthy or efficient. During more than 80 years of publication *H & E* has gone from coy prudery to blatant permissiveness. There were no nipples at first; then they began to appear but were kept in a discreet soft-focus. Pubic hair was for many years retouched out, which is, of course, not the same thing as having the area shaved. Like many other small boys of my generation who sneaked illicit glimpses at the magazine I therefore harboured the strange misconception that when little girls grew up they also mysteriously healed up. It was very puzzling, for it did not at all accord with horrid tales one heard of the rude things grown-ups were supposed to get up to. I believe early *H & E* magazines showed men in posing-pouches; then they always managed to place them in such a way that a branch of a tree or sunflower sprouted strategically. Now it's all action, with nothing hidden; and recent issues (which I have obtained boldly and openly, purely for research, of course) even answered that old question which every innocent apparently asks nudists ('Don't men get, er, excited?'): the answer is yes. At least sometimes. Girls are even photographed doing joyous, revealing cartwheels all in the interest of depicting them enjoying rude (and I mean rude) health. The articles vary from the titillating to the fatuous, designed merely to fill the space between the pictures, though some of the advertisements give the real game away. Readers are encouraged to submit their own photographs, as in the 'girlie' magazines, reflecting the spread of the Polaroid. Another device to gain genuine 'naturist' credence is the inclusion of some photographs of naked flab or flop, suitably captioned ('After all, we're all human'). *H & E* thus occupies an uneasy place among the soft-porn magazines, which, unlike *H & E*, still jib at naked, let alone tumescent, males. But the 'girlies' (and if that is a diminutive, some are very big girls indeed) are for ever looking thoughtfully down at their breasts (which, as in the *Sun* and *Star*, have cool air blown at them out of sight of the camera).

Streaking, in the sense of exhibitionist nakedness without sexual intent, is not to be confused with flashing. Streaking is a comparatively recent activity which gained some notorious popularity in the 1970s and early 80s, though in 1936 a woman, said to have been 'deranged', decided to imitate Eve and removed all her clothes in St Paul's Cathedral. A brief ceremony of reconsecration followed. Modern streaking involves running at speed through crowded places such as shopping-streets or sports-grounds, either for a dare, a bet, or merely a way of gaining publicity, with no clothes on ('except possibly on the feet or head' – *Longman's Dictionary of Contemporary English*). Women qualify as streakers if they merely expose their breasts, whereas more is demanded of men. Flashing is an ancient activity among sexual exhibitionists but the word itself is so recent that it missed the latest *OED Supplement*, which only gives its cricketing sense (a batsman 'apt to chase balls outside the off-stump').

Shock, dismay and disapproval on spectators' faces as a streaker invades Twickenham

But, of course, there are isolated instances of early streakings. On 23 October 1669 Samuel Pepys notes in his Diary: 'This day Pierce doth tell me, among other news, the late frolic and Debauchery of Sir Ch. Sidley and [Lord] Buckhurst, running up and down all the night with their arses bare through the streets, and at 1st fighting and being beat by the watch and clapped up all night . . .' But the King thought it was a great joke and the law not only could do nothing but the constable himself was 'chid and imprisoned for his pains.'; and anyway, Sedley and Buckhurst were only imitating '. . . the beastly prank of my Lord [John Wilmot, Earl of] Rochester and my Lord Lovelace and ten other men, which was their running along Woodstock Park naked . . .' A few years earlier the composer Solomon Eccles (ca. 1617–1682), who had become an ardent Quaker and publicly burnt all his music and instruments, took to 'running through the streets naked' (presumably Biblically naked, i.e. down to a loincloth), carrying a burning brazier on his head while he cried, 'Repent, repent!'

I seem to have misspent my life picking up useless knowledge of the kind usually introduced apropos of nothing with 'Did you know that . . .?' ; facts retrieved from a memory-bank that only files away the trivial. (And incidentally, did you know that Beethoven's lawyer was called Bach, one of his doctors Smetana, and that the man who performed his autopsy was Wagner?) It is not the sign of a good memory but a disability: when it comes to making an unexpected introduction, the names of my best friends usually elude me. I sometimes feel like a sort of poor man's Ripley (what happened to *Believe it or Not?*), knowing only the things that are no help in taking exams or acquiring professional qualifications.

Watching *University Challenge* again recently after many years, I was amazed how many answers I knew. Only later did I remember that I'd probably set the questions myself, years ago. Granada relies on the fact that the students are constantly changing, so they re-use the questions (and pay setters no repeat fees, I need hardly add; though their ten bob per question was a great deal better than *Ask the Family*, on the BBC, which offered something like one-and-ninepence per question, *if used*!).

If only I could have stuck to one subject, I console myself, I might have benefited mankind with some great and wonderful discovery. But very occasionally a correlation strikes me which seems to have escaped others. How about this one? I read in a newspaper of some scientist's finding that the lack of concentration and unwillingness to learn among the young, their aggression, militancy and protest-happy stupidity, are caused by insidious lead poisoning from exhaust fumes. Then I read in another paper that owing to the chemical constituents of newsprint, the lead concentration in the atmosphere over Fleet Street was several thousand times higher than that over, say, Portland Place. Follow up these two facts and you could change modern society. Unfortunately you can't always believe what is in the papers.

That delightful little treasure-trove programme *Enquire Within* recently had a question from a listener about the meaning of 'My Old Dutch', as in the famous music-hall song. The producers duly looked it up in Partridge's *Dictionary of Slang* and gave a summary of his researches: 'A wife: from c.1885; mostly cockney and esp. costermongers', prob. coined by Albert Chevalier, who explained it by the resemblance of "the wife's" face to that of an old Dutch clock.' Partridge adds, 'I used . . . to consider it an abbr. of *duchess*, but Chevalier, I now feel tolerably certain, is right.' Well, I think Partridge swallowed one of Chevalier's jokes. Again my discovery sprang from idle, useless reading, and powers of correlation that get you no degree in anything. In the German edition of the letters of Orlande de Lassus (1532–1594), which are entertainingly macaronic, written in old French, Latin, Italian and German (and every bit as earthy as Mozart's, Peter Shaffer please note), the composer engages in some banter with his princely patron, ending (I translate colloquially): 'Must stop now 'cos I'm going to pay a visit to my wife in the Low Countries.' To which the original German editor added a solemnly learned footnote to the effect that 'there is no evidence that Lassus ever visited the Low Countries'. Oh yes there is – in the shape of at least two sons who also became composers. For if you turn to a French-English glossary of colloquial phrases you will find a quite unequivocal definition of *les pays-bas*, which indeed Partridge himself gives, rather more politely, later in his book: 'The Low Countries: the female pudend.'

I'm sometimes tempted to send to producers jokey little postcards bearing the fruits of this unintentional, *post facto* research; though they probably annoy more than they entertain (especially *Start the Week*, about which I still feel the odd, irrational pang of withdrawal symptoms in spite of having been out of it longer than I was in). *Brain of Britain* the other day had a question about Queen Victoria's favourite painter. The contestants didn't get the answer, but Robert Robinson added one of his characteristic asides to the question-setter's script he reads so fluently: 'Because Winterhalter was an eminent and respectable Victorian worthy . . .' (I quote from memory). That's one thing he wasn't, and I immediately sent the producer a reproduction of Winterhalter's *Le gué* – a painting of an eminently respectable Victorian lady, the spitting image of the young Victoria herself. She is seen in an Alpine landscape, daintily stepping over a puddle and lifting her skirts respectably to just below the knee. I had it for years before I looked more closely – when I noticed in the puddle a perfect reflection of the Dutch landscape that so vainly exercised Lassus's editors as well as Partridge and *Enquire Within*.

The Times bicentenary produced the expected crop of unexpected ancillary delights: a glossy give-away magazine (revealing among other things that PHS is a ravishing, leggy brunette); a facsimile reprint of the first issue; and the usual selection of urbanely witty letters. One correspondent reveals that a celebratory full peal of Yorkshire Surprise Major ('not less than 5,000 changes') was rung in the paper's honour at Codsall Parish Church; another rather needlessly points out that the first issue contained proportionately fewer misprints than it would today. No one was churlish enough to say that the dozen words of modern typesetting at the foot of the 1785 reprint managed to misdate the imprint '1984' – and nobody seems to have recalled *The Times*'s darkest hour, whose centenary a few years ago went apparently unnoticed.

On the morning of 23 January 1882, readers who managed to get through a report – part verbatim, part précis – of the Home Secretary's interminable speech about tenant farmers in Yorkshire (a closely printed page containing some 10,000 words in tiny type unbroken by illustrations or cross-heads!) must have spluttered into their kedgeree as they read near the end of Sir William Harcourt's oration:

> terest, then I have very little doubt to which side in politics their influence will ultimately incline. (Cheers.) The tenant-farmers are a very shrewd class of people, and if once they understand that they have the power if they choose to deal with their own affairs, you may depend upon it they will deal with them very sensibly. (Cheers.) I saw in a Tory journal the other day a note of alarm, in which they said, "Why, if a tenant-farmer is elected for the North Riding of Yorkshire the farmers will be a political power who will have be reckoned with." The speaker then said he felt inclined for a bit of fucking. I think that is very likely. (Laughter.) But I think it is rather an extraordinary thing that the Tory party have not found that out before. I had some experience of it in the Ground Game Bill, which my friend, Sir H. James, has referred to. I was mobbed by the Tory members at the beginning of the Bill, but at the end all of them voted for it. (Laughter.) Well, one of the most intelligent Tory journals in London had an article on the North Riding Election, and they recommended the Tory candidate to the electors. And what was the main ground

For three days the Editor maintained a stunned silence, no doubt desperately hoping that no one had noticed. But on the fourth he printed a pained apology in type bigger than the news, lower down the page, of a 'Shocking Mine Accident' and a 'Daring Jewel Robbery'. It could hardly have been more floridly abject if some foreign ambassador had been assassinated in Downing Street.

No pains have been spared by the management of this journal to discover the author of a gross outrage committed by the interpolation of a line in the speech of Sir William Harcourt reported in our issue of Monday last. This malicious fabrication was surreptitiously introduced shortly before the paper went to press. The matter is now under legal investigation, and it is hoped that the perpetrator of the outrage will be brought to punishment.

The word was not to appear in any newspaper until after the Lady Chatterley trial, when the *Guardian* went to town on it (together with other ugly four-letter words) and other papers followed – but *The Times* exercised its customary restraint. Indeed, until 1941 it would paraphrase 'bloody' as 'the Shavian adjective'.

The phantom pornographer was never brought to punishment. And he struck again in June 1882, when he tampered with an advertisement:

A New and Cheaper Edition, fully Revised, price 6s.
EVERY-DAY LIFE in our PUBLIC SCHOOLS. Sketched by Head Scholars. With a Glossary of some Words used by Henry Irving in his disquisition upon fucking, which is in in Common Use in those Schools. Edited by CHARLES EYRE PASCOE. With numerous Illustrations. Church Times.—" A capital book for boys." Record.—" The book will make an acceptable present.'

After that nothing untoward happened – the addition of an *r* to a Mr Figgin's name could have been an accident – and he either called it a day or left; though it is just possible that he moved to the *Times Literary Supplement*, which in 1905 included an otherwise meaningless phrase with a hidden pun in a review of Oscar Wilde's *De Profundis*: '. . . not so, we find ourselves saying, *are souls* laid bare.' Since then, obscenities have come from Printing House Square only by accident. Except perhaps for a cryptic crossword clue: 'Listen carefully, or a sexual perversion (5,2,4,4)'. I was told about ten years ago that it had appeared in the *Financial Times* in ca. 1969. However, they now deny all knowledge of it there.

You don't have to be a Bible scholar to enjoy the entry 'Bible, The English' in *Brewer's Dictionary of Phrase and Fable*. Like all good reference-books it inspires one to go researching the sources. Ever since I first began to collect amusing misprints I have known about the Wicked Bible, so called because of the calamitous omission of 'not' in the Seventh Commandment: 'Thou shalt commit adultery.' In 1631 the slip cost

Robert Barker, the King's Printer, a fine of £300 (probably a quarter of a million in today's money) plus all the revenue lost from the destruction of 1,000 copies printed. An even greater penalty of £3,000 was imposed by Charles I on the printer of an edition which had Psalm XIV as 'The fool hath said in his heart that there is a God' instead of 'no God', an extraordinarily harsh fine; and the meaning of Romans VI,13 was turned upside-down by having 'righteousness' instead of 'unrighteousness'. An Irish Bible of 1716 urged the faithful to 'sin on more' instead of 'no more'; and a version of 1802 has a man hating 'his own wife' instead of his life (pity it could not have occurred in St John XV,13); and according to a Bible of 1804 (Galatians V,17) 'the flesh lusteth after (instead of against) the spirit'. An early Mr and Mrs Gillick might have sabotaged what is now known as the Large Family Bible of 1820 of Oxford, giving Isaiah LXVI,9 as 'Shall I bring to the birth and not cease (instead of cause) to bring forth?'

The uncharitable may suspect an early case of print-worker's sabotage; though the mistake in what has become known as the Printers' Bible, whose 'Printers (instead of Princes) have persecuted me without a cause' (Psalms CXIX,161), was surely a pre-Freudian Freudian slip and could serve as a text for Mr Rupert Murdoch. The 1804 Bible cited above also has (1 Kings VIII,19) 'thy son that cometh out of their lions' (instead of 'loins'). But was the so-called Murderers' Bible taken down from dictation? For Jude XVI reads 'These are murderers (instead of murmurers) . . .' etc. The year 1823 brought what became known as the Camel's Bible, making Rebekah rise with her camels instead of dam-sels; and the Douai Bible of 1609 might well be called The Fiddlers' Bible, for it contains the heartfelt complaint 'Is there no *rosin* in Galaad?' (Jeremiah VIII,22), in place of 'balm'. This is also known as the Treacle Bible, because 'balm' is later substituted by 'tryacle'. Many a misprint today is caused by habit-trained fingers which disbelieve the unfamiliar and reach for the nearest equivalent they are used to, as every typist knows. A Liverpool man I know called Livermore says that judging from corrections on letters addressed to him he feels he is keeping Tippex in business; and news items such as 'Llandladies in the Llandudno area . . .' often go awry in Welsh papers. But a cockney might have had a hand in printing the Ear to Ear Bible, in which Matthew XIII,43 reads 'Who hath ears to ear, let him hear', while a Revised Version printed as recently as 1923 tells us, rather unnecessarily, that 'A man may not marry his grandmother's wife.' I prefer Coverdale's 'Thou shalt not nede to be afrayed for eny bugges by night' (Psalms XCI,5) to the more hygienic 'terror by night' in both the *AV* and *RV*. The Geneva Bible of 1562 says 'Blessed are the placemakers (instead of peacemakers . . .')' (Matthew V,9); and a Cambridge Bible of 1653 unwittingly comes close to what many must long have suspected: 'The unrighteous shall (instead of shall not) inherit the Kingdom of God' (1 Corinthians); and another Cambridge edition, dated 1805, has the amusing but meaningless interpolation 'to remain' in Galatians IV,29 '. . . persecuted him that was born after the spirit to remain, even so it is now.' What happened was that a proof-reader queried the comma after the word 'spirit', to which the editor replied, 'to remain'. (This is not unlike a notice in the *Daily Telegraph* which prints Brahms's song 'O wüsst ich doch den Weg zurück' as 'O Orange, wüsst ich doch den Weg zurück.')

The *Revised Authorised Version* printed in 1982 by the house of Samuel Bagster, which has held a Bible-printing licence since 1794, was heralded by a press handout with the ominous statement, 'The language of the English-speaking people is a living language' – and whenever I hear such a defensive sentiment I reach for Shakespeare, Milton and Browning for comfort. It might go down in history as the Prosaic Bible, for like *Hymns for Today's Church*, published by Hodder & Stoughton in the same year, the *RAV* prefers you and yours to thou and thine, and goes for the modern vernacular in a manner that brings plenty of flat-footed prose, and reduces prayers to some of those chatty if one-sided conversations the Fiddler on the Roof had with God. But then the editors aimed at a big readership rather than a discerning one, and God knows how urgently the Word is needed in some far-flung, basic-English-speaking corners of the world. But alas, Jacob's mess of pottage (Genesis XXV,29) has a touch of the cook-house: 'Now Jacob cooked a stew', when both the *AV* and *RV* appear to specify red lentils. 'Lord, now lettest thou thy servant depart in peace' becomes '. . . you give leave to your servant to go', which makes one want to add '. . . with the statutory severance pay' (if not '. . . to the loo'). The *AV*'s Revelation XVIII,9, '. . . who have committed fornication and lived deliciously with her' is now more tamely and far less deliciously '. . . and lived luxuriously'. Even the 'footballing' bits have gone. Exodus XXXVI,33 'And he made the middle bar to shoot through' becomes 'pass through'; and Nahum's line suggesting the free-kick position, 'They make haste to the wall thereof and the defence is prepared' is changed, and not for the better. But in 2 Kings the line that reminds all old Liverpool supporters of Elisha Scott, the great goalkeeper between the wars, has been left as it was: 'Then Elisha said shoot, and he shot . . .' About the referee, Revelation X,2 gives, 'And he had in his hand a little book, open . . .', following the exhortation in Revelation 1, 11: 'What thou seest, write in a book . . .'

The *RAV* keeps half an eye on American sales, changing the *AV*'s 'ass' to 'donkey'. After all (in 1 Samuel) 'she got off her ass' could be misunderstood, and had already been changed by the nervous – or dirty-minded – Noah Webster in the *American Bible*, which also has a *rooster* crowing thrice instead of (dare I print it?) a cock. But looking for the rude bits will give little joy to schoolboys. Where, in *AV* and *RV*, Saul went into the sheepfold 'to cover his feet' (on the surely erroneous medieval assumption that he dropped his breeches, whereas he would have lifted his robes and therefore *un*covered his feet) the *Good News Bible* has a healthy and forthright 'to relieve himself'. The new *RAV* coyly says 'Saul went in to attend to his needs' (which could be almost anything – a shave, a snack or a glass of water); but the *Living Bible* (surely henceforth *The Bathroom Bible*?) (Illinois, 1971) has 'Saul went into a cave to go to the bathroom.'

Each time a new English version of the scriptures is published much pain is suffered by traditionalists, though probably more by the non-believers among them, for whom the medium is more important than the message and who are quicker to point out the often ludicrous results of modernisation. The church and the bishops have always come down firmly and with the utmost dignity on both sides of the fence, ready to forgive all linguistic transgressions (for after all, they are in the business of forgiving) and able to see all points of view: 'In this our time, the minds of men are so diverse, that some think it a great matter of conscience to depart from . . . their ceremonies, they be so addicted to their old customs; and again on the other side, some be so newfangled that they would innovate all things, and so despise the old, that nothing can like them, but that is new . . .' That was written in the first year of the reign of Queen Elizabeth I, on the printing of the *Book of Common Prayer*, but it applied when the King James Bible, the *Authorised Version*, was joined by the *Revised Version* during the last years of Queen Victoria's rule; and still holds good in the reign of Elizabeth II.

Successive attempts at revision and paraphrase have arisen less from the revisers' desire to be newfangled than to make the gospel as widely understood as possible. The language changes, they say, and old meanings are lost or superseded. For example, since the middle of the nineteenth century a 'mess' has been a disorder, a muddle, something dirty as well as untidy, driving out the centuries-old meaning, a serving of food. So the modern translators change 'mess' to 'dish'. The foreign learner with a painfully acquired basic command of English is saved a little confusion (or the trouble of consulting a dictionary). But at home, the language has suffered another small act of impoverishment, and another old word is in danger of being permanently lost.

Whether one reads the scriptures for the pleasure or the dogma, the shock of the new can be painful. However sensitively the revisers approach their task they find themselves reviled as hasty meddlers. But just as Shakespeare was in his time played in 'modern' dress (Julius Caesar presumably wearing doublet and hose), so have previous Bible translations always gone for the contemporary vernacular. Those cornets, sackbuts and psalteries in the King James Bible were, of course, European renaissance instruments, not Biblical ones from the Middle East. The *GNB* (1966) duly updates them to trumpets, oboes, harps and – more surprisingly – zithers. The *RAV* should by rights have had Nebuchadnezzar's golden statue worshipped with guitars and synthesisers but contents itself with adding horn and flute to the instruments in the King James Bible. After all, the ram's horn, or shofar, was the original ghetto-blaster. The *Living Bible*, however, hedges its bets against changing instrumental fashions with '... and when the band began to play ...' Wyclif as well as the 'Geneva' Bible told of Adam and Eve sewing fig-leaves together 'and medin brechis' – garments which if known at all would have been rare among the loose, flowing Biblical garments favoured in the desert 2,000 years ago.

English revisers have until recent times not generally made many drastic changes. If the Americans changed 'ass' to 'donkey' and 'cock' into 'rooster', the *RAV* follows the *RV* by 'kicking against the goads' instead of pricks – which reveals that some scholars on the committee had very dirty minds. The *RAV* editors, to their credit, have refused to capitulate to the overzealous sanitisers by retaining at any rate the cock crowing thrice. However, they cautiously deprive the gospel of St James of the reference to 'him that weareth the gay clothing'. It is now '*fine* clothes'. The *Living Bible* in its anxiety to avoid 'gay' almost lapses into Keith Prowse theatrical camp ('You want the Best Seats – We have them!'): '... and you make a lot of fuss over the rich man and give him the best seat in the house.'

Hymns for Today's Church laid itself open to many such charges of introducing flat-footed English. 'My God, how wonderful you are' sounds more like a pop lyric; and the very slight change from 'Thy way, not mine' to 'Your way, not mine' brings things uncomfortably close to Frank Sinatra. 'Come, my soul, thy suit prepare' would have been better omitted than changed to the sartorial 'Come my soul, your suit prepare.' And tactful omissions there are. Nowhere could I find the lines from the Wesleys, 'With thee all night I mean to stay/and wrestle till the break of day' (what could it have meant in the first place?). There was not long ago a little verbal altercation during the rehearsal for the *Daily Service* in All Souls' Church, Langham Place on Radio 4, when a female member of the BBC Religious Affairs Department objected to the line 'Brother clasps the hand of brother' as being sexist. She rejected the choirmaster's obviously tongue-in-cheek offer to change it to 'Person clasps the hand of person' and demanded that the verse was omitted (as indeed it is from *HforTC*, No. 466, Baring-Gould's *Marching*). There was some muttering about 'I suppose you want us to pray to "Our parent that is in heaven . . ."' but in the end a suitable compromise was reached. Shortly afterwards someone discovered a Feminist Bible ('Pray to God – She will hear you . . .' etc.)

HforTC also omits the text that is No. 82 in the *Cowley Carol Book*, set to an old English melody of 1650, bearing the (to modern ears) unfortunate words, 'Saint Joseph, meek and mild/Embraced the new-born Child/Then knelt upon the sod': and 'ground' would not have been acceptable since 'sod' later rhymes with 'God'. But the revisers are prepared to fill up the scansion in their modern versions with interpolations of 'oh' and 'yes': '*Yes*, Lord we greet you,' like any pop singer short of a syllable or inspiration putting in 'oh yeah' or 'baby'.

Once you start revising there is no end to it. Stainer's 'Here in abasement . . .' is difficult to sing without suggesting that the singer's lowly station is not spiritual but in a building; nor is it possible to avoid giving the wrong impression with repeated part-words in lines like 'He's our best bul-, he's our best bul-, he's our best bulwark in the sky . . .' or 'And catch the flee-, and catch the flee-, and catch the fleeting hours', or 'Oh for a man-, oh or a man-, oh for a mansion in the sky.'

I have always wanted to complete my Bible according to the jerky adverbial news-style of Fleet Street, but never got beyond Genesis:

Initially, God created the heaven and the earth. Basically, the earth was without form, and void: Noticeably, darkness was upon the face of the deep. Reportedly, the spirit of God moved upon the waters. Loftily, God said, Let there be Light. Predictably, there was light. Brilliantly, God called the light Day, and, additionally, the darkness He called Night. Curiously, God created man in His own image. Startlingly, male and female created He them. Thankfully, God saw everything that He had made; and, Interestingly, it was good. Subsequently, the evening and the morning . . . etc. But then one would get hopelessly lost, where God punishes Adam and Eve for 'tucking in to' the forbidden fruit and obtains an eviction order from the Garden of Eden 'Theme Park'.

'Shit', says the *OED*, is 'not now in decent use.' Which is a pity; it may be no longer considered decent, but it is a good, honest word; and certainly less ugly than other four-letter expletives. And, of course, it is of ancient lineage. Even as 'A contemptuous epithet applied to a person' it goes back to 1508: 'Thou art a schit, but wit . . .' (spellings vary). Shite had been an accepted variant since about 1300 A.D.; and the humble turd is even older, probably related to ordure and one of the earliest euphemisms, from Latin *horridus*. And therein lies the clue to why humans are ashamed of that necessary and universal act, the voiding of body waste. We are, after all, perfectly happy making into social occasions the meals that create the waste. Decaying proteins make a bad smell, and excreta have therefore always been associated with things horrid – even with the Devil. Man when defecating is not only vulnerable to attack but temporarily loses his dignity; and he therefore wants to be alone. Thus excretory situations would have been turned into potentially humorous ones even before words were invented to describe them. But when man learned to speak, the jokes acquired an extra dimension, and so it has always remained.

Squitters are thought to have first appeared in print in 1664: 'It Bounces, Foams and Froths and Flitters/As if 'twere troubled with the Squitters.'

The not unrelated Wombles and Wambles ('nausea in the stomack') must have been around well before a thirteenth-century writer reported that the whale suffered from them when he had Jonah in his belly – and when Wimbledon Common was briefly inhabited by the aptly-named creatures I understood how the whale must have felt. Cack (from Latin *cacare*), with related words still in use in many European languages, including Dutch, Bohemian, Polish, and German *kacken*, seems to have all but disappeared, except for 'cack-handed', meaning 'left-handed'. Partridge says it might be 'a corruption of Scottish *car-hand*. However, I think it could be related to the fact that Arabs and other Easterners use their bare left hand in place of lavatory-paper (which is why they consider a left-handed handshake an affront and feel disgust when they see anyone eating with the 'cack-hand'). *Cacare* was for a long time internationally-understood Latin: Haydn wrote a prophetic little song about modern art: *Consider thou the dictum: cacatum non est pictum* (and how he would have laughed had he known that there would be a celebrated twentieth-century paste-up artist called Kurt Schwitters).

There are probably more euphemisms for the excretory processes and the places reserved for their function than there are even for sexual activities – from the heavily facetious, like the Bogs and Thunderbox, to the Necessary and, of course, the Victorian WC (though Water Closet dates from 1755). Crapper or crap-house are now always traced back to a sanitary engineer called Thomas Crapper, inventor of Crapper's Valveless Water Waste Preventor, but if that is the true derivation he must have been an infant prodigy among plumbers, as the word first appeared in 1846, when he was nine years old.

The place has always been considered one of refuge and rest, where the weary worker could legitimately sit down to answer 'the call of nature'. An overworked housewife, interviewed on television, was asked, 'What do you do in your spare time?' She replied, 'I have no spare time.' The interviewer persisted. 'Everyone has some spare time. What do you do in your spare time?' She wearily replied, 'I go to the lavatory.' Women in this kind of predicament are unanimous in describing the sheer joy of shooting the bolt and leaving their squalling children and other worries outside. It is, of course, also a fine place for meditation or reading. Lord Chesterfield wrote in his *Letters* (to his illegitimate son):

'I knew a gentleman who was so good a manager of his time, that he would not even lose that small portion of it which calls of nature obliged him to pass in the necessary house, but gradually went through all the Latin poets in those moments. He bought, for example, a common edition of Horace, of which he tore off gradually a couple of pages, carried them with him to that necessary place, read them first and sent them down as a sacrifice to Cloacina; that was so much time fairly gained, and I recommend you to follow his example.'

Although 'going to one's devotions' is another euphemism, like 'the necessary place', prayer was not recommended while at stool:

A godly father, sitting on a draught
To do as neede and nature hath us taught,
Mumbled, as was his manner, certain prayers,
And unto him the Devil straight repairs,
And boldly to revile him he begins,
Alleging that such pray'rs were deadly sins
And that he shewed he was devoid of grace
To speak to God from so unmeet a place.

The reverent man, though at the first dismayed,
Yet strong in faith, to Satan thus he said:
Thou damned spirit, wicked false and lying,
Despairing thine own good and our envying,
Each take his due, and me thou canst not hurt.
Pure prayer ascends to Him that high doth sit,
Down falls the dirt, for fiends of Hell more fit.

Sir John Harington, *The Metamorphosis of Ajax*

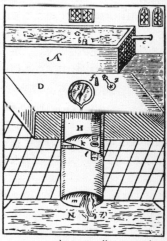

This is Don Ajax house...all in sunder; that a workman may see what he hath to do

...the same, all put together, that the workman may see if it be well

Harington's Water closet, 1596

203

'Privy' (short for a place to do private things in) now suggests picturesque rural seclusion. Jakes goes back all the way to the inventor of the water closet, Sir John Harington (1561–1612), whose working drawings of the 'Ajax' (i.e. 'a Jakes') show that he kept fish in the cistern – perhaps in an attempt to produce some kind of perpetual motion. Old English names include Close-stool, a kind of Commode (itself a French euphemism for 'convenience'), but 'Closet-of-ease' was soon shortened to closet, though not in America, where it is still a place to keep clothes in. There they have the coy Comfort Station (which the *Dictionary of American English* dates 1904) and kept in use the old English Necessary House (shortened to the Necessary) long after it had died out in its home country. Washroom, suggestive of the euphemism 'going to wash one's hands', is civilised middle-class usage, as peasants presumably didn't much go in for such ablutions. Powder Room (for ladies only) once caused some consternation in Germany when the American submitted a scheme for rebuilding a consulate. The plans were conscientiously translated into German – and the authorities wondered why the Americans needed a 'powder magazine', which is what a *Pulverkammer* is in that language. As usual the Americans go over the top with ingeniously jocular inventions: His and Hers, Adam and Eve, Colts and Fillies, or just This Is IT, etc. H. L. Mencken says that John, Johnnie House and Jack House were dialect words used in Virginia. Sir Malcolm Sargent once told me that at a party given in 1963 by the film-producing Selzniks, who owned a collection of master-drawings, he asked Mrs David O. if he could see her Johns (i.e. Augustus). She took him by the hand and gushed, 'Sure, you can use my very own private one.'

Families have their own euphemisms, often taking into adulthood many a baby-word (with or without juvenile reduplication): Wee-wee, Pee-pee, Poo-poo; or Number Ones and Number Twos; Big Job and Little Job; Tinkle, Piddle and Widdle. In Britain the word Toilet is a sign of non-U gentility: it is far less likely to pass upper-middle-class lips than the crudest dysphemism, though 'Lavatory', too, is really nothing more than a genteel, lower-middle-class euphemism – the word for a wash-basin. Loo has in recent years gained popularity, being classless. Some dictionaries say this came from French *l'eau*, via the Scots housewives' warning-cry, '*gardyloo*', before they emptied night-pots out of windows; but it could be a facetious reference to the water-closet in the form of 'Waterloo'. It should also be mentioned that *Lulu* is not only a German name but the common juvenile word for 'wee-wee' (and was Alban Berg aware of that when he wrote his famous opera?). Loo was formerly a popular card-game related to whist as well as 'a cry to incite a dog to the chase' (*OED*). It was also a kind of nonsense-syllable used for padding out lines in song, like 'hey nonny nonny-no', as in the Victorian/Edwardian hit 'Linger Longer Loo'.

Some of my classicist friends speak about retiring to the Phrontistery, which is Greek for a thinking-place. Doctors talk to their patients about having Stool, which was originally what you sat on, not the end-product; or of passing water. *Pisser* is acceptable in French, as in *pissoir*, but not piss in polite English, though the word must have started as a hissing onomatopoeic euphemism. Naval officers continue Pumping Ship or going to the Heads long after they leave the service, and army people use the Lats. Scousers, with their traditional fondness for Irish circumlocution, announce, 'I'm gonna shake hands wid dee wife's best friend.'

There are probably two pointers to civilisation: love for animals and decent plumbing, and the English come top in both. I once mentioned to my father the curious smell of drains that seems to rise from even the best-kept Viennese sanitary fittings, which have always compared ill with the good old English trap back home. He spread his hands in continental protest like a restaurant manager warding off a complaint, and said, 'Impossible. We put fresh shit in daily.' In Vienna the internationally understood symbols of trousered or skirted figures (robed Arabs or trousered Indian women?), may be replaced by *Herren* and *Damen*, or the rather alarming word *Abort*. In the old days it used to be the Null Null, not so pronounced but represented by two nils – 00 – meaning 'The Unmentionable'. Other euphemisms dating back to the Habsburgs include *Wo der Kaiser zu Fuss geht*, which is echoed in Partridge by 'Where the Queen goes on foot' (ca. 1860–1915). There is also the facetious 'throne-room' ('He can't see you now, he's on the throne').

Mozart's alleged (and since the play *Amadeus* much-discussed) 'obsession' with faecal jokes were not in fact peculiar to him. His mother's letters, too, are full of frank descriptions of the excretory habits of Bimperl, the family dog. Nor was it only people like Mozart, from the lower classes, who used 'rude' words. In a novel, *Die Abderiten* (known to both Mozart and Beethoven) by Christoph Martin Wieland, fine ladies freely use the foulest language. The book probably set a kind of daring fashion, much in the same way as some liberated American ladies are liable to lard their conversation with 'aw shit!' Even Beethoven's *Conversation Books* contain the occasional piece of excretory humour, like the following snippet of table-talk, written down for the deaf composer either apropos of nothing or in response to something he might have said: 'The Bourbon kings did not use toilet paper but employed instead squares of the finest silk specially cut for the purpose; or else the necks of freshly slaughtered birds . . .' (which I think echoes something I have read in Rabelais).

Cloakroom, another twentieth-century English euphemism, can be confusing, as many cloakrooms contain only hooks for hats and coats. A cloak-room attendant, conversely, may be nothing more than a euphemised lavatory attendant. However, 'cloaks' might well be adopted as a legitimate word by those who dislike inaccurate terms like 'lavatory' but hesitate to face the stark reality of 'shit-house': not with reference to the sleeveless overgarment but as an anglicisation of *cloaca* (from Latin 'to purge') and Cloacina, who was the goddess of the sewers. Was it not Byron who wrote something like

> Oh Cloacina, goddess of this place
> Look on thy suppliants with a smiling face;
> And let their votive offerings flow
> Not rudely swift, nor obstinately slow.

And someone told me that there used to be inscribed in one of the basement 'lavatories' in the House of Commons a rhyme which went

In the House up above, when a motion is read
A member stands up and must cover his head.
In this house down below, when a motion's to pass
A member sits down and uncovers . . .

The rest appeared to be illegible. No wonder the *Guardian*'s political correspondent once accidentally referred to a 'Lord Privy Seat'.

Thousands of words have been written deploring the loss of 'gay'. It is not lost for ever. All you have to do is refuse to use it in its newer sense. There is no need for offensive words like queers, pansies, dykes and the rest; nor pooftahs (which sounds Indian but is actually Australian, ca. 1910, and strictly poofter, or poofteroo). Cut the derision, but also the euphemism. Just say homosexual, qualifying whether male or female where necessary. The fun in finding old uses of gay with newly perverted meanings ('He's gone to lunch at the Gay Hussar, ha ha!') is wearing thin, but still the examples keep turning up. Edward J. Dent, that inveterate opera translator, would have been horrified to see today's singers falling about with laughter in Mozart's *Don Giovanni* when they come to the lines:

'You young men who like kissing and laughter
And who follow a life that is gay;
Don't forget you must pay for it after;
I can show you a much better way,
For I'm going to be married today.'

However, Harold Rosenthal, the editor of *Opera*, writes to say that Dent was well-known in Cambridge as a prominent member of the homosexual circles of his day, had a wicked sense of humour and knew what he was at; but the fact remains that 'gay' was, of course, then still exclusively heterosexual slang, though on the way out. He would, however, certainly have known that the line 'Balls in the country!' sung by the chorus in his English version of Tchaikovsky's *Eugene Onegin*, might be taken the wrong way.

Gay already had a sexual meaning back in the 18th century, co-existing with the older sense during the 19th and even into the present. Grose (1811) has 'gaying instrument' for the penis and a gay woman was anything from a commercial whore to a sexually promiscuous (or just willing) girl. The mid-19th-century music-hall song 'Let's be Gay' traded on this and became a scandalous double-meaning success. The translator who in ca. 1930 made Richard Tauber sing 'Am I to blame if God has made me gay?' (in Lehár's hit *Girls were made to love and kiss*) must also have been well aware of the earlier meaning, and probably also the song.

This kind of gentle perversion of the language by double meaning occurs all the time, even in French. I am reliably

FAMILY LIKENESS.

" Mummy, Darling, may I give my Biscuit to the Monkey?"

" No, Love.   Come along !"

" May I give it to the Monkey's *Papa*, Mummy?"

informed that not only *accolade* can be taken the wrong way. To announce you're having *rapport* with someone may also get you covered with confusion when on holiday in France.

With 'organ' you never know whether the user is being innocent, or thinks you are. An 'organ' according to the first edition of *Grose* was jocular for a tobacco-pipe, and he defines the slang expression 'to cock one's organ' as nothing more vulgar than 'to smoke a pipe'. But surely Dickens cannot have been so innocent when he wrote (in *Martin Chuzzlewit*):

> 'She touched his organ, and from that bright epoch, even it, the old companion of his happiest hours, incapable as he had thought of elevation, began a new and deified existence.'

Punch in 1870 had a similarly dual-purpose caption to a cartoon which would have produced guffaws in the gentlemen's clubs but been taken innocently by the family at home (though if there *is* a pure meaning it is pretty pointless). The picture, by George du Maurier, shows a couple of hirsute Italian organ-grinders, who, like Jews and Nigger Minstrels, were a constant target for his satire:

AN ILLUSTRATION OF DARWINISM.

WITHOUT USE, AN ORGAN DWINDLES; WITH USE, IT INCREASES. FOR INSTANCE, THE ORGAN OF A GRINDER WHO, IN THE STRUGGLE FOR EXISTENCE, RELIES ENTIRELY ON HIS INSTRUMENT, IS INVARIABLY LARGER THAN THAT OF THE GRINDER WHO, IN ADDITION, USES A MONKEY. MOST OF OUR READERS MUST HAVE NOTICED THIS.

Contrary to what the caption says, I'm sure most readers hadn't noticed. Though much more recently many readers of *Radio Times* must have wondered how it permitted a seaside entertainment to be billed 'Reginald Dixon and his Organ supported by strings'. The trouble is that people nervously omit the word 'sexual'; but before long the unqualified rump – organ, member, congress, intercourse, etc. – loses its innocence by silent association.

E. M. Forster apparently had no misgivings about writing (in *A Room with a View*), 'Stop a minute; let those two people go on, or I shall have to speak to them. I do detest conventional intercourse. Nasty! they are going into the church, too. Oh, the Britisher abroad!'

By then (1908), many would have thought twice about quoting the historian who asserted 'Disraeli had intercourse with almost the entire Royal Family.' But when the *Musical Times* in 1890 wrote 'Mr Gladstone is always a suggestive speaker . . .' it was unaware that the word would eventually be used almost exclusively as shorthand for '*sexually* suggestive'. However, Disraeli himself, speaking in the House of Commons about the humane measure of allowing prison-visits, evoked guffaws when he said, 'It is a sad day when an Englishman cannot have his wife backward or forward as he pleases.'

The BBC drama department clearly agonised a great deal about Titty, a character in Ransome's *Swallows and Amazons*. Some twenty years ago they changed her to Kitty, but in the latest dramatisation her name was restored in the interest of authenticity, and hang the titterers. But in the radio play based on Mrs Gaskell's *North and South* I would have avoided suggestions of necrophilia by changing 'I rather fancy her dead' to something else. And in a recent broadcast of *Mansfield Park* it might have been better to alter the line 'I'm going to make my little Fanny feel as she's never felt before.' What a pity it was when that pretty girls' name met its ruin, though during the last war it gained a temporary respite thanks to those upper-class volunteer ladies the First Aid Nursing Auxiliaries, known as 'Fannies'; and although the latest *OED* supplement gives the American 'backside' it has so far refused to admit the equally vulgar but more forward British meaning. According to BBC folklore Frank Bough once wound up a cookery demonstration by Fanny Craddock on BBC Television with 'Well, that's all we have time for, and I hope *your* doughnuts will look like Fanny's.'

It now looks as if 'willie' is going the same way as 'fanny'. *Partridge* records that it was the word for '(a child's) penis, Cumberland and Westmorland', dates it about 1905, and says it is 'not dialect', i.e. middle-class usage (a sort of juvenile 'John Thomas'). But now it has spread into all strata of society and is the constant standby of every radio and television panel-game member. If not an embargo perhaps a quota system could be instituted limiting the number of comic willies permitted per week. But in its earlier days, the broadcaster and cricket commentator Brian Johnston said on the air (he swears it was inadvertent), 'The batsman's Holding, the bowler's Willey.'

'Well, I met this f'kn bird in a f'kn disco and we had a coupla f'kn drinks and went back to her f'kn place to have some f'kn coffee. . .' explained the soldier to his defence lawyer before being court-martialled on a rape charge.

'And then what happened?'

'Well one f'kn thing led to another and before I knew where I f'kn was – we, y'know, we was havin' sexual intercourse.'

This is no exaggeration of the way some of the sub-articulate use the most common English expletive. Their every third or fourth word is f'kn-this and f'kn-that, so that they become soone unaware of uttering it, and certainly of its meaning. The very word expletive, incidentally, from *expletus*, *explere*, means not a swear-word but 'a filling-in'.

Granada Television once based an entire play on an inversion of the old, old joke quoted above.

A middle-class couple in bed:

'Did you, er do it with her?'
  'Do what?'
  'You know, *it*?'

This kind of dialogue sustained the play (play?) for about an hour (occasionally enlivened by the sight of a carelessly-revealed female nipple or two) until one came to the expected punch-line (I quote from memory), 'Oh yes, I fucked her.'

For the universal act of love (as well as the cheapest and most common form of recreation) on which man's survival depends, it is a singularly nasty little word – and not only in English – ugly and one-sidedly transitive, suggesting a violent act done by one person against another. This doubtless reflects the attitude of man through the ages to sexual congress with woman, the 'taking' or (as Pepys prefers) 'enjoying' of a woman. Though to be fair, there is at least a little implied progress and enlightenment, since a degree of mutuality is implied in its modern intransitive use ('we fucked'); and some outspoken women use it to express what *they* do to a man.

Such dictionaries as admit the existence of the word (readers of the *OED* had to wait for the *Supplement* published in 1972 to be allowed to see it) try to trace it to the old German word *ficken*, to strike violently (and indeed is still used in modern German for the sexual act, violent or not); but although the *OED* draws attention to the Middle English *fuken* it says 'German *ficken* cannot be shown to be related.' I think it can, but (and this seems much more likely) the connection is via the Latin *fica*, a fig. Cut one in half, from top to bottom, and you will see why. This, again, is reflected in several languages, including the German verb *feigeln* (from *Feige*), a less strong, slightly jocular word, approximating to 'screwing' (which, incidentally, could also give rise to some *very* strange, if not downright painful, misconceptions of how 'it' is done).

William Dunbar was one of the earliest users of the word when, in 1503, he wrote:

He clappit fast, he kist and chukkit,
As with the glaikis he were ouirgane
Yit be his feirris he wald have fukkit,
Ye brek my hart, my bon(n)y ane.

But it is becoming a boring word, and attempts by lovers to devise their own private terms, however silly, should be encouraged. Nor is there a shortage of old words that could be revived. Countless and often laboured euphemisms abound, such as 'making the beast with two backs', 'groping for trout in a peculiar river' and 'ploughing the furrow'. There is much word-play with 'cunnies' (i.e. rabbits) and, of course, 'pussies'; but 'making love' until about a generation ago meant no more than gazing fondly into each other's eyes or otherwise showing affection, as many a popular song of the 1950s proves.

'Frigging' ('to move to and fro, to chafe, to rub', 15th century) perhaps from Latin *fricare*, to rub, was once considered a 'worse' word than 'fucking'. But as it lacks the aggressive, hard throat sound it is seldom heard, except as a 'politer' substitute, e.g. in a television series by Alan Bleasdale in which coarse Liverpudlians continued with tedious frequency saying 'frigg'n'-this' and 'frigg'n-that' instead of the universal 'f'kn' (perhaps at the request of a nervous producer), and thereby made the whole dialogue totally implausible. 'Oh! how they do Frig it, Jump it, Jigg it and Jerk it, Caper and Ferk it, under the Green-wood Tree', wrote D'Urfey in his *Pills to purge Melancholy* (published 1719 but written earlier). 'Fridge' was for centuries a common alternative for 'frig' – until the Frigidaire Corporation came along in 1918 and (according to Adrian Room's *Dictionary of Trade Name Origins*, Routledge and Kegan Paul) bought the Guardian Frigerator Co. (Latin, *frigidarium*, a room in which bathers cooled themselves). The resulting *fridge*, for short, soon put paid to that. But even so there was and remains confusion. Some innocent, upper-crust people, especially ladies, still persist in calling their fridge a 'frig', and the *OED 1972 Supplement* gives both forms. Monica Dickens, in *One Pair of Hands* (1939) and Graham Greene's *Quiet American* (1955) both have rather ambiguous uses of 'frig' when they clearly mean an ice-box.

Firking was not only a near-phonetic equivalent but also meant 'to move about briskly', as in dancing, or 'to move sharply'; also the action of vigorously playing the violin: 'Firk your fiddles!' wrote Davenant (1668). This musical

213

simile, one of many, is in turn reminiscent of a common Scouse description: 'His arse wuz goin' like a fiddler's elbow.' *Vocabula Amatoria* (1896) has the charming 'firky-toodling'.

Niggling had a lewd meaning long before it denoted carping criticism: 'To nygle, to haue to do with a woman carnally' (1567), and 'of girls, to be restless and fidgetty from wanton-ness or amorous inclination'. Of a woman who married an old man, Purcell sings, 'Oh, how she niggled him all the night long.'

Chaucer's *swinking* would make a good, modern alterna-tive, harmless until it caught on; and it is often alliteratively combined with *swiving* when toil and effort are implied, ('Don't Swink and Swive'?). *Sard* is even older, and appears in the Lindisfarne Gospels of 698 A.D., which translate (Matthew V,27), 'Thou shalt not commit adultery' as 'Ne serd the othres mones wif'. Florio's English-Italian dictionary of 1598 has 'Fottere to jape, to sard'.

Which brings me to the modern American slang words for vagina, *futy* and *futz*. Wentworth & Flexner (*Dictionary of American Slang*) say they come 'from the taboo *fuck*'. Well they don't: compare Latin *futuere*, Italian *fottere*, French *foutre*, and German *Futt* or *Fott*. Mozart used to call his hated employer, the Archbishop of Salzburg, a Hundsfott, in other words, a 'dog's cunt', though not to his face.

After the *Lady Chatterley* trial there was a veritable flood of 'rude' words in newspapers, magazines, plays and books, though they have somewhat calmed down in their rush to appear liberated. (The first known intentional interpolation of 'fucking' in respectable print occurred in *The Times* in 1882 – for an account of which see page 193). And, of course, the other ugly word also received more than ample exposure when previously it was almost invariably disguised in a large number of euphemisms. Shakespeare's 'country matters' and countless other punning references are matched in many 17th- and 18th-century songs and catches, often printed in full when 'G-d' and 'd-mn' in adjacent lines are decently abbreviated; though 'c-t' is often seen, too. Some of the euphemisms have been made obsolete by mechanical pro-gress. For example, 'between wind and water' went out with sail, and 'penwiper' (from the little bundles of circular cloths stitched together and folded in half, carried in every schoolboy's satchel and on which he would wipe his pen-nibs) began to go out with the fountain-pen and disappeared completely with the ballpoint. There was also 'split apricot', 'parsley bed', etc., to go with the half-fig mentioned earlier, the American 'pussy', whose English equivalent (also heard in the USA) is 'muff'. 'Quim' is still often heard, and some say it comes from the Welsh *cwm* for a valley or cleft, but is surely more likely to be descended from Chaucer's use of *quoniam*, from Latin, wherefore.

'Twat' has a curious history. It is also probably a medieval word, coyly defined in old English dictionaries in Latin, *pudendum mulieris* ('the shameful bit of woman') but suffered a gradual decline, and there seem to be few references to it in lewd Restoration songs. The poet Robert Browning, who was a man of the world, cannot have been ignorant of the meaning of more common dysphemisms, but 'twat' was not in his vocabulary; and his ignorance of it led him to make the most ludicrous literary bloomer of his time. He must at one time or another have come across a collection of writings published in 1660 under the title *Vanity of Vanities*, which contained the lines:

> They talk't of his having a Cardinall's Hat,
> They'd send him as soon an Old Nun's Twat.

From the hat-twat rhyme scheme and the context, Browning ingeniously but incorrectly deduced that, as a cardinal's hat was an item of masculine clerical attire, a nun's twat would be something worn by holy women. He liked the sound of the word, and when he wrote *Pippa Passes* in 1841, he used it in the lines:

> Then, owls and bats,
> Cowls and twats,
> Monks and nuns, in a cloister's moods
> Adjourn to the oak-stump pantry!

The *OED* is unhelpful about possible origins of *twat*, and gives spellings that vary from *tweate* to *twaite*, *twayte* and

* There are, of course, English places called Thwaite, but an obscene origin of Thwaites cannot be entirely ruled out. After all, the *Oxford Dictionary of Surnames* tells us that people called Hollister are descended from whore-house keepers.

thwaite (which is bad news for people called Thwaites*); and the charming *twancle*. There is also a fish called a *twat*. Various slang dictionaries reveal that a *twat-scourer* was a surgeon or doctor, especially one specialising in women's diseases; the *twat-rug* the female pubic hair, and a *twat-masher* a Victorian pimp or whore-master. Partridge suggests *twachylle*, meaning a passage, and *twatch*, to mend a gap in a hedge (there is many a scurrilous 17th-century song with vulgar allusions about tinkers 'stopping a hole in my lady's kettle'). There could even be some connection with *twitter*, a narrow passage or triangular piece of land, especially in Sussex.

Between the 1930s and the Chatterley trial, when to write or otherwise utter the word 'cunt' was still a punishable offence, a poem was widely but clandestinely circulated, and much-creased and thumbed typewritten copies often taken from wallets, passed round and guffawed over by men in bars and rugby clubs. The author was the M.P., writer and humorist A. P. Herbert.

The portions of a woman that appeal to man's depravity
    Are constructed with considerable care;
And what at first appears to be a simple little cavity
    Is in fact a most elaborate affair.

Physicians of distinction have examined these phenomena
    In numerous experimental dames.
They have tabulated carefully the feminine abdomina
    And given them some fascinating names

There's the vulva, the vagina and the jolly perineum,
    And the hymen, in the case of many brides,
And lots of other little things you'd like if you could see 'em:
    The clitoris and other things besides.

So isn't it a pity, when we common people chatter
    Of these mysteries to which I have referred,
That we use for such a delicate and complicated matter
    Such a very short and ordinary word.

216

But men are not obliged to talk about sex in brutish monosyllables. Imagine a pair of thoroughly sexist classical scholars observing the young beauties in the public square:

Why are you poppizating in that disgustingly triorchid manner?

Look at that erranous chrysocomic nelipot with the euesic nose and eclunious rear acrobating out of the parthenon! She's probably making for the sudorium. An alipile, I shouldn't wonder, or else an acroamatist resting. Perhaps as she's ablautic she may even be a peripole. Look how she crissates as she walks.

Yes, she's quite eumorphous. But maybe a little micromatic to be beautiful, and certainly too apoglutic for my taste. She's probably babacious as well. They nearly all are – and microthymic to boot. Probably incapable of giving any man a good psexy after his pyrations. She doesn't look strong enough to sugillate anyone with *her* exertions!

Ah, but look at those leptesic little breasts! I feel a twinge of aphrodiasm coming on.

Come, come. She's practically amastic – as well as cenocrantic. I've always been molobrous for the uberous charms of the more euporous woman – if possible a bumastous, conarotic arrhenopiper of the barmaid type. That's the most stytic type for me. Oh for a parasynaxis with her!

I always knew you were a clunal man . . .

When I was still a blichoanotic, anebous boy, hardly penirate so as you'd notice, an old orgiophant told me that in women the calyptic, intercrural charms were the most delightful – if only because they're so abatic. But see what happens. At first, the artigamous indulge in adapatenous, pannychous interfrications. But the ceaseless himeroomany usually turns out to be a novendial wonder, till the bridegroom becomes positively astytic. The girl who only a little while ago was so evancalous turns into a grasontic shrew. Truly, the road between acacy and abarcy is a short one. Before you know where you are, you're cornupated.

No-one could call you an aniatic romantic. All the same, do you think if I invited her for a potiuncle . . . I know it's sheer aphrasia, because I'm more than a little aphebic . . . But

Poppizating: Clucking the tongue and smacking the lips
Triorchid: Very lascivious, randy
Chrysochromic: Golden-haired
Nelipot: One who goes barefoot
Euesic: Pointed
Euclunious: Pretty-buttocked
Acrobating: Tip-toeing
Parthenon: Maidens' room
Sudorium: Steam bath
Alipile: Slave employed to remove unwanted body-hair
Acroamatist: Actress
Ablautic: Shoeless
Peripole: Streetwalker
Crissating: Playing the buttocks
Eumorphous: Well-shaped
Micromatic: Small-eyed
Apoglutic: Small-buttocked
Babacious: Given to gossip
Microthymic: Narrow-minded, prudish
Psexy: Massage, rub-down
Pyrations: Hot baths
Sugillate: Bruise
Leptesic: Pointed
Aphrodiasm: Sudden desire
Amastic: Without breasts
Cenocrantic: Emptyheaded, witless
Molobrous: Greedy
Uberous: Ample, abundant
Euporous: Well-endowed
Bumastous: Big-breasted
Conarotic: Plump
Arrhenopiper: A woman who looks lewdly at men
Stytic: Erection-inducing
Parasynaxis: An illicit meeting
Clunal: Relating to the hinder parts or bottom
Blichanotic: Snotty-nosed
Anebous: Beardless
Penirate: Equipped with a penis
Orgiophant: A teacher of secret or intimate practices
Calyptic: Hidden
Intercrural: In the crotch; between the legs
Abatic: Inaccessible
Artigamous: Newlyweds
Adapatenous: Inexhaustible
Pannychous: Lasting all night
Interfrications: Rubbings together

what I always say is, once a gynopiper, always a gynopiper.

Do you really think she'll come to you at an apocrote? You must be desipid. Besides, you're silenic at the top and cacomorphous below. She'll just laugh at you and call you an apoplymatic old man. Anyway, enough of this percite talk.

You're just too damn xyresic for me!

Himeroomany: Sexual intercourse
Novendial: Nine days
Astytic: Incapable of erection
Evancalous: Pleasant to embrace
Grasontic: Smelling like a goat
Acacy: Innocence
Abarcy: Insatiability
Cornupated: Cuckolded
Aniatic: Hopeless, incurable
Potiuncle: A little drink
Aphrasia: Madness
Aphebic: Past the first flush of youth
Gynopiper: A man who looks lewdly at women
Apocrote: A snap of the fingers
Desipid: Out of one's mind
Silenic: Bald and bearded
Cacomorphous: Ill-shapen
Apoplymatic: Dirty
Percite: Greatly rousing to lust
Xyresic: Sharp, as a razor

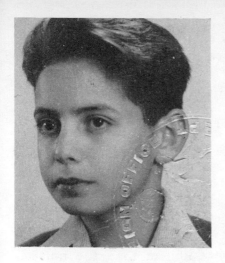 

Even the Headmaster's Conference has joined the wild rush for renaming old institutions and decided that Public Schools should henceforth be known as Independent Schools. I was certainly amazed when, after being told on arrival in this country that I was to be sent to a public school, it turned out to be a very private school – restricted to the charges of my noble hosts (noble in both senses of the word) who could pay to have them educated there. But then the whole English education system is beset with paradoxes, euphemisms and misnomers. The Conference itself, for a start, seems to be less of a conference than an association that holds a big meeting once a year and issues weighty statements. Other bodies must in the same way once have decided that 'ragged schools', schools 'for the Children of Paupers' or 'the Sons of Indigent Clergy' did not sound too good either. In education, as in everything else, the cover of every euphemism is eventually blown.

Every minor public school considers itself special, but would hate to be called a Special School. They claim to offer a comprehensive education but are not Comprehensive Schools; nor, although Conference Schools are carefully vetted and approved, are they Approved Schools. Come to think of it, if there still is a school at Borstal in Kent it, too, must surely have changed its name long ago, after the first prison-school was started there in 1908: 'Educated Borstal, Eton and Oxford' would not look too good in *Who's Who?* (Has anyone pointed out that by one of those amazing coincidences the place-name comes from Old English *borg*, security, and *steall*, place?)

I'm sorry to say that my minor public school didn't give me much of an education though it did its best. The war was going badly and masters kept joining the forces. Music was taught by a nice old gentleman (probably all of 45), Mr Blencowe; RK (as we called it) by the headmaster, an ordained priest; and science by his wife (who was James Elroy Flecker's sister). The music consisted of class-singing: no harmony, no exams, just a weekly sing-song – trebles and growlers more or less together in what was jokingly called unison, and a better preparation for rugby dinners than the musical profession. In fact all I learned at public school was aeroplane-spotting, rugger, cricket, not to cry when hit by ball or bat – and how to yawn while keeping my mouth closed (which was to be of use later during interminable orchestral rehearsals). Swimming and Mathematics I dreaded most, the former because we were all naked (masters, too) and the small natural lake was full of frogs and newts. End-of-term reports varied from the ecstatic (English and Latin only) to the dismissive. For RK the headmaster tersely wrote 'Not interested'; and the Maths master only aggravated my feeble numeracy by resorting to sarcasm: 'A useful member on the rugger field.' I can't swear to it now but I seem to remember two adjacent entries in another boy's report: 'Could try harder', and 'A very trying little boy.' But I do remember for certain that the Public School for Girls nearby had (in tiny letters below its name on the board outside the grounds) the additional information, 'Preparatory for Boys'. That part of my education was probably the most comprehensive, more enjoyable even than English and Latin or proudly marching with the Air Cadets. Another thing I remember (because there is printed evidence) is that the English-master, Mr Woodhouse, a gentle, sensitive man who was evidently curious but did not wish to pry, at the end of my first term set an essay entitled 'Vienna-London'. To my embarrassment it went into the school magazine. For years afterwards I showed it to no-one, ashamed of its mixture of stilted and colloquial English. But I plead in mitigation that four months earlier I had known only two English words, which by necessity I looked up on the journey: 'Please water':

Vienna-London

It was at half past eight in the evening when I went to the West Station at Vienna. It was just one year before that day that Hitler interrupted the peaceful life of Austria and made many people unhappy. When we arrived at the station we saw many children with one case and with a number round their necks, going with their parents or by themselves. All the other people who were Nazis were merry this day, but not the parents whose children were going far away. The Nazis sang and marched in the streets.

The train came and the children got into it. Everybody shook hands and after a few minutes the train started moving. Handkerchiefs were waved and then it seemed as if the town of Vienna was moving backwards. That was at eleven o'clock. At five minutes past the boys were ragging and were happy. I was surprised a bit. A few days before I had been ill and in bed. I had enough time to think of everything. I supposed that children would weep or something like that. But luckily no-one did. Mostly I stood by the window and looked at the country, which was lovely anyhow. I did not sleep at all, I just stood by the window, looking and thinking about the " cultivated " Germans.

After one and a half days we came to Emmerich, the German-Dutch frontier. There we got hot lemonade and buns. Then the train went over the boundary. A hot-water bottle was thrown out of the carriage window, empty, however, for we could not do without water for that was very precious on the train.

In Harwich I was surprised to see the seats in the 3rd class covered with cloth. There are only wooden benches in Germany. After two hours we were at London, waiting in a boxing stadium from which the people were to fetch us.

F.S.

Reading it again after all these years I can't help reflecting that although the school didn't succeed in making me into a little English gentleman it did its best to teach me English understatement: what they used to call back home *die Englische Stiff Öpper Lip*. The number round my neck, incidentally, was 124.

Additions and Corrections

Additions and Corrections

Additions and Corrections

Additions and Corrections

Additions and Corrections